When You're DONE Expecting

By
Parul Agrawal
&
Over 100 Global Moms

parul.agrawal@asu.edu
Nirvana Wellness Publishing

Ordering Information:
Quantity sales. Special discounts are available on quantity purchases by corporations, associations, and others. For details, contact the publisher at the address above.

Please download your FREE gifts that come along with the purchase of this book from "**www.whenyouredoneexpecting.com**."

Contents

Finding Balance as a Woman and a Mom

The Greatest Teacher- Motherhood!

Heart-to-Heart, Tete-a-Tete

The Art of Parenting

The Different Phases of Motherhood

Mom, You Can Overcome Your Fear

Infertility, Death, Adoption & Hope!

Mom, You are Brave & Strong!

Mom Challenges, Struggles & Triumphs

Raising Healthy Kids

A Collection of Poems For Mom's Soul

Dedicated To

All Past, Present and Future Mothers!

Acknowledgements

The compilation of this book is a result of concentrated efforts of various individuals without whose help "When You're DONE Expecting" wouldn't have been possible.

My sincere gratitude goes to all the Authors who contributed their time and expertise to this book.

I would also like to acknowledge the valuable contributions of the editors, formatters and initial reviewers regarding the improvement of quality, coherence, and content presentation of chapters. Thanks to Jewel Eliese for suggesting the title of the book, to my business partner Ewa Ramparte for her design and marketing advice, to my business coach Noam Kostucki for expanding my vision beyond what I thought was possible, to my husband Ankur Agrawal and to my children for their continued support during the conception, creation and launch of this wonderful book.

Finally, I would like to Thank all the Mothers for everything they do for their children and for the World.

"A mother gives-up the most important things in her life so her children could take on the most important things in their life. Thank YOU Moms!"

Foreword

I had a troubled relationship with my mother. She was in search of the cowboy life, so we were on the move a lot. I spent many nights sleeping on a bedroll by her car. Mom called it camping. You would call it being homeless.

As an adult, I had a heart for helping children. I began a career as a Motorcycle Officer with the Arizona Highway Patrol. I was on a 10 man squad that worked the whole state of Arizona and when we had some spare time, we would visit the grade schools and talk about bicycle safety. The kids were more interested in our motorcycles than bicycle safety, but it was good public relations.

In 1980, I met a seven-year old boy named Chris. He changed my life. Chris had terminal leukemia but he had a wish, he wanted to be a motorcycle officer like his heroes Ponch and Jon from the hit TV series, "CHiPS. The Arizona Highway Patrol made that wish come true, making Chris the first and only honorary Highway Patrol Officer, complete with a custom made uniform, troopers hat, badge and his motorcycle uniform wings.

Tears streamed down his mother's face as she watched him run around like a typical 7-year old child and play on the police motorcycles. He lived his wish. For this one special day, his mother had her son back. A few days later, Chris passed away.

Chris was my inspiration to create and co-found the Make-A-Wish Foundation, a non-profit that grants the wishes to children around the world who have a life-threatening illness.

No mother is perfect. Not mine, not yours, and not even you. But they each carry a wish. It doesn't matter which country they're from, their culture, or the color of their skin. They hope their children will have a childhood of joy and free of worry. They dream their child will grow up safe, healthy and happy.

This book will give you a look into over 100 real mom's lives from across the world as they live through the trials of motherhood. They will inspire you with passionate true stories that will break your heart, make you smile, and help you realize you are not alone. They know the fears you face while raising your kids. They feel the same aching love for their children that you do. These 100+ moms understand you.

Many people call themselves supermom's, but I call them genies. From incredible miracles to simply making peanut butter and jelly sandwiches, mom's grant wishes every day with love and gentle strength. They create magic. This book is a wish for you to become a part of this wonderful and terrifying life called motherhood. Read and join them in this journey.

Frank Shankwitz
The Creator and A Founder of the Make-A-Wish Foundation

Introduction

When You're DONE Expecting is a compilation of stories from women all around the world.

Each shares her own story about the challenges and triumphs she's faced as a mother or daughter. Some tell tales of the day their precious child was born and lessons they learned in their motherhood journey, while others weave stories about finding the perfect work–life balance to raise conscious children in this tech-driven society.

No matter what kind of mom you are—a stay-at-home mom, working mom, mompreneur, teenage mom, birth mom, adoptive mom, single mom, or grandmother—motherhood is an experience that ties us all together.

We may live in different corners of the world, have different value systems, cultures, or religious beliefs, but we all speak the same language—the language of Motherhood. Every mother has similar fears and challenges and a beautiful desire to provide a loving and supportive environment for her children.

So join us on the laughter-filled, tear-inducing journey full of endless twists and turns... called Motherhood.

Let these women warm your hearts with tender moments that make up their experience of being a mother.

Parul Agrawal
Founder & Chief Editor, Alpha Female Magazine
Publishing Director, Alpha Female LLC.

I am a Mom

Wishes From The Divine Mother
by Naomi Pereira

I am the Divine Mother here to wish all of you brave warrior Mothers a very happy day today.

It took a very special type of human to choose motherhood in the current energies on earth. They were all equipped with a different understanding of what it would entail and most of all the qualities we looked for was the ability to accept and create change, to relearn old ways of motherhood acquired from ancestors and love love love.

The early 60's mothers have been the instruments of change...birthing the type of human that was required at that stage of this life changing ascension process you are undergoing. The first mothers gave birth to the innovators, the challengers who were born to break down the old stagnant ways and introduce new ways of thinking and doing things. This was the hardest. The mothers chosen were strong endurer with the two pre requisites of change and love in their hearts plus a heavy doze of strength for their children who would stop at nothing to break down the old patterns of existence. They suffered much to do this along with their children. They are one who went out on marches and stood up to authority.

And this is why they were chosen.
And they never gave up!

Then came the mothers who bore the ones who came to lay the new foundations. To challenge people to a new way of thinking...to make acceptable different ways of life and sexuality and religion. And these mothers suffered because their children were different..they were ostracized and looked down upon and thrashed by the old ways of rigidity. These mothers fought for acceptance for their gay children, and differently-abled children and started foundations for others like them.

Many of these children who came were pure starseed energies and suffered to exist amidst the hate and negativity on earth...many opted out through the process of suicide.... their energies were too sensitive for the world they were born into. And they were judged as weak and their mothers endured that. But they accepted and still loved unconditionally.

And this is why they were chosen.
And they never gave up.

And now we have the mothers who have birthed and are birthing the newest ones. The ones who will show us the way. Again alien energies...sensitive souls, some from other planets and constellations getting used to the darkness of our earth..struggling to make the adjustment necessary. And they have mothers who have chosen to evolve and accept the role change.....that their children will be the teachers and they will be the nurturers and the support system to create the environment that these new ones will need to factor what they came down to do.

And so, yes it has been a challenging experience being a Mother in this age on earth. The problems of motherhood being different and more challenging than ever experienced before. Because you are giving birth to the new world. Your wombs have borne and will bear the movers and the shakers and the game changers needed at this time on earth. And sometimes you will not understand them or even resonate with them and they will drive you up the wall with their ways and their thinking and stretch your limits of endurance, patience and tolerance. But you will love them.

That is why you were chosen
And this why you will never give up.!
I SALUTE YOU MOTHERS!
You are the wombs of creation seeding the new world!

What greater honor can there be?
You are so loved and honored.
You have a special place in our hearts
KNOW THAT AND BE BLESSED!

I AM,
THE DIVINE MOTHER OF ALL.

Counting with Kisses
by Jewel Eliese

A middle-aged nurse mops the concrete floor with an old gray shirt. My bed is flat and lumpy. The hospital room is European style mixed with Soviet influence. It makes me feel like I have been transported to the 1940s. A wounded Ukrainian soldier should be recovering in this bed, not a simple American like me.

Maybe I should go home even without my husband? The hospital would be more sanitary there. Safer.

I make myself relax against the patterned pillow and try not to think about things I can't change. I want to simply enjoy these pain-free moments. Staying still as the doctor stuck the spear-like needle in my back during a contraction was almost impossible. But it was worth it.

My Ukrainian husband, Lyu, has a wrinkle between his brows from recent frowns. He once wished he could go through the pain for me. I believed him. He looked so helpless watching me. Now his eyes wear a cautious, hopeful smile.

I rub my oversized belly. I just want my baby to be healthy. I dream of counting and kissing ten pink fingers and toes. Still, I can't help but wonder what he'll look like. Will he have Lyu's wide hazel eyes and heart-shaped lips? Or will he have my near-black hair and pale skin? My heart jumps in anticipation and worry.

My stomach muscles harden. Not a contraction. A push. I did NOT do that.
"I'm pushing!" I tell Lyu. Without a sound, he's out the door searching for the doctor. My stomach pushes again. It feels like a wave of water

running across my baby bump.

My numb legs feel like they belong to someone else as Lyu and the doctor carry me over to the birthing area. My new robe has brown smeared on it; surprised, I remove it. What if it smells? A part of me is embarrassed; the rest of me is focused on birthing a human.

The bed—if you could call it that—is maroon leather. It has foot straps and bars for gripping. My heart pumps loudly in my ears. I feel like there should be a director barking out orders for a horror movie. But once I am settled in, my husband gives me a reassuring grin.

I can do this.

Ukrainian women in green scrubs surround me. My doctor, a beautiful woman with a kind face and intelligent eyes, stands in front of my girly bits. She speaks, but I don't understand enough. Lyu translates, telling me how to sit, how to push, and when.

It's time.

I push as they count, "Odyn, dva, tre!"

I can feel the veins under my skin, and my face flushes with heat.

"Good!" Lyu says, holding my hand. "A little harder this time." I wonder how.

"Push!" I do. More forceful this time, but I don't know if I'm doing it right.

"Better," he translates.

A middle-aged nurse—our mopping lady—places her hands by my ribs where my bump begins. When I push, she also pushes.

"It hurts," I tell Lyu.

The nurse answers in a tone even I understand. "Yes, yes it hurts," I imagine she says.

"No, my skin!"

Her chubby fingers reposition and the pinching pain is gone when I push again.

"I can see him," Lyu says, smile wide. "He has some hair." I half laugh, half sob.

The doctor speaks to Lyu, nodding slowly. It seems serious and my heart starts to flutter. Is there something wrong with the baby? What if the cord is wrapped around his neck and he can't breathe? Maybe having the baby here was a mistake. Maybe I should have had our son in an American hospital. Alone.

My breath comes out in bursts.

Lyu catches my panic. He smooths my hair and explains they have to cut me on the next push—an episiotomy. It sounds terrible, but my brain doesn't have enough compartments to think about it.

"Now."

I grab the plastic bars and strain muscles as hard as I can. The doctor snips. My hips shake. A baby cries.

That was the last push already?

My son is placed on my bare chest. I let out happy howls; my voice doesn't sound like me. The baby is so big. His slightly blue body is covered with white film and crimson blood. His nails are long like Dracula's.

They take him away, and I realize I never let go of the bars to hold him. I am still gripping, my knuckles white.

The middle-aged nurse takes him under the warmer to be checked. My husband follows. It's just me and my doctor as she stitches me back together.

I want my baby back. I need to see him. Is he OK? What if there is something wrong? My fingers tremble.

"How is he?" I call across the room.

"Beautiful," Lyu answers. A baby sneeze echoes around the room. It reminds me of Simba from The Lion King. I laugh and sob once more.

Once the stitches are finished, my healthy eight-pound baby is brought to me. My hands have no trouble cradling him this time. Lyu kisses my forehead as I stare at the new addition to our family.

My baby looks at me, squinting in the new light. I stop breathing. He has a button nose with a light pink birthmark hidden in the side, wide almond-shaped eyes, and heart-shaped lips. I don't know if he looks like me or Lyu. I don't care. He is perfect.

He ripped my heart from my chest on his way into this world. Now it belongs to him. Every moment of agony, the long needle stabbed in my back and each annoyance from the past nine months has been worth it. He is the reward for my suffering, a gift from God I can never deserve.

I lay my head back on the patterned pillow once more. Everything happened just as God planned. I was able to have my husband by my side and a healthy baby.

A tear of joy crawls down my cheek. I kiss each of my son's ten pink fingers.

Author Bio:
Jewel is a mom of two goofy munchkins and the wife of a serious, yet comedic husband. When she's not playing with her kids or making soup, you can find her snuggled up on the couch with a beverage and a pen or book in hand. She is also the creator of Write away, Mommy, where women become better writers and mothers along with her.

Website: **www.writeawaymommy.com**

Motherhood Mash-up
by Ruthi Davis

Dear Confessional,

From the moment that I held my first child and was privileged enough to gain the extraordinary title of mother, I knew that just about every facet of my life was about to change drastically. You see, motherhood isn't just a title and a responsibility—it's an evolution that will rock you to the core and test every ounce of your character and might from the get-go.

Between those glorious moments of stepping on a curiously sharp Lego mid-hallway, to placing your iPhone in the fridge and juice in the pantry in an exhausted mommy mishap, we don't give up. Even when you've caught the school's epidemic of the stomach bug and all you want to do is curl up in the fetal position, your title and responsibility never waver. From the projectile poop of a newborn all over your clothes to the flailing four-limbed tantrums mid-aisle at the store, somehow moms just manage to keep moving forward through bedtime, each day, when you stop and wish that time would just slow down. I must admit, this journey is an incredible ride of highs and lows, and twists and turns that I honor, even during my Darth Vader voice moments.

To all dedicated mothers:

I am proud to stand by you and with you, knee-deep, in this all-consuming, all-draining, and all-empowering journey that is parenting.

Regardless of what style of momma you may be, we are all the same in our intention to parent for the best interests of our kids. So today I feel privileged to salute each of you, because moms just deserve a lot more hugs and even more appreciation for this epic ride called parenting. Whether you relate to one, all, or none of these mom categories below, I bet you at least know someone who does.

- **Energizer Mom** who is a high-speed doer and doesn't pick her head up for a breath between the endless piles of laundry, dishes, supermarket runs, dinner prep, class mom duties, and limitless errands. She is virtually a magical fairy who seamlessly keeps the home and family together and doesn't take a breath, until her eyes start crossing and closing while putting the kids to bed.
- **Suited-up Mom** who juggles professional and home life like a pro, even when her suit is hiding the morning milk stains from her daughter's flying cereal bowl. She just does it all, from lunch boxes to status meetings, weekly reports to spelling tests. She's got this.
- **Frazzle Dazzle Mom** who may not always be on time and often arrives to school in her pajama pants, she tries so hard. She's always in a rush, in a stumble, in a frazzle, and so very lovable as she is always learning and doing her best.

Celebrate your perfect imperfections with this Motherhood Mashup, perfectly contrived from the famed words of the United States Constitution. We mothers mostly make up the fabric of our homes and family. We deserve a little extra boost besides those push-up Wonderbras, so please enjoy this momma salute.

Constitution of Motherhood
(Original text by James Madison, Mash-up by Ruthi)

We the Mothers of this brood,
in Order to form a more perfect Union, establish Justice among competitive siblings,

ensure domestic Tranquility when kids won't share, provide for the
common defense during tired tantrums,
promote the general Welfare with clean underwear and warm
meals, and secure the Blessings of Sanity to ourselves
and for the Well-Being of our children,
do ordain and establish this Momma Constitution
for the United Function of the Family.

Whichever kind of mother you are, even if it's not listed here, I commend you—from stretch marks to cellulite, saggy boobs to cesarean scars, varicose veins to dark under-eye circles, gray hairs to 30-something acne, this one's for you. From girls'-night-out-venting to date night drink-a-thon, Zumba dance booties to toned limbs, Photoshopped selfies to breast implants, botoxed wrinkles to personal training, I applaud you.

No matter what path you take to embrace your flaws with your inner and outer beauty, we all wear this badge of motherhood in various forms. No matter what you look like or how you manage this most important commitment,

We are all Supermoms.
Celebrate your perfect imperfection!
And remember—
We're all in this journey called motherhood together.

With Love,
Ruthi

Author Bio:
Ruthi Davis is a global multimedia editor/writer, author, speaker, consultant, business/brand strategist, founder of Superfly Supermom and SuperKids Chronicles, and frequent contributor for Thrive Global, The Huffington Post, Bonbon Break, Red Tricycle, and Scary Mommy.

Her Superfly Supermom brand quickly garnered global reach through her candid and informative blog and overall brand mission to encourage a powerful journey of self-empowerment through humor, sincere emotion, and practical strategies. For nearly two decades, Ruthi has reached audiences worldwide and worked with Fortune 500 (Top 50) companies on multi-faceted advertising/marketing campaigns through copywriting, brand development, and business strategy.

Website: **www.superflysupermom.com**

Number Two
by Alicia Power

I had my first baby a few months after I turned 40. I wanted a home birth so badly. I never even toured a hospital "just in case." My husband David and I found a midwife, took a childbirth class, and did as much as we could to be prepared. I made two music playlists, one mellow and soothing and another full of energy and power. Our midwife and her assistant loved the playlists and said we should have more babies. I was set and determined not to go to the hospital, but after all efforts failed I ended up transferring there and having a C-section.

Nevertheless, we were both healthy, she breastfed just fine and I recovered. When I became pregnant again almost a year later, I was thrilled to have another chance at a home birth. I was 3 or 4 weeks pregnant with Caleb when Analeigh turned one, but we didn't tell any family until after her birthday celebration. I didn't want even an ounce of attention taken away from her. There would be more than enough attention taken away from her in the future, I figured.

I took care of myself as best as I could during this second pregnancy while working full time and being mom to little Analeigh. She and I were very, very close. David was a huge help as he stayed home with her while I was at work. He had been laid off 6 months or so before her birth, which was truly a blessing for our family. He even brought her into work each day to visit me and nurse at lunchtime while he took a walk. Analeigh nursed until I was in my second trimester.

One evening she just got up after nursing a bit and asked for milk in a cup. I was ready to continue as long as she wanted, but she made it easy and decided she was done on her own.

I loved nursing her so much, maybe even more because I was away from her during the workday. I was thrilled I would get a chance to do it all again with a second baby. I interviewed a couple of midwives and explained the situation with Analeigh's birth.

Apparently her head had been cocked to the side and her chin back instead of tucked, which made it difficult for her get into the right position. I was encouraged to try home-birthing again, as there was no evidence to indicate the positional issue would reoccur. I was fit and active and super healthy. I exercised every day I could, even if it was just a little bit. My body was well nourished by the prenatal vitamins I had continued to take while Analeigh nursed. David helped immensely by cooking simple, healthy meals for us at home. We found a doula we adored, which we had not done the first time around. I was so grateful to be having my second baby at age 41, at home, with no pregnancy difficulties other than some sciatica, in the cool, calm, enveloping wrap of winter. I felt very peaceful and blessed.

Caleb announced his impending arrival by giving me gentle infrequent contractions for a day or two first. Midwife Janet said these small contractions every hour or so were his way of taking it easy on me and slowly moving into position. It was the weekend before Martin Luther King, Jr. Day. He would be right on time. I was grateful and joyous and went with them without even saying very much about it to my family. My parents visited and entertained Analeigh. I felt like we were graced by many, many people.

When labor finally ramped up, my parents came in the night and took sleeping Analeigh to my sister's house as planned. I remember saying to David, "Get Analeigh out of here." I knew I needed her out of the house in order to feel free to make any noise or movement I wanted without being afraid I would upset her. I did not want her to need me and be unable to tend to her. I remember stomping my feet, moaning, and swirling my hips. David and doula Rebekah held me up by the arms. Midwife Janet walked in and laughed, saying, "You're not even going to wait for me, are you?" The way she said it, so lightly, filled me with confidence that what was happening was exactly right for the moment and exactly what was needed, even though I had no idea how this baby was going to come out of my body. Caught in the tornado of birth, it is only possible to be in this moment. The next one and what it may bring are too unfathomable to consider. Caleb was born in that very room, without the need for any medications or procedures. I held him in absolute awe immediately afterwards. There was a small blob of goo on his forehead, and I felt a fear it might be a disfiguration. They told me to talk to him. I made a conscious decision to put this fear aside.

"We did it," I said to him softly, "you and I. You were great. We were great. We did it. You are here." Only after looking deeply in his eyes and fully accepting him completely in love and gratitude exactly as he was did I move to brush the goo from his forehead. It came right off.

We had done it. I had done it. He was here. I could hardly believe I had done it, but I had.

There were many other steps to take that early morning with the midwives, not all fun but certainly easier than birth itself. The futon in the front room was set up to be a bed for Caleb and myself for a few days. I was instructed to do nothing but nurse, sleep, and care for Caleb. David was instructed to bring me food. Finally our beloved doula and midwives left. After a short while, family came.

My mother carried Analeigh in. "Baby Caleb!" Analeigh cried, twisting around in my mother's arms to see her new baby brother. "You did it," my sister said, full of admiration. Her two children had been born in hospitals. Everything was glowing and beautiful. I could not have asked for a more perfect outcome. I was so satisfied and happy.

Eventually everyone left, and David, Analeigh, Caleb, and I were alone. David was getting me something to eat, as instructed. Analeigh was dancing around the kitchen delightedly. Caleb was sleeping in my arms. I was on the futon looking into the kitchen, hungry and waiting. I heard the sound of granola spilling. Analeigh loved granola. I noticed her picking some up off the floor and eating it. It seemed like she was really having fun sneaking food off the floor.

What a great game!

"She's eating food off the floor," I said to David from the other room. I thought he probably couldn't tell, as he was busy getting me food. I don't know why I thought I should tell him. It was just a fact, like telling someone there is something behind them so they don't fall over it. I thought my tone was calm and nonjudgmental. I really had no energy to be bothered by such behavior at this point. It was not ideal for her to be eating food off the floor, but hardly a problem. We had just birthed our second child successfully at home, and I could not ask for anything in the world except food, which I would be getting soon.

David came out of the kitchen and leaned against the wall. I watched as he slowly slid to the floor, his head in his hands, sobbing. My emotions were spent, but I felt pangs of surprise, dismay, and disappointment at a distance, as if in someone else. We had done so much, prepared so well, had so much success. We were finally in the clear only to drop fully into complete chaos. We had meals in the freezer, but we had not given a thought to what it would really be like after Caleb's birth. There is nothing that can prepare you for holding a baby you can't put down while your one-year-old begs to be picked up and cries when you can't.

I saw that David was overwhelmed. Birth is an intense emotional process, and men have understandably fewer tools to manage it than women. Yet I was the one who gave birth, I was the one he was supposed to feed, I was the one supposed to do nothing but take care of the baby for days. He was supposed to take care of me and he was on the floor crying with his head in his hands. I felt so completely vulnerable: baby in arms, toddler uncontrollable, myself hungry and helpless. Every mother has moments like that. There were more to come in my future.

This one put a chill into my core that truly, contrary to all preparation and expectation, I was on my own with no one to help. The feeling of that moment has never left my heart.

Author Bio:
Alicia Power helps women heal from their birth experience, supports them in their role as a new mother, and prepares them for their return to work. Birth can be traumatic. Recovery on all levels is essential to face the demands of postpartum life, especially when returning to work. Alicia's been there! Her experience and unique healing system are tailored to support individual needs.

Website **www.healthechasm.com**

My Children...My Dreams Come True
by Kiya Bonilla

From as early as 7 years old I can recall wanting to be a mother. The teenage years swept in; hormones were high and inhibition was low. So I engaged in shameful promiscuity. I was full of shame and convinced myself that God would punish me for my sin by making me barren.

These thoughts plagued, punished, and pursued me for years. However, that was before I knew the God of unconditional love, mercy, and grace. That was before I completely left religiosity and welcomed a personal relationship with Jesus Christ. That was before I realized that my sin struggles and imperfections were evidence of my humanness, not failure. In 2003, during my junior year at Long Island University, I met the God of unconditional love, mercy, and grace!

It was a highly stressful period of time in my life. I was a nursing student who was dedicated to succeeding. Succeeding at becoming a nurse was my own way of "redeeming myself" for my past and present struggle with fornication. Becoming a nurse would prove to me and everyone around me that I wasn't a total failure. Therefore, I did whatever it took to do well, and one too many sleepless nights and early mornings led to me missing my menstrual period for 8 months. After a visit to my primary care physician's office, it was discovered that my issue was stress. I had to make a major change. My first step was to have a much-needed conversation with someone I'd seemingly abandoned over the past several months. . . God!

"Father, I know I haven't been one of your best-behaved children. I've fornicated and still struggle with fornication now. Please forgive me and help me to change. I'd understand if you say that I deserve your punishment, because I do, but I'm seeking you for your mercy. My menses have been gone for 8 months and I'm not pregnant or ill. I thank you for allowing stress alone to be my issue and nothing more serious! These past several months I've been so focused on becoming a nurse that I haven't read your Bible and I mostly talk to you only before exams.

Please forgive me. If you allow my menses to return to a normal cycle, I promise to read my bible before I study for my nursing exams and to pray every day. I also promise to never again take pain medicine for my menstrual cramps. You have my word, Lord, so can you please bring my menses down? Lord, as you know, I suffer with the fear of not being able to have children; can you also give me a vision, a dream, or a sign to let me know if you will allow me to have children or not? Thank you, Lord. I love you! In Jesus's name I pray, amen."

I went to sleep after I prayed, lying side by side with my fiancé Percy. And that very night I had a dream. I dreamed of a little girl who looked a lot like me, yet way more beautiful, delightful, and intelligent. She played peekaboo with me as scenes from her life from birth to approximately 4 years old were shown to me. In the end of the dream, I held a birth certificate, on which I wrote the name: Nyla. I woke up amazed, in shock and excited all at the same time. Nyla was my gift from heaven revealed to me in a dream. I woke up knowing for sure that God chose to show me his mercy rather than his wrath. I was and will always be eternally grateful. 6 years later Nyla Sabrina Bonilla was born, exactly as I dreamed her to be. She's my literal dream come true!

After the dream about Nyla I was satisfied, content, and grateful to be mommy to her alone. However, without asking for another dream or another child, 6 months later I dreamed of a little boy who resembled my fiancé Percy, dressed in blue and sleeping peacefully in a bassinet. When I woke up, I just knew the Lord was sending me another child, this time a son. I knew then that God's mercy truly does endures forever! I told my fiancé Percy about both dreams and we settled that when we got married we would have 2 children. 4 years after my dream about the baby boy in the bassinet, Percy Emmanuel Bonilla III was born, exactly as I had dreamed. He is another one of my dreams that came true.

My husband and I were content. We believed our family was complete! We had our 2 promised children and we couldn't ask for more! The only problem was neither of us consulted with God to find out if HE was done with us having children. We only considered our will and plan for our lives. Both of our children were born via cesarean section, so we were further convinced that it wasn't safe for me to have many more deliveries. We were done, or so we thought!

It was 2012, Percy III was 5 years old and Nyla was 3 years old. I woke up from an afternoon nap and heard myself speaking these words as I came out of my sleep, "You will have a child and you will name her Faith." I was lying on my husband's lap at the time. I recall hearing the words I spoke and knowing they didn't come from me; I knew it must have been from God.

So I repeated it again in amazement and to share what I heard with my husband. In response he said, "God spoke to you, not me!" He may not have believed it then, but I believed it was true from the moment I said it. So I surrendered and waited. He may say I harassed him about having Faith, but I'd say I gently reminded him from time to time that what the Lord spoke must come to pass. It was early in January of 2013 when my husband called me from work and said, "This is the year we will have Faith." I couldn't believe my ears and I asked him if he was serious, and he was. In that moment I knew God had done a miracle!
Strangely, the night before he told me his decision to have Faith, I had another dream. It wasn't about a girl named Faith. It was a handsome

little boy who remained very close to me the entire dream. I wanted to believe he was my grandson, because I just couldn't imagine how hard it would be to get my husband to agree to a 4th child. So I kind of asked the Lord to please make him my grandson. Without getting a reply from God, I moved forward and did my best to forget about this little boy and focus on getting pregnant with Faith. But another dream came of the same little boy; this time in the dream, he called me mommy.

I then bargained with God. . . "Okay, I would love to have this precious little baby boy as my own, Lord, but please let him be born after Faith. I've waited so long for my husband to agree to have her, and if we have a son before her, I'm not sure if I could get him to agree to have another baby. " Again the Lord was silent. And again after the 2nd dream there was yet a 3rd dream of the same little boy. And then a few weeks later another dream! 4 dreams in total until the day I found out I was in fact pregnant with a little boy. It was him, the boy of my dreams. He was born on January 20th, 2017; we named him Percival Emmanuel Bonilla. Another dream come true.

The good news was before his birth my husband had already agreed to try one more time for Faith. Initially he was opposed to the idea, stating his concerns about me having 4 cesarean sections. He had a good point, but I knew that if the Lord would allow me to get pregnant then he would see to it that I'd safely deliver and live to enjoy his promise to me. One day during a conversation with a friend about my husband's hesitancy to have another child, she said, "You know that God can change the King's heart. " It was those words that stirred my faith to believe again. And that is exactly what happened, God changed my husband's heart and he agreed to try one more time for Faith. In a few short weeks, on January 30th, 2017, I am expected to deliver our promised princess Faith! I am the evidence and the reality that dreams from heaven truly do come true!

Our children are not only dreams that came true, they are evidence that God is real and HE rewards those who diligently seek HIM! Thank you Jesus for your gifts from heaven to my husband and I! We are eternally grateful to YOU!

On this earth where I temporarily reside,
I've found a light that I cannot hide.
HE's given me such beautiful and sacred things,
From the treasury of his throne 4 human beings.
There's no greater love to me. . .
Than 10 toes on 2 feet.
Than hearts in my womb that joyfully beat.
There is nothing in this world that can compare or compete. . .
With birthing into reality God's dreams for me!
To live the life HE chose for me!
Whenever I am low or feeling down
I think of my children and my joy abounds.
My gifts from God. . . my angels on earth,
My children give this life so much of its worth!
With love for my children and all of humanity.

Author Bio:
Kiya Bonilla is a follower of Jesus Christ and is also referred to by her Facebook page name: Souljah For Jesus. From the tender age of 14 years old when Kiya made Jesus Lord of her life, she had the desire to learn and teach anyone who would listen about God's grace and mercy. Her Souljah For Jesus page is an extension of that desire. She is the wife of Percy Jr., and mother of Percy III, Nyla, Percival, & Faith. Kiya and her husband own and operate PKB Bookkeeping & Tax Service Corporation. She is also a Registered Nurse.

My New-Mom Epiphany
by Durga Mamidipalli

I was a first-time mom and 10, 000 miles away from extended family in India. I did not know what to do with this tiny creature in my hands, and neither did my husband. I had thyroid issues, post-delivery blues, and perhaps mild depression too.

I went through so many scary nights. I remember sitting in my purple pjs. I scrolled through YouTube and googled for advice. How to give a bath to a newborn. What to do when they were not sleeping or cranky.

My TSH (Thyroid-stimulating hormone) reading was 0.07. This was far below the normal 0.4–4 range. In 3 months, it went up to 10. I was on a roller coaster with my emotions. I had no physical stamina to handle anything. I felt hopeless.

I was so scared to leave my baby with a babysitter and go to another room and sleep. I had no idea why I felt that way. I'm still uncertain if my feelings were normal. My moods swung back and forth. I felt like a caged tiger.

I judged myself and criticized what I was doing every moment. I always wanted to do much more for my baby and was never satisfied with what I was doing for him. I used to feel that I was not a good mom. Sometimes I felt so disconnected from myself and my baby. In this turmoil, I was not sure where to get help. If I went to the doctors, they would put me on depression medication. I felt it would cause other complications. I had a few close friends who did not mind my mood swings. I leaned on them for support and suggestions. Some of their suggestions worked and some made the situations much worse.

I regretted leaving my shining career to take care of my baby. I felt stuck with him 24/7 with no other thing to do in my life.

One day, sitting in the backyard, I watched the water fountain and looked at the blue sky for hope. I had an epiphany. I remembered spiritual practices like praying, chanting, yoga, and meditation. I acquired these from my parents and spiritual teachers. I ignored them now, thinking that I could not practice them when the baby was around, as he consumed a lot of time. But I realized that I could do at least some to fit in my schedule and gain a little benefit, even if I could not practice them all.

That moment was a wakeup call and I started chanting, which my baby enjoyed as well. This made me more motivated to do my meditations at least 3 to 4 minutes for every hour. I set up a timer on my cell phone and just followed it. My previous thought was, "how will I meditate for 20 minutes when my baby is awake?" Now, since it was only for 4 minutes, I would keep him in my lap or swing. I would sit in my brown chair next to his swing and meditate. If he cooperated, I would go on a little longer, and if not, I would reduce the time.

Instead of feeling bad that I could not do more, like wanting to clean up the mess in my house right away, return phone calls, fold the laundry, and so on, I started feeling thankful for whatever I could do. I observed that the way I saw my world started to change. I realized that there were so many things for which I should be grateful. I had my beautiful backyard. I had my amazing neighbor. I had my caring friends and loving husband. And it was a blessing that my newborn was a calm baby. I did not appreciate these blessings when I was going through my mental and physical struggle.

Within 6 months, I started appreciating the things I was doing for my kid. Maintaining his cloth diapers. Making all his food at home. Giving him Abhyanga (Ayurvedic Oil massage). Taking him to the park and to play dates. I was meditating, laughing with him, reading books to him, and talking to him a lot.

My feelings shifted from despair to joy. I was proud of my mothering skills. I was giving him all the love, attention, and care that he needed at that point of time. I felt fulfilled that I had conquered my monkey mind. I could live in the moment by being persistent with my practices. I was completely able to accept my present moment and be happy with my baby. I might not have been perfect or efficient, but I had a connection with my baby. My baby and I were the most contented and happy people in the world.

As my thyroid levels came back to normal, I could manage my toddler without exhaustion. I started my Life Coaching career. I was happy being able to follow my lifelong passion as a profession.

Now when I see new parents, my heart goes out to their struggles and I am pleased to share my way of getting through them. My situation was abnormal due to thyroid complications. But talking to various moms through several years I see the issues to be similar. Either we are less confident when we are new moms, or we are more nervous or paranoid with the daily activities regarding taking care of a newborn, or just tackling any problem. All it takes is a few deep breaths, an inner soul search to find out what gave us strength in the past. That is how to conquer our trials.

If you do not have any experience, close your eyes and take a few deep breaths in and out for a few minutes every waking hour. You will see your strength multiply to overcome your challenges.

Author Bio:
Durga Mamidipalli is a born intuitive, spreading healing and spirituality since very young age, she has touched many lives all over the world. Durga has a Master's in Computer Science from US. She is a certified

relationship coach as well as a yoga and meditation teacher. Durga is also a Martma Therapist and a senior Art of Living teacher. She is a regular contributor for publications like Thrive Global and My City 4 My Kids.

Website : **www.befreecoaching.com**

The Battle...
by Nicholle Caldwell

"Motherhood is a blessing."

"It is the best thing to ever happen to you."

"You will cherish these moments forever."

It is what everyone tells you. It is what you are "supposed" to feel. But what happens when you feel like the Universe was crazy for entrusting you with a child?

Sometimes I feel like the best mother on the planet! I feel I was born to do this and feel like supermom. Checking everything off my list, house is clean, meals prepped, time for my business, time for me, and everyone is happy. YES! I feel like I just scored a winning shot at a basketball game. I feel like the queen of my castle! It feels amazing when I am doing what I love with the people I love. My heart feels so full, like a toddler's belly after their favorite meal. My point is, when life is good it is good. When motherhood is good, life is great! I feel like the "battle" is over. Victory is mine! Or so I thought... until my toddler daughter threw a home-cooked freshly prepared meal to the floor, only to watch the dog eat it. In that moment I felt a small defeat. But these kinds of things happen, right?

That's what I tell myself. I give myself a pep talk, clean up, and remind myself it is nothing personal, I am born to do this and keep on going. I got this. My daughter chose me. I am fit for this. In the same breath my daughter is hitting the dog after countless reminders of "gentle hands," and I lose it and yell at her to "STOP hitting the dog!" I can't believe I just yelled at my daughter. Even though I have told her over a 100 times (ha, maybe more like a thousand), she is only a child. She's learning. I'm the adult. I can't believe what I just did. Will she remember this? Will she be scared? What is she thinking of me? Does this make me a bad mom? What would people say?

This was my internal battle: to stop judging, criticizing, and overanalyzing everything I did or said and to be more gentle with myself. With my daughter. Give myself the same grace I wanted her to give herself. Let go of the way I thought things should be and appreciate what is. Let go of these expectations of myself and just love. Show compassion and be compassion.

Motherhood has taught me the biggest lesson of all, and that is to love myself. By loving myself, I'm being an example for not only my daughter, but my community and anyone who comes into contact with me. I truly believe that all change starts by going within ourselves. It begins with being willing to take a look at our past hurts, triggers, and be honest about what we would like to change.

Honesty is the best policy. Only by being truly honest with ourselves can we begin to create a life we truly deserve and love. As we love ourselves more and more, it ripples out into our families, friends, communities, and throughout the world.

Love is the most powerful tool. So I choose to use it wisely. As I battled to love myself, love was the most powerful tool that has made the biggest impact in all areas of my life. As I have loved myself more, my world has shifted. My family is more loving because I am more open to giving and receiving love. I wasn't able to receive all the love they offered because I had walls up. I was closed off. I had to face the internal battle to love myself. I was at war with myself.

Initially I thought it was about everyone else. I thought my partner needed to change or my daughter needed to comply more. That was not the case. Each time I was suffering it was because of me. It was due to my thoughts. If I didn't feel good, I can guarantee I was thinking about something negative. Something that was out of alignment with my soul's truth.

I have learned through this journey of motherhood that the best thing I can do for my family is to love myself more. And that means putting myself first. Something I didn't learn growing up and I feel society in the past taught us otherwise. You may have been seen as selfish if you weren't putting everyone else's needs first. Maybe even looked down upon. Yes, sometimes motherhood requires putting our family's needs first; however, we have to make ourselves a priority. It can be too easy not to when caring for others.

I am here to tell you the answers you are seeking to feel better about yourself, about being a mother, and having a purpose, boils down to SELF-LOVE. Focus on making yourself happy and everything else will naturally fall into place. It is a paradigm shift. A new way of being. "Doing" is a way of the past. It's about being the mom you were born to be. Rising into your power and creating a life you love. I didn't believe this before, but I am living it now.

Motherhood has been the best thing to happen to me. I found me. I can be me. I can serve my purpose and be the best mom I can be. I have realized it is about being real. It is about progress and not perfection. I have the power to stop the internal battle at any time. It is something I created. I know the negative self-talk and the comparison will come up again, and I am ready. I am equipped with the most powerful tool of all: Love. With the power of Love and God, all things are possible (including motherhood).

You are doing an amazing job!

Author Bio:

Nicholle Caldwell is an Intuitive Healer, Psychic Medium, Spiritual Guide, and International Speaker. After having breastfeeding challenges and suffering with postpartum depression after the birth of her first child, she began her journey of self-healing and self-discovery, uncovering her natural talents, abilities, and life purpose. Through the journey and life-changing lessons of motherhood, she built a new relationship with herself and developed a connection with Spirit. She discovered her passion and purpose is to guide sensitive and empathic children and Mothers along their journeys to self-healing and to support the development and connection to their intuition.

Website: **www.momgelic.com**

The Intentional Mom
by Nikki Van Strien

**"When you get right down to it,
intentional living is about living your best story."**

— John C. Maxwell, *Intentional Living: Choosing a Life That Matters*

When I became a mom, I completely lost who I was. I left my job as a teacher to be a stay-at-home mom. I didn't want to miss out on any part of my children's life. But I had no idea how taking care of someone else for 24 hours a day could suck the life right out of you. The first few weeks home with the baby were so exciting. Everyone wanted to visit and meet him; there were cards and gifts, phone calls and messages with best wishes. Everyone shared their wonderful advice on all things baby. Eventually that special treatment tapered off, my husband went back to work, and reality set in.

Life with a six-week-old is not pretty or desirable. There were a lot of tears (from me). I felt so incredibly alone. Life was a huge repeat of changing diapers, nursing and laundry, with not much sleep in between. My husband had to travel for work and those weeks were the absolute worst. There were days we couldn't even make it to the mailbox, let alone actually leaving the house. I was a wreck.

Day by day, things got a little better. It felt like a deep spiral that slowly unwound for that first year until I was back on solid ground. When I got back to the surface, I felt like a different person. I felt so much stronger. My mantra for a long time was "I made it through the first year, I can do anything." My priorities were different afterwards. I cared a lot more about other people and especially other moms. I cherished those new mom friendships like a sisterhood. But my baby always came first; there's a fierce, loyal bond between a mother and her firstborn. A symbiotic relationship; you created them and they created you.

Becoming a mother is a beautiful process when you can relax and accept the change. I'm still working on figuring out who I am again. I am now living life with intentions. Not just drifting or letting other things dictate my direction. I keep a journal and find time to be alone with my thoughts for a few minutes a day. I choose to be blessed by my children instead of annoyed by them. I focus on the lessons they teach me: patience, strength, compromise, following through. They simplify everything and make life so clear.

I create my own measure of success now. They are things like, Did I laugh with my kids today? Did we do something nice for someone today? Did we thank God for our blessings? Did I listen to my husband? Did I smile at people out in public? Do my kids know I love them unconditionally?

If you can wake up each day and be intentional with your thoughts and your words, you can find the joy in the journey of motherhood. Make your daily mantra things like "I'm going to be positive; I am a good mother; my family is a team and we work well together." Write it on the bathroom mirror, stick notes up on the wall. Our thoughts become our words, which become our reality. Be intentional to be true to yourself. After all, what would you teach your kids to do?

Author Bio:
Nikki Van Strien is a work-from-home mother of two. She is passionate about helping other moms get their happy back by creating a positive community of work-from-home moms.

Website: **www.bizmomsblog.wordpress.com**

Motherhood Is Bliss
by Ruchika Rastogi

My child was born. And seriously, I had forgotten all my pain, my depression, and even my stitches—about which I was complaining about a few seconds ago. Suddenly, my whole world was in front of me. I just wanted to have a glimpse of my baby, my sweetheart—only for some moments at least, as I was still not completely conscious at that time. My half-closed eyes couldn't stop me from trying to lift my body so as to lift my visible, smiling part who had then become a separate being altogether. Miraculous it was, indeed!

Wow! Salute the sense of motherhood. It's special. It really is. I swear.

I sensed the girl in me had taken a back seat and the motherly, emotional, but strong lady wanted to peep out.

Just after returning home from the hospital, I managed to take care of his diapers, his feed, his emotions, his sleeping time, his potty time, his pain, and everything. Few days back, I wasn't able to take care of myself, was dependent on everybody for my needs, and just after his birth, as if some magic had happened, I became capable of taking his care along with myself.

The process of cultivation of dreams had started. How to raise him? How to stand by him? And most importantly, how to instill moral values in him?

Being a teacher, I had always aspired for both my children to have good moral values along with strength and confidence to face any adverse situation.

In modern society, where everybody is progressing—be it in the field of technology, education, behavior towards girls or the cultural beliefs or virtues of people, one thing that's not progressing at the same pace is VALUES.

Sometimes, we become so engrossed in making our child successful that the value part is ignored and thus lead to the ignorance of our whole being, which is not even realized by us.

Therefore, it's very essential to instill the moral values in the child from the very beginning.

Values like respecting elders and women, helping others, sharing things with others, caring for other family members are the building blocks for a successful family as well as for the success of an individual.

I would like to quote a few lines from my own novel—A Mystical Majesty-the woman: "Most underrated yet overly said word today is Values"

Everybody knows, yet everybody ignores Values. Mother teaches but the kids forget: Values

The school preaches, still not followed—Values.

Values symbolize the culture, the background, and the character of an individual, the society, and the country as a whole.

Honesty, trust, friendship, sharing and truth are the values, that are imbibed from childhood, and shamefully, the followers are too few to be seen by naked eyes.

It would be overwhelming, if, we, as individuals, should respect the dignity of these values, thus laying the foundation for a better tomorrow, and yes, a respectful tomorrow.

So, according to me, the values aren't the medicines that can be taken directly with water. They are either taught or learnt. Learnt, not only in the class but also from the surroundings, i.e., from school, home, other children, but value-givers are the parents, always. Thus, again, to become a good role model for children should be our priority and necessity, simultaneously. Indeed!

Phew! So much I have learnt yet so early. Thanks to my kiddos. They have made me what I am today. And definitely, I'll try my best to guide them, to facilitate them, to motivate them at every step as I can cover.

Author Bio:
Ruchika Rastogi is a Post Graduate in English along with B.Ed. Currently, she is working as a teacher in a reputed school in Delhi. She loves to travel and experiment with new things in life. Writing has been her passion for a long time. It has given her strength and shown her the illuminating path whenever she got stuck in any darkness. Her romantic endeavor with writing got somewhat fulfilled when her first book got published—*A Mystical Majesty, the woman*.

Facebook Page: **www.bit.ly/2jW7bYH**

Once You Become a Mother
by Kelli Matonak

Before I became a mom, I had it all figured out. The manners my kids would have, the veggies they would eat, the chores they would complete. It would be freakin' fabulous. The most fabulous part would be what great listeners they would be. Bounding into action on my first polite request. When you are a good mom, you have good kids. It's that simple. I would bake pies (I don't even like pie), exercise every day, have a tidy home, and have endless patience once I became a mom. Little did I know, I would soon be converted into a greasy-haired, chicken-nugget feeding, coffee-toting scream monster.

My story is simple, and still there is nothing about motherhood that has turned out as I painted it. There is just so much that no one tells you. The anxiety, the swelling, the first post-partum poop. Who could forget those weird but awesome giant net underwear and super bleed pads? Even though no one has asked me to sign it yet, I am convinced there is some kind of gag order that comes around requiring new mother signatures. They certainly don't tell you that in one moment you can experience pure joy, fear and dread, especially in the early evening facing another long and colicky night. No one ever told me how desperately I would need a break but how fearful and anxious I would become the minute I got one. But I'm getting ahead of myself.

My family and the mothers before me never warned me about the transition between woman and mom. They didn't tell me that once you become a mother, you die and are reborn in the very same body. They left out that giant part that confesses that the old you will be shattered, and although physically recognizable, once you become a mother, nothing about your life would ever be the same.

It should have become clear the moment my baby girl was handed over to me. All slimy with a perturbed look on her face. This sounds ridiculous, but I had a feeling of overwhelming shock that she was a real, live baby. Doctor visits show you ultrasounds, and you hear the heartbeats. You feel the kicks from restless feet, punches of wild outstretched arms. All of these glaring neon signs paled in comparison to that first demanding moment of eye contact. She was real, and that one look from her said it all. Her dark eyes and concentrated stare, in that moment she was telling me that I was her mama. She was telling me that I was going to have to pull my shit together and get the job done...forever. Her eyes said it all. In that moment, I already loved her beyond my known ability, and on the spot I was willing to die for her. She owned me, and she knew it.

No one tells you that this tiny human will break you a million times before their 10th birthday and that you will love them fiercely anyway. They don't tell you that it never really gets easier, just different. I became a mother 10 years ago, and added another daughter 4 years ago. I lost a pregnancy in between. Throughout this decade so many things have changed, but my role has remained the same. Tired yet hopeful, and somehow when I need it most, the energy comes. Some days I think I'm doing a good job. Others I feel I'm failing miserably. Always, I want to do better. You will never be satisfied, because the job is never done. You tackle one problem, you get a new one. Once you become a mother, you never get comfortable.

In these 10 years, I've been a working mom, a stay-at-home mom, and am now a work-from-home mom. They are all incredibly hard for different reasons. As a working mom, your heart aches for time with your kids. You know you are missing out on all the little big moments. You never feel like you are giving anything 100%. As a stay-at-home mom your wallet aches along with missed opportunities money can provide for your kids. You endure loneliness (even though you are never alone), repetitiveness, over-exhausted patience with very little intellectual stimulation. And you lose yourself a bit. Still, you never feel like you are giving anything 100%. As a working-from-home mom, starting a new business, everything friggin' aches. Never, have I ever, felt like I am giving anything 100%.

My daily struggle is mainly holding on to my sanity. Homework, sports, girl scouts, church, chorus, dance. The tasks are endless. I am not an overachiever, I promise you. In our culture, this is the norm. Our family is far from perfect, and I refuse to hide the mess that we are. I want our home to be our sanctuary. Their safe place where no discussion is off the table and no dream should go unshared. That includes them telling me that I'm annoying them. That life is unfair. That someone broke their heart. That school is hard. They should always show me all of their flaws, because I will always love them unconditionally, and help them with a vengeance. We cope. I hold on to the friendships of my fellow moms for dear life. There is no way I could do this without them. Whether the days are amazing or suffocating, I always count my blessings. There is always something to be grateful for. My kids are healthy, happy, and safe.

Always: gratitude, coffee, and wine.

My husband has been the provider for our family for almost 6 years. He keeps terrible hours and comes home with buckets of stress. Without family nearby, we depend solely on each other. Sometimes we bark at each other but are quick to forgive, and do our best. He is my best friend, and I'm happier each time he walks through the door. Unless he comes home and complains that I left the vacuum out. Then I want to punch him in the throat. Still, I go to bed every night grateful to have him. We actually are living our dream. This is the life we dreamed up 16 years ago, when we ourselves were just babies.

This growing-up business is hard. I'm reminded of the speed of time by growing feet and falling teeth. I don't long for the days of infancy, but want time to slow down. The cracks in their childhood cocoon get bigger as they become more aware of what this big, scary, amazing world has to offer and inflict. I find myself constantly balancing between being completely honest with them and withholding what I think they are not ready for. They don't want to know the world for what it is. And frankly I don't want them to, either. In certain cases, ignorance is bliss. Mean girls, boyfriends, hormones, illness, death, sex, sexual predators, STDs, social media bullying, suicide, drugs, and alcohol.

It all sounds great, doesn't it? Ha! Yeah, like a terrific advertisement for birth control. If I knew then what I know now, would I do it all again? Yes. Hell yes. A hundred times, yes. Because even with all the uncertainty and heartache, my life is joy. My home is a place of laughter. There is hilarity in fart parties at the dinner table and slipped bad words from a toddler's lips. There is peace at TV cuddle time every night and beauty in living-room performances of Dancing with the Stars. There is so much joy in being a mother.

What is easy? Loving them. Loving them is easy. Laughing. Dear God, I had no idea I would laugh this much. Being their cheerleader and encouraging them is so darn easy. Admiring the ridiculous sense of humor they get from their dad. Viewing the world from their eyes. Witnessing their new experiences and traveling with them to new places. All easy, so very easy.

So often I think of other mothers. I envision mothers with similar circumstances, and the parallel lives we live. I know without uncertainty there are millions of moms just like me, doing their best with what they have. Though I am far from wealthy, I think of the mothers who do this gig completely on their own, paying the bills, sending their kiddos off to day care or with a neighbor after school, scraping every penny and depending on the state to close the gaps a little. I pray for mothers who struggle to provide their kids with the most basic sustenance like clean water, food, and medicine. Mothers who fear the very real possibility of violence and leaving behind children to raise themselves on the dirt streets should something happen to them. Mothers who cross borders desperately searching for some chance of safety. My heart breaks for them. And the mothers of sick children. Who pray for clean scans, organ donation, a new treatment, pain medicine that works. A certain hell I am blessed to know nothing about. I am blessed to be an American. Blessed with the opportunity to go into debt to provide for my kids. Blessed beyond words.

No matter what the circumstances are, being a mother means you never get to give up. With each new challenge you have to get it together and figure it out. You don't get to give up because it's too hard. It's the hardest thing you've ever done because it's the most important thing you have ever done. Once you become a mother, it can never be undone. You can walk away, but you are still a mother with a child that desperately needs you. If you lose your child, you are still a mother with a child in heaven. It's not always easy, but it's always worth it. Once you become a mother...

Author Bio:
Residing in south Florida, Kelli is an entertainment blogger and self-proclaimed laughter addict. She enjoys sorting Barbie shoes, perfecting her British accent, and snuggling with her police officer husband watching *The Walking Dead*. Her two daughters, ages 10 & 5, keep her on her toes and provide hours' worth of entertainment and rejected meals. Kelli also spends her time devouring books, climbing mountains of laundry, exploring Pinterest wins and fails, and finding ways to make her family's life on earth more delightful.

Website: **www.crazyeverafter.com**

Dear New Mother
by Meela Meadows

Dear New Mother,

Welcome to a very special clan. With open arms I welcome you to a tribe that will both confuse and empower you. Motherhood is a difficult journey, and there will be many ups and downs that will test you, and may even consume you. Take comfort in knowing that somewhere out there, in this massive worldwide community, there are mothers that are going through the same joys and sorrows.

You will never be alone in this journey, because we are all here, every mother that has ever been and ever will be.

We are blessed to have a part of ourselves walking outside of our bodies. We get to see this being become something greater than ourselves. Some of us will always seem to be better at it than others, but it is important to remember it is only an illusion. Every mother will struggle. Every mother will cry and scream and worry over every little detail. We will all give more of ourselves than we should, and we will all find comfort in that familiar exhaustion as we search for a few minutes of "me" time.

When you become a mother, you give up everything of yourself, whether you realize it or not. Having a human within is a difficult and painful job. You must not let others dictate to you the mother you should be. You'll know. I promise you will know what kind of mother you are once you meet that baby for the first time.

At that moment, that single, most joyous moment, the world around you will cease to be a bother, because you hold the world in your hands. You nurse the world, you raise the world, and you love the world, that tiny everything that consumes your every waking moment. You may find this to be the most difficult part. After all, you've never had to be responsible for another human's welfare. This will lead to doubt and questions you may not have answers to. You may reach out to others who won't understand, and you may feel more alone than ever.

Do not despair, dear mother. We have all felt this. Every one of us will have a moment where we feel we can't go on, but you will find that you are stronger than you ever thought you could be. You are more powerful than you could ever imagine. You are cultivating a beautiful soul, and you are blessed to see them blossom. Never doubt that you are capable. Never blame yourself for not being perfect.

Perfect is useless. Life is messy; you should embrace it as the joyous journey it was meant to be.

You will be tired every day, but you will be more fulfilled than you have ever been. You will go to bed exhausted, and wake up ready to do it again. Those gorgeous new eyes looking at the world will harbor a perspective that can't be taught anywhere else. Children look at life with innocence, and it is our job to teach them how to exist in a world that won't always be kind and gentle. We teach them through our perseverance, through our actions, and the way that we cope with our own emotions and needs.

Motherhood is beautiful chaos that you couldn't imagine being without. It's uncontrollable, it's unpredictable, and it will be more than you think you can handle. But as the years go on, as the diapers pile up, the bottles get washed, and as the sleepless nights begin to get better, you will see, dearest mother, you CAN do this.

Trust in your instincts. You have them. Trust in your heart, because it is walking outside of your body now. And it doesn't matter if you gave birth to that baby, or if you adopted them into your life, that is still a part of your heart walking around, seeing the world for the very first time. Teach them to love, to accept, and to be better than yourself. Teach them to never stop exploring, never stop asking questions, and never hate. Teach them to love themselves inside and out. Teach them to reach out, and share their compassion with others like you do for them every day. They will learn this just by watching you proudly wear the mantle of motherhood.

Embrace this new identity, dear mother, because it is one that is full of honor and beauty, and there is always beauty in the mess of motherhood. Love those chaotic days, and never stop believing that you are a great mom. Every day will not be perfect. That's OK. You'll get through it. You are an amazing woman. Never let anyone tell you otherwise.

With much love, admiration, and support, **The Mothers of the World.**

Parenting: Baking the World a Better Place
by Ruchi Kalra

Sharing my experience on parenting and a reminder that these big kids that we have now were also tiny little angels just a few years ago.

As I sit down with my cup of chai this morning, the usual rituals of hurry up, get your jacket, the bus will be here any minute, did you brush your teeth, did you pick your jammies off the floor, finish your milk, put the plate in the sink, eat your vitamins PLEASE, hurry up the bus is nearly here... my hubby gives me the look of, Are you possessed, babe? and mind you, this is a daily look! That gets me to start thinking of the big picture, but before I can think of the big picture I have to go backwards and realize I need a few more snaps of the past to carry me forward!

I have to be honest and say the first time I found out I was pregnant I was not only scared but not sure I even wanted to be there. But after a few weeks, when I thought I was going to lose the baby, I realized I wanted it more than anything in the world. The first time I felt that flutter, and the kick, was a feeling that I still miss, one of my sweetest, most exciting memories. I walked around every day feeling so special to be carrying this magical thing inside of me. I felt like a baker hoping my creation would turn out just right as long as I didn't open the oven in the middle.

After many trips to the ER with pre-term labor, I was able to keep the baking going 39 weeks. Out came this tiny yet amazing being, and I was so in awe with what we had baked together!

Needless to say, the first few weeks were the hardest I've have had to endure. They sleep so little, they poop so much, they cry incessantly, the projectile explosions... from both ends. Did everyone forget to mention this small minute minuscule detail to us? If they had mentioned these little facts maybe I would have slept a little more (even though a rib was piercing my stomach), gone out to eat a little more and maybe, just maybe, I might have been a little better prepared. But then again is anyone really ready for the most daunting, challenging, but perhaps most rewarding task ever? This little thing was amazing but a lot of hard work, looked deceptively peaceful but generated so much chaos. Chaos that I now look back at with such fondness and such familiarity. I have to admit at one point as I mistakenly walked into a wall in the middle of the night feeling like a zombie from the Night of The Living Dead, I was ready to take this precious little bundle back to the hospital and say this was not my kid. She is fair and has eyes bluer than the Caribbean ocean waters. There must be some sort of mix-up, and they gave me the wrong cake... oops, I mean baby! I am Indian, for God's sake! We have brown or black eyes, where did these come from? But she was short and she was hairy, so we convinced ourselves she was our little muffin.

Six weeks later her first beautiful smile made it all worthwhile. Every week after that was a sense of growing enjoyment and pleasure like no other: the first words, the first laugh, the first steps, the first hugs, the first tears. There were so many firsts, and still continue so... For many years after that, every time someone said, "Guess what... I'm pregnant," I heaved a sigh of relief and thought, thank God it's not me.

But then we decided to bake another cake... crazy, I know. It's amazing how our brains are wired. If we were not wired this way, most parents would be one and done. But here we were willing to go down the road again... and we ended up with a blue-eyed baby boy! But this time there was no questioning, as we knew this little bundle of joy was ours! By this time now we knew the drill of eating, sleeping, crying, pooping, throwing up. We had become smarter and faster in our knee-jerk movements on how to dodge incoming objects such as projectile vomiting during diaper change times—sorry, a little graphic, but when you are a parent of a newbie, your world becomes topsy-turvy and no topics are off limits... even with strangers.

The big change this time around was watching our older child react and adjust to the colossal shift in her world. It was beautiful to watch her discover this feeling of joy for the little one and to see the love in her eyes every time she looked, held, or kissed her little brother—priceless.

Now I realize after nearly 18 years since the first baking process started that the baking didn't stop there. It is an ongoing continuous process of decorating and icing, and I am realizing that this process may soon be coming to an end and my cakes are going to have to be ready for the presentation at the bakery.

I feel that if we raise two individuals that maybe are not the most talented or the smartest and don't go to the best Ivy League schools but are kind, nice, caring, and respectful human beings, I have succeeded as a parent—we have succeeded as parents. I feel in this world today, yes, it's important to be yourself since it is so easy to lose oneself, but at the same time is it just as important to be a good person. My hope is for them to be self-confident and know that they are capable of doing anything, and I mean anything. They just need to believe in themselves and their capabilities. I want them to find their passion in life and follow it. If there is passion, everything else will fall into place. Their passion is what is going to carry them through the tough times when they think they just can't go on anymore. There is a calling for everyone, and we need to help find that calling!

As a parent we hope and pray that we are steering our kids in the right direction by giving them a good set of values and beliefs. They are in our kitchen and it is up to us how we want to decorate them without compromising their true flavor in the process. We have to make sure our decorating complements each individual cake, as every cake is different. If every cake looked and tasted the same, life would be so boring—well, life would be a little boring.

Every parent does the best they can do with the information that they are given at that very moment. Some kids do grow up and blame their parents for what they did and did not do—how one sibling is loved more than the other. But is that truly possible? Is it? If one had to choose which leg they liked better, would they be able to choose? We need both our legs to walk; they are both just as precious. Sometimes as adults we forget what our parents must have gone through to bring us up.

The sleepless nights, the throwing up, the tantrums, worried sick nights with sick kids—every parent has done their due diligence, so why does one assume that we are doing such a better job with our kids than our parents did? The parenting style has changed over the years and that's just a part of progression of the culture. We try to be friends to our kids whereas our parents were too busy trying to achieve a better lifestyle for their kids.

I am who I am today because of my special parents. We don't and haven't always seen eye to eye. But then they are parents and I know they want the best for me. They have sacrificed a lot in life to make me what I am today. They have given me everything in life I have ever wanted and needed. They have been my friends to the extent that they knew how. And over time I have come to realize that everything that I used to fight with them about growing up, they were right in their decisions.

I left home at a young age for a better education, and sometimes I wish my parents had been selfish and kept me with them for a while longer and not sent me to the US. As they get older, I think of the inevitable... and my heart breaks and wonders what the solution is. They are thousands of miles away... Is there a viable solution when something happens? And if so, what is it? I truly love them and cherish them with every shred of my heart!

I feel if I am half the parent to my kids that my mom and dad were to me, I will be the Head Chef in the best bakery in town!

Hmm... a slice of cake sounds good right about now.

Author Bio:
I was born in India, brought up in Africa, and have lived in the US for over 30 years. I am a spicy blend of Indian, African, and American culture. I have done a lot of schooling—graduated in Math/Computer Science, an MBA in Marketing, 3/4 of a MS in Information systems (Crazy, I know). I have been married to my best friend & soul mate who is the love of my life for over 20 years and cannot imagine a day or moment without him. I have two amazing kids aged 17 and 14 that make my life a wonderful experience and teach me something new each and every day. I have a passion for so many things: cooking, baking, crafts, interior decorating, traveling, photography. I am what I am today because of my parents. My parents and my hubby are my rock—they keep me grounded to this confusing yet amazing world.

I am More Than, "Just a Mom"

Witnessing Our Lives
by Aditi Wardhan Singh

Our five-year-old son dreads that trip to the train station and those words, "Dad has to go to New York to work. " His two-year-old sister replies consistently with "Where's daddy?" and wakes up more often those nights. To children who don't understand the concept of time, it is an extremely long four days.

I fear that upcoming but necessary week too. I have to pick up the strings that he usually holds up, most importantly my sanity!

In the beginning it is so much more difficult. Sure, I try to plan ahead and get the house cleaned, groceries bought, bills paid (by him), and deal with all my chores so I can concentrate on just being there and not worry about the trivial things. But it is still tough to juggle. They miss him so much. And get bored. I take them out more often and keep them busy. But the first few months, I forget myself. Simple things like wearing the right shoes or eating take a back seat to making sure the kids are appeased.

As always, I adapt, and things get much better. Meals are planned in advance and the kids accept begrudgingly that this is something that will happen every so often.

And then I notice a disconcerting thing. When he's gone, everything seems to be super organized. Outings and days preplanned. Toys are picked up as they are played with. Everything is cleaned as it gets dirty. Life is like clockwork. The routines get followed impeccably. When he's gone, even the kids also are more cooperative. When I mention their extra insubordination in his presence, he laughs and asks, "You want me to go away again?"

The day after he arrives, the house gets messier by the minute, the days are unpredictable. I am kind of getting too used to him being away. He likes things a certain way, and I too am getting used to my "too-organized" life. My frustration at having to constantly clean builds, and we bicker. Till I realize we are becoming two parts of a family, living parallel lives. In love but not in tandem.

I wondered for months about this difference. Till one day, my wandering mind has an epiphany. The house isn't clean because I let things go when he's around. I let things go because I would rather be watching them or living life with them. This realization leads me to think of other things that are different in a positive way when he's around.

- There are more toys lying around, because he and the kids play with toys I don't usually think of.
- When I'm too tired to deal with them, he takes the kids out.
- Any anger I feel subsides when he acts funny and says, "Cool it. You don't want to burst!"
- When I'm busy cleaning/organizing like crazy (I literally go into a frenzy), he reminds me to take a much-needed break.
- When I watch too much TV, he tells me to write/create instead.
- He loves me when I don't feel very lovable.
- When he's there, the kids are more sure that a No just might turn into a Yes (happens quite often when there's another perspective involved).
- He bears the brunt of half the kids' million "whys" and "hows" when he's there.
- All our outdoorsy adventures happen thanks to his interests.
- He ensures I have time to give to event-planning or hosting or choreographing or participating.
- We have tea time with a lot of conversation that's NOT about the kids (on purpose).
- He reminds me to eat on time, go on walks, shop for and pamper

myself.

- The house is so much more full of noise; most of it is actually laughter!!
-

In essence, he fulfills what I cannot. He is the yin to my yang of parenting and my own life. Our house becomes a home on the days when we are all together.

When I decided to be a stay-at-home mom, it was because I wanted to witness my children's milestones firsthand. I wanted to be the one to mold their formative years. For them to know that I am always there for them. It is what I wanted. It is what I did. Spending time with them makes me happy.

Of course, I never expected it to be the challenge it is. Being a stay-at-home mom is a job like any other that you learn each day. Without any extended support system, you are left scrambling to understand how to manage doing the simplest tasks while having kids vying for your attention. You are not just their first teacher, but their doctor, driver, entertainer, organizer, chef, personal shopper, etc. And these are not tasks that you are perfect at balancing automatically. Every single minute you prioritize. Teaching the kids the simplest tasks has you striving to find the best way to get them to do it.

Through all this, if you are lucky, there is one person who can provide relief to your endless day. That is your partner. They are the ones that support you in holding the kid, cleaning up the puke, taking turns waking up for feeds, and leading the charge when you run yourself tired or sick into the ground. They are the ones who help with thinking up new ideas when your own brain gives up in teaching the children something new.

Many a times this same person starts coming after kids, food, and house. Gentleman that he is, he understands that you have your hands full already, and so tries to share as many responsibilities as he possibly can. But let's face it. A father's brain works differently than a mother's. He will know when to take the kids to hospital. But he may not know which shoes the kids need in which weather. He will know the kids are cranky when they are hungry but he may not know that they will not touch a different kind of bread than they are used to eating. He will know what the kid needs to be doing but may not know the easiest way to get them to do it.

This is the inherent reason why kids tend to scream, "Mama!!" when they need something. And oftentimes, slowly but surely we start feeling that we are doing more than they are. And this is the reason why the "I do more…" battles start slowly. Unknowingly you start taking each other for granted.

Two of you in unchartered territory, caring for lives that are more precious to each of you than your own is one of the hardest thing any relationship undergoes. A couple learn a lot about each other after marriage, but having a child and bringing it up on little-to-no sleep shows both of you sides of each other that are not pleasant, to say the least.

But your love for each other is what your children witness daily. The fact that your partner is making sure you are cared for in sickness, pampering you when you need it, respecting your opinion, and putting up with your bad days is essential to their well-rounded upbringing. Being together is one of the cornerstones that make for great parenting. Those actions that you do for/with each other are what children use as a compass to guide themselves through relationships they come across in their lives. Healthy arguments teach them to respect the opposite sex and to know the value of their own self-worth. Simple acts of affection tell them that they are surrounded by love. Most importantly, they learn that it is okay to be themselves with people who care about them. In fact, someone who truly loves them will celebrate everything they are.

My spouse is not only the witness to the trials I go through in raising my children, he is the one reminding to not lose myself while doing it. He is not just my other half or better half, he helps me find parts of myself even I didn't know needed to exist.

Author Bio:
Aditi Wardhan Singh works from home as a mom of two and writes for many blogs, like Huffington Post, Thrive Global, Richmond Moms Blog, etc. She is also the founder of the web magazine Raising World Children, which aims to help families achieve a broad worldview and thus find that perfect balance of modern thinking, culture, and heritage. Her passions include organizing, dance recitals,and event-planning.

Website: **www.aditi.ws/SilverLinings**

I Am Mom, Hear Me Roar!
by Megan Heit

Sometimes, in the very early morning, I find myself awake before anyone else. In this peacefulness, I daydream about starting my day slowly with some gentle yoga stretches, and sipping my hot tea by the bay window. Ahhhh, relaxation. Sometime during this fantasy I drift back into sleep again. Twenty minutes later I am awoken by the sounds of 2 blood-curdling screams from my children wanting out of their cribs, and my alarm clock blaring. In a panic, I quickly roll out of bed, noticing I'm late. I step on a diaper that must've been left there during one of my son's 4 a.m. feedings. This is when reality hits me.

BEEP BEEP BEEP. My alarm clock continues to go off as I run from room to room corralling kids like a circus act. My two-year-old daughter is convinced that 32 degrees is not too cold to wear her princess dress, and my son wants to nurse one last time before we leave. As I'm buckling in car seats and kissing my husband goodbye, I get in my car and realize I haven't even looked in the mirror yet this morning. I glance in the rearview and notice I have mascara smeared down my cheek from yesterday, and I can't help but laugh. My daughter says "you're booty-full, mommy" from the backseat and a tear rolls down my cheek. It is now that I remember to breathe.

This is my life now, but it wasn't always like this. Just a few years ago, I was 21 years old and living on the beach. I was soaking up the sun by day and bartending at night. I was living the ultimate carefree life. I moved back home to Pennsylvania for winter break with plans to move back that summer. But you know what they say, "If you want to make God laugh, tell him your plans." Those next few months swept me up like a rip current as I fell in love, got married, and found out I was pregnant. Before I could blink, my life was completely changed, and I admit, I felt lost. And scared. And probably every emotion a person could ever feel. But as the winter faded, so did my fear. I felt a connection to this little life inside me, and felt wonder for the first time. I was really going to be a mommy!

On March 4th (the only day of the year that is also a command) I gave birth to my daughter, Dandelion Rain. She was the most beautiful thing I'd ever seen, my little wildflower. I held her hand, kissed her head, and breathed her into me. It was like I'd known her forever. An inner fierceness flowed through me. I had become a lioness ready to roar at anything that would try to come between me and my baby. On that day, two people were born: a daughter and her mother.

The next 8 months flew by. When the initial excitement passed and visitors slowed down, we found ourselves alone together while everybody was at work, trying to figure it all out. It was during these quiet moments we learned the most about each other. As she reached every milestone, my heart grew heavier. My baby was growing up, and there was nothing I could do to slow her down. Then I found out I was pregnant... again. I collapsed to my knees. This can't be right, I'm not ready! She's still a baby!

Could I handle another one? Could I possibly love another child this much? I wept at the loss of our alone time ending and a new dynamic starting. I wept because I was terrified. I wept because I was exhausted. And eventually, as time passed, I wept because I couldn't wait to meet my baby boy.

Nine months later (ten, if you want to be honest!), our little Sonny Bunny was born! Blonde hair, blue eyes, and the biggest grin I ever saw. His name fit him perfectly: he was a beam of light that shone on every dark thing left in my life. Now time went even faster. I felt like a little girl swept up into a tornado as I watched the months, years, just fly by me like seconds on a clock. Hikes through the woods, movie nights, and tickle fights. We bonded, and became a family. All 7 of us.

Before I confuse you, let me back up a little. When I met George, I found out he had children from previous relationships. And when I married him, I vowed to love them as my own. Initially, I was scared. I never babysat, I was an only child, I knew nothing about kids! But I loved him so much, and I understood they were a part of him that I would learn to love, too. As time went on, and our bond grew, so did my love for them. As a co-parent, it's hard. I mean really hard. I never know if I'm doing the right thing or if I'm stepping on anyone's toes. But, at the end of the day, I consider them my kids and I will fight for them and love them unconditionally.

At the peak of my loneliness as a stay-at-home mom, I stumbled into a job counseling pregnant and breastfeeding women. It felt like a sign from God. It's hard to leave my babies every day, but I'm grateful for the chance to support other women on their journey. And it has come to be my newest passion in life! I've laughed with these women when they realized their shirt was on backwards, I've cried with them when they realized how alone they feel. I'm not sure which is harder, being a stay-at-home mom or a working mom. But regardless of our specific struggles, we are part of the "secret club" known as motherhood. Our journeys are different, but our destination is the same.

If you were to ask my family or friends, they'd tell you I'm an amazing mom. But sometimes I don't feel like it. I cave in and give my son a lollipop when he throws a fit in the store. I barricade myself in my room while all the kids run and scream circles throughout the house. I have felt touched out, exhausted, and ready to quit. But sometimes, in between the craziness, a miraculous thing will happen. My son will waddle as fast as he can down the hall and wrap his arms around me as tight as he can. He'll pull away and wrap his toothy grin around my chin, his way of giving me a kiss. Flashes of moments that brought me here flood my brain: wrinkly toes, curly hair, little squeals of excitement, and the word "momma" said over and over and over again. This Christmas, my stepdaughter told me for the first time she always knew I was the one for her dad, and is proud to have me in her life. It's because of these moments that make every other unbearable moment a little more bearable.

But motherhood is not just the big parts. It is mostly the in between moments, the everydayness, that define us. We brush teeth, make beds, and play dinosaurs, even when we don't feel like it. These are the things we don't give ourselves enough credit for. And when I'm feeling lost, I collapse in the arms of my own mother, still ready to take on the world for her own baby. And her mother holds her. Holding their once small babies. I realize that being a good mother isn't a destination that we eventually get to, but a journey that reveals what we are all here for, what connects us all: *love*.

Sometimes, late at night I sit in my toy-covered living room and wonder how I got here. I look out the window and imagine running far, far away. I eventually drift off to sleep and dream that I am a free woman. I dream that I am lying on a beach somewhere all by myself, with no kids. It is then that I wake up to the sound of my son crying. It's 4 a.m., and he's ready to nurse. A sigh of relief... it was only a dream.

Author Bio:
Megan Heit is from small town Pennsylvania where she and her husband George are raising their family. She is a breastfeeding peer counselor. She is also taking online classes at the Southwest institute of Healing Arts in Tempe, Arizona, pursuing her dream in holistic wellness. In her free time, she loves reading, gardening, and upcycling. But, most importantly, spending time with family. She and her husband love to learn about sustainable living, and plan to turn their love of nature into a business in natural healing.

D Is for Disruptor: The Evolution and Revolution of Motherhood
by Cheri L. Philip

Words cannot begin to describe the awesome and sacred role that is Mother. The truth is that most of us have no idea what kind of mother we will be and the drastic transformation that occurs between being a pregnant woman and then... a Mother.

Your life is forever changed and you will never be who you were before you brought this other person into the world.

But that is the true alchemy and wonder of it all—that transformation from simply being an individual, to an individual who begins to literally grow new life inside her body, to an individual who is then able to completely support that life with her own body for many months after giving birth to that new life. Each mother is reborn herself when she gives birth. In the process of giving birth, she will sacrifice her own life for that of her child. It is sobering to think that each time a woman gives birth, she risks death. We don't often think of it this way, but the ultimate gift that only a [human] woman can give is life.

Motherhood has shifted tremendously in the last 10 years. Concepts of tradition and modernism have been melded in ways we never thought possible, but what does it mean to be a mother when there is access to so much more... of everything?

The 21st-century mother can occupy anywhere between 10 and 100+ roles in a given day. I have been asked whether I miss my 9–5 job as a social scientist and my time in academic research. In the early days and weeks after my son was born, I would have said "Yes, terribly." Now, I cannot imagine my life at any kind of 9–5.

From Professional to "MAMA"

What changed? Everything. This tiny human transformed my whole way of thinking and living. I instantly went from a professional and the title of "Dr." when fielding inquiries from the public and government officials to "Mama." And it has remained this way for the past 7+ years.

I have gone from research psychologist, to mother, to fulltime homeschooling educator, to educational entrepreneur (along with an incredibly brilliant spouse and partner) in the blink of an eye. Though it has been a roller coaster ride at times, I could not imagine my life without the two men who mean the most to me, my son and his father. They are twin souls, really, and I literally cannot see one without seeing the other. We are truly an interdependent team, and I am amazed when I consider how much we have grown together over these 7+ years. It has not been easy, but the daily moments of pure joy cannot be quantified in words or numbers.

"So, when are you going back to work full time?" "You can't possibly waste all those years of school, a Ph. D. from one of the top universities in the country, to just babysit?" Yes, I was repeatedly asked this question (with slight variation) in that first year of motherhood. Couldn't I? Waste all those years? Would it be a waste of a few degrees and most of my life to not be a professional researcher, scholar, and professor? The answer to all of these questions is a resounding "No."

On the contrary, it would be a waste to not take a pause, to consider what kind of contribution I would make if I did not devote myself fully to a job that just may be the most important role I will ever hold. If we are really honest with ourselves about this singularly most important job (mother) we will ever perform in our lives, does that not require that we rethink everything we thought we knew?

When I entered graduate school at the University of Michigan, it was stressed to us "first years" that we must "give up" the luxury of time to fully devote ourselves to one of the most rigorous training periods of our lives. The only way to make groundbreaking discoveries and better understand the human condition was to immerse one's self in the process. So why should my approach to successfully executing the role of mother be any different than that of successfully executing the role of psychologist?

It turns out my approach was not different at all. I fully immersed myself in the role of mother the same as I did when training to earn my Ph.D. The beauty of my mothering journey is that I was able to employ my research skills at every stage (from breastfeeding tips to exploring the best tech and traditional learning tools) and in the process learned to become an educational disruptor. One who found a new way of approaching teaching (and learning) that has begun to uproot traditional methods that have gone unquestioned for decades. The result? I, along with my husband as the ideal partner, have raised a son who is: studying college chemistry and physics, has perfect pitch and a deep grasp of various musical genres, and reads various subject matter at the high school/college level. So, after having been invited to lecture at Duke University, we have demonstrated that early science mastery is possible.

My entire life was disrupted for the better when my son entered this world. And, because of my wholehearted embrace of this most worthwhile profession of Mother, the universe has opened.

Fast-forward from 2009 to 2016, and my family is boarding a plane to receive a private tour of the largest physics experiment in the world at CERN (The European Organization for Nuclear Research)-one that is exploring the very beginnings of our universe—in Geneva, Switzerland, by a seasoned physicist working on the ATLAS Experiment. With a flurry of interviews upon our return answering questions like

"How did you do it, and how can we do it?" we are poised to make a mark on the world of education that many thought impossible. And our 7-year-old has been named CERN's ATLAS Ambassador with the task of sharing the love of science and physics around the world. Disruptors, indeed.

Author Bio:
Cheri L. Philip, Ph. D. is a Mother, Wife, Social Scientist, Author, Entrepreneur, Homeschooling Parent, Apple-Certified Teacher, Educational Strategist, and Artist.

In addition to her book Asian-American Identities: Racial and Ethnic Identity Issues in the Twenty-First Century published in 2007, she has continued to break new ground along with her husband. As a small business, they have blazed a new trail in education. They were profiled by the Washington Post after their visit to CERN (The European Organization for Nuclear Research) in Geneva, Switzerland, where their 7-year-old son was named a CERN ATLAS Ambassador.

Website: **www.robesongroup.org**

What Do You Do All Day?
by Rebecca G Vijay

What do you do all day? Well, I am a Facilitator, Knowledge Giver, Mompreneur...

I am often asked by people (well-wishers and otherwise), "When do you plan to return to work?" and the favorite one—"What do you do all day?" Externally, I smile and say that I am taking a break, at least till my younger one joins school. Inwardly, I wonder why I should have to explain to them or justify my decision to work or not. Also, how or why it would make a difference to them either way.

About me:
Well, let me share a little about myself. I was born a mother when my premature twins were born in April 2009 and died a mother when my firstborn went back to his Maker on the third day. I raised a preemie survivor (who is now in primary) while working long hours with a lot of help from my family and am now raising a toddler, having quit a lucrative position with a leading publisher.

You might ask, why quit your job? Many mothers continue to work and raise their children well. They sure do, and do an awesome job of it. But each mother has a list of variables that decides her actions. Mine was to take a leap of faith and trust in the LORD that HE would provide for all our needs and sit back and watch my buds bloom.

My motherhood and work experiences:
To clear the semantics war and to list my motherhood experiences:
* I am NOT a housewife (nope, I checked! I am not married to a house).
* I have been a working mother who worked for 10-12 hours a day

and still brought work home.

- I have been a mother who sent her two-year-old to a playschool and in a few days ended up having to hospitalize the little one due to febrile convulsions.
- I have been a touring mother who has left behind a little one for many days with very little contact, as she could not communicate on the phone well.
- I have been a work-from-home mother who has tried to concentrate and produce results, while the little one is at his crankiest best and the constant rescheduling of deadlines would be driving me nuts.
- I have also been a stay-at-home mother who has taken care of the kids, the house, the cooking, the husband, and others (don't judge the order)...
- Currently, I am a friend, knowledge giver, confidence builder and booster, study explorer, homework specialist, crafts artiste, recreational buddy, television and movie controller, rule enforcer, tear drier, fight breaker, bather cum bubble maker, fellow wanderer, culinary taste introducer, baker of treats, mobile phone app decider, blank check/unlimited credit card, habit maker, and hold various other job responsibilities and important job portfolios in my children's eyes.
- Every mom's priority is her child: As you can see, in the fight of the mothers, I have been on almost all sides, so I understand the points of views of each side. I firmly believe that there are no right or wrong choices. Every mother's child is her priority and she considers the various aspects of her life and then takes the decision whether to work or not.
- The ones who choose to stay at home might work for more hours and not get a break and feel guilty about not earning, not being independent, not growing, not having adult company, and many other things that the brilliant human mind is capable of imagining.
- Those who go out to an office to work are also pretty liberal with injecting themselves with guilt doses and consider all the

moments and milestones that they would be missing and the constant worries about whether the caretakers are taking good care of their child.

- The ones working from home would be consuming doses of guilt amid taking care of the kids and trying to maintain a tight ship to produce quality work and submit them on time, while the well-wishers query about the house not being kept well despite her being at home all day!

I am a Facilitator:

I call myself a facilitator. I do not DO any thing for the child, but facilitate them to do it themselves. I do not write for them or draw for them or think for them. I am teaching them to handle their responsibilities and duties themselves without having to depend on anyone.

I would rather have an independent child who can think for themselves and take the correct decisions in life rather than one who is always looking up to the mother to know what to do or how to do it. How long can one finger-hold them? Children need to be able to spread their wings and fly. If they fall once or twice, wipe them up and send them back. The tears will dry, the wounds will heal, but the joy of doing something by themselves will never cease, and the confidence that comes from knowing that they can do that themselves will be worth the weight in gold.

I do not believe in rote learning. Unless one understands what one is trying to cram, one forgotten word might start an avalanche rolling and the child shuts down in panic. Once the child learns the concept and its application, the sequence would become intuitive and the words would be building blocks that they can fashion whichever way they like and build an amazing building. All it needs is a good foundation.

A knowledge giver:

I am a knowledge giver. I take them shopping and make them count; take them to movies and get them to tell colors & shapes and read the subtitles; take them visiting friends and have them spell out their friends' names; bake their favorite treats and ask them to help mix the batter or butter the mold or cut the cookies into various shapes; get them to help out with the washing by putting in or taking out clothes from the washing machine or helping to put them out to dry in the clothes stand; or wipe the spill with a cloth; and so on and so forth.

Learning is not limited to books; overall learning is what makes a child a creative thinker and problem solver.

Life as a mompreneur:

In the various stages of motherhood that I have been through, I like my current phase as a mompreneur a lot. I have published my first book about the loss of my son (My Angel in Heaven), have written the first draft of a YA novel, have my own website and blog, and am starting my creative services company.

I am occupied with the little "work" that I am doing, and at the same time I am at home to cater to the various requirements of charts and tests preparations and learning this and that. I am able to make learning fun for my little ones and can teach them in various situations. It does not have to be preachy or teachy. It does not have to be limited to a table and chair. The entire point of studying/learning is that the child understands the concept and is able to apply it in different settings.

Our little secret!

Let me let you in on our little secret. I just click pictures of the concepts that need to be learned or the worksheets on my phone and we are ready to learn. We have learnt in the car, in the park, in front of the television, in a movie hall; the setting is not important.

Memorizing spellings is a fun game anywhere, and once the kid learns *night*, they can obviously know *right, light, bright, might,* etc. Similar sounding words are all the more fun and you can keep adding to the complexity of the word. *And,* then *sand,* then *stand,* then *strand*— you get the picture, right?

Learning number concepts is all the more fun in outdoor settings: the number of cars going or the number of swings in the park or buckets of popcorn and glasses of cola that we have ordered (corny, but fun!) You can add them or subtract them or multiply them or use whatever concept needs to be focused on. You don't need to sit with books for that. Every moment can be a learning experience, and if applied practically, it will be embedded in the mind for a longer time than just trying to cram it. Every child just needs a guiding hand, a shoulder to lean on, and someone to cheer them on. Moms and dads are cheerleaders for their child and buck them up!

And yeah, back to the million-dollar question, so what is it that I do all day? I just facilitate and help the kids learn and shuffle knowledge learning building blocks together the whole day. And yeah, for the record, I don't "work"!

Author Bio:
Rebecca Vijay is an author, mommy blogger, freelance editor and designer, with two young children and an angel in heaven. In a career spanning a decade and a half, she has worked in various industries and was heading a commissioning team in OUP when she took a break to spend time with her kids and explore ways to make a difference. She is a NaNoWriMo 2016 winner and has brought out her first book – My Angel in Heaven (hyperurl.co/MyAngelinHeavenPB).

Website: **www.rebeccavijay.com**

I am an
Entrepreneur Mom"

From Welfare Mom to Entrepreneur
by Ana Garcia Grande

"Get yourself a good lawyer so you don't get sideswiped."

I laughed, thinking he was joking. He made it clear he was serious, and it was confirmed when he arrived at our home to pick up his belongings later that day.

As I watched him leave, I wondered what would become of me and my children now. I was 6 weeks pregnant and had a two-year-old girl to feed. It was in this moment that I felt the weakest I had ever imagined a human could feel. It is one thing to feel physically weak, but when your entire soul aches, that is incomparable.

How quickly things had changed. Together we had decided I stay home, so I left my career in the government in order to raise our daughter. It is important that in this society I stay true to my beliefs and ideologies—for me, not placing my children in daycare was one— and was lucky to have someone who supported my views. I told myself if my mother was able to do it alone while working from home in a third-world country, so would I in an advanced first-world one. I did, however, work at a grocery store every night until midnight; although it wasn't a desk job I was happy because it fit into my schedule and allowed me to spend the day raising my child. Most weekends, while my then partner would care for our child, I would work for a company that hosted princess and hero parties for kids. I had to do all this in order to keep some income coming from my end and still stay true to my heart as a mom. I was also taking some courses to open my own home daycare center and bring in more money while raising my children and saving for our dream home. And now there he was leaving with no real explanation, just a bunch of excuses.

I had been through worse in this lifetime. I am not one to stay down for long, and sure enough I bounced back almost immediately because I had a child watching me and I needed to stay strong. I am so thankful to live in Canada, as we have so many amazing resources and help for all kinds of people from different paths of life. I jumped online and did my research for help and found out about something called legal aid. I had never heard of it and was able to quickly sign up and secure myself a lawyer. My daughter and I were suffering a lot of emotional hardship, I needed to be healthy in all aspects for my unborn child and for my sweet little girl, and so I looked into financial aid for single moms, which I qualified for. The downfall was that it is a dollar-for-dollar system, which means any penny that comes to your pockets must be reported and is discounted from your financial aid check. The night shifts at the grocery store made no sense, and I quit. I went from an independent career woman to a stay-at-home mom to welfare mom—and as ashamed as I was, it was what I needed to do for my sanity, to be my best self and be present for my daughter. I had to put my ego aside and focus on what my children needed right now—they needed me.

Our rent was over a thousand dollars, and although the first one or two months the father paid half, it was of absolutely no help because of the dollar-for-dollar rule, therefore not only did I have to put all and the only $500 per month I was given, but I was basically in debt for every penny he put towards the rent. By the second month I was facing the hard reality that I would be evicted and indebted to the financial assistance office for over a thousand dollars.

With intense pain from my high-risk pregnancy and tears running down my cheeks, I immediately sprung into action and started packing. I simply had no time to waste. I was going to see where I would leave or donate our things to, and with no place to stay, I would have to go to a shelter. It was a scary time for me; I couldn't bear the thought of my daughter in a shelter, so I asked around who would rent me a room for the little amount of money I had. A godsend friend from childhood offered we stay with her mom, as she lived alone. So we rented a bedroom there until we could figure things out.

The wait list for housing is about 5 years, but as always I was not going to just sit there. I contacted as many resources as I could that could help us advance the process. I wanted to secure a home before my baby was born. Sure enough, 2 months before he was born, I received a call not for one but TWO homes to look at, so not only were my wishes coming true, my hard work in advocating for ourselves paying off, but I also had CHOICES. My daughter and I settled into our small 3-bedroom home and welcomed a little miracle boy shortly after.

Although many hospital visits came for both baby and I, we survived and all were happy and healthy. My daughter was thriving and I had never felt this alive and free before.

Life brought many obstacles along the way after the birth, and I am ever so thankful for each one, as they all left me with many lessons and made me so much stronger. And I did not let anything stop me from my main goal, which was to get out of financial assistance and be my own boss.

Fast-forward five years later, my kids are happy, I myself have healed, I am no longer on financial assistance, and have an online business in health and wellness through which I get to empower other women through their individual journey as well as mentor them in starting their very own home-based business.

I am a true believer that when you truly want something, you go for it and you WILL get it; when you really believe it will be better it surely will be, there simply is no other option but to move forward and be your own hero.

You must believe in your own capabilities; all that you need lies within you, you must simply ignite it.

Author Bio:
Ana Garcia Grande is a mother of two, blogger of "A life of fairy dust and sweat," a place where she shares her experiences, obstacles, and views in order to help and inspire others in their own personal journey. In addition to writing, Ana is also an entrepreneur who not only mentors others through a happy, healthy lifestyle journey, but helps guide them in starting their own online business and provides guidance to make their own goals and dreams a reality.

Clawing My Way to a Better Life
by Denise Damijo

As a mother of 5 children with 3 children under the age of 2 years old; my worst fear is to not be an exemplary role model for my children. I not only just want to be an exemplary role model but my core desire is to build a lifestyle for my children that they never want to stray from. Before I get into that, let me give you a little bit of my history.

I was born to parents that weren't parent material, and unfortunately, other than my grandmother on my dad's side, I had no one else desire to take me in. My mom was the parent that was MIA, and her side of the family was also just that until we were reunited when I was 28 years old. So for my youth, foster home after foster home and group home after group home was my way of life. I had children early but I was still determined to create a better life than what I had. I had to do better because I knew that there was better for me.

Now, I must admit that it was definitely a challenge being around drugs, being taken advantage of, and being abused. But to give you a better understanding of what I went through as a 16-year-old girl, let me explain how a typical holiday looked through my eyes. I showed up at Thanksgiving dinner with a huge knot on my forehead because he had hit me with a metal pole prior to arriving there.

I had been kicked down stairs, punched, threatened with guns, and even had my family threatened if I ever decided to leave him.

Eventually, I did make it out... only to repeat the cycle a few more times before I was able to finally break it.

The unfortunate part was that the damage had already been done before I was able to finally break the chains of bondage that bound me to a life of abuse and feeling like I was worthless and unwanted. Looking back, I know that the only thing that kept me alive and kept me going day after day was God and my unwavering desire to see my dreams come true.

As my two eldest children got older, I missed out on a lot of things because I was working two jobs while finishing college. They couldn't stand the fact that I wasn't there and they couldn't comprehend that I was truly working hard and striving for higher heights for them as well as myself. They wanted what they wanted right then and there and at that time I just couldn't provide it for them.

The decisions that I had to make cost me more than what I bargained for. Even though I was able to keep the lights on, a roof over our heads, and food on the table, they blamed me and was upset that I created that life that they had to live.

They wanted things that I just couldn't give them, and each and every day it broke my heart.

But I couldn't give up. . . I had to finish the mission that I had set out to accomplish.

Years and years passed as I prayed and believed in something bigger and better to happen to us and for us. I completed my degree but was disappointed when I found out that it was basically useless. I couldn't get through doors because I had no experience. I couldn't get experience because no one would give me an opportunity, and I had to settle for dead-end jobs that were, again, barely paying my bills.

I know I had to tell my children no, more than 10,000 times. What truly hurt me was that all they wanted to do was be and feel like normal kids, and I felt so helpless because I couldn't even meet their simplest desire.

In 2012 I finally got married to a man that I loved and admired and he felt the same way. I thought my life was going to just miraculously get better, but that was far from the truth. I didn't realize that because I was not really raised but I basically raised myself and I never really had people tell me or show me what marriage was all about and really how to play that dance, I struggled. We both did... He was stuck in his foreign ways of doing things and I was stuck in fairytale land when we were supposed to be creating the marriage that had a strong foundation and was uniquely tailored to who the both of us were.

The one thing that was on my side was that I was a fighter that wanted to truly give my marriage an opportunity to succeed, and so was my husband. So we fought for our marriage, made lots of mistakes, learned about each other, and grew together. Doing that led us to eventually develop a beautiful marriage and also having three amazing children together on top of the two I already had.

I would have never imagined that I was going to have three more children. We had agreed on two more, but God saw fit to bless us with a set of twins in our second full-term pregnancy.

Life was getting better and I knew that there was even better and more out there for us, and all we needed to do was keep seeking it. So throughout the course of both my pregnancies, I kept working on and in my business that I started literally right before I found out that I was pregnant with our first child together.

To most, it might sound too risky to have started a business after you just found out that you were pregnant, but the problem was I had just put in my two-week notice to my bosses, who were prejudice. I felt like I was in the twilight! I'm not kidding! They made jokes about having a German manager and a black girl and they couldn't wait to see who was going to win. That was actually one of the more milder jokes they told. Not to mention cussing me out. I couldn't believe the environment that I was in. So yes, I was happy to run out of there.

I had a little bit of money to play with and at that point I knew that it was now or never. I chose the NOW and I jumped. I was terrified, and in trying to make my family better I invested in whatever I believed that was going to render me the results that I truly needed and desired.

Unfortunately, I ended up investing in coaches, programs, materials, and services that cost me around $80k cash, not credit. That amount didn't even include the expenses of doing business. It was only a little bit of money and now I was crushed because I pretty much spent it all and I felt like I had nothing to show for it. I thought I had something that I could create my business and lifestyle with, but it just wasn't happening for me.

After two years of really trying, I was exhausted, broke, marriage failing, and suffering from my second pulmonary embolism in 13 months.

The only thing that was good in my life at the time was God and my children, and even at that time I felt hated and forsaken by both. Even though I had those feelings, I also had the feelings of still believing in them and desiring to really see my dreams be birthed into reality. So I decided to do something huge, and scary.

I decided to be all in! It was a no-brainer for me. I was already losing it all, and if I was going to lose, I was going to go out with a bang. I was going to put in everything I had so at least I could look my children in the eyes and honestly be able to tell them that I did my best and it just wasn't good enough.

Well, it turned out that me saying that never became necessary, because from my desire to provide my children with a better life, the sleepless nights, the hard work, the never giving up, the determination to succeed, and the investments that I made in myself and in my business, I started winning. My business started making money and I started to see things in my business happen that I only dreamt of. I love the business and lifestyle that I'm creating for myself and my children.

My journey is not over yet but I'm enjoying it. My marriage is in a beautiful place, my children are recovering and our relationship is much better, and life is great!

My advice to anyone who will listen is that each and every one of us has a desire, a goal, and/or dream, and it is not always going to be easy to achieve. Be willing to fail, but fail forward, not backwards. Fight for it, believe in it, and never give up on it, because reaching it is so worth the fight.

Author Bio:
Denise Damijo has currently resided in Texas for the last 10 years. Throughout all that she has been through and overcome, her foundation rests in the faith of God's divine plan for her life. She believes that she has a huge purpose to impact and help nations of people in their business and lifestyle journey.

Website: **www.denisedamijo.com**
iTune: **Momapreneur's Grit Podcast**

From Wife to Mom to Entrepreneur
by Cara Brzezicki

When I was young, I always saw myself as a mom. The more the years went by, I became scared to have children. My husband and I had great jobs. I had waited eight years for my husband to propose! I knew I was supposed to be with him from the moment I met him.

Starting a family seemed scary, especially since I finally was able to marry my husband.

Two years after we married, I became pregnant. I was so scared that I would not be a good mom. I had prayed that if I was supposed to get pregnant then God would give me a baby. At least I had the higher power believing in me! From the very beginning of my pregnancy I was very sick and I threw up multiple times a day.

I was already a pretty thin gal, and after the first fourteen weeks, I lost 10 pounds! I had many spurts of nausea throughout my pregnancy, but did not throw up again. After my son was born, like every other parent, we had no sleep. From the minute my son was born until he was about six months old he screamed nonstop. I know parents say that their babies scream all of the time, but I am not exaggerating and am truly being honest.

The only time my son would stop screaming was if he was nursing or riding in the car. My husband and I would have to gallop throughout our home to help keep him calm. He barely slept, and neither did my husband nor I. There were times when I would put my screaming son in his crib, shut the door, and sit outside his room and cry. I knew that being a parent was going to be hard, but I never expected it to be this hard. I loved my son so much, but I did not know what to do. For the longest time I thought my son did not like me.

After he turned about six months, he was able to crawl and move around. The screaming finally stopped! He still cried all of the time and had many meltdowns, but at least he was not screaming.

As he became older, we would notice meltdowns more than normal kids his age. The littlest things would set him off, like not being able to get his shoes off, or having his socks on. By the time he was three, the meltdowns were so bad that it was suggested to go get my son tested for SPD (Sensory Processing Disorder).

We had him checked and he had a very mild case of SPD. His occupational therapist stated that it was mild and suggested play therapy. I took my son every week for months for his therapy. The occupational therapist taught me how to handle the meltdowns and how to prevent them. I read many books and did a lot of praying and now you would not even know he suffered from it.

My husband and I are very blessed because our oldest son was such a mild case. SPD is much more common these days, and many children have it very severe. I thank God every day for the blessings He has given my family and I.

When my son was a little over one, I became pregnant with my second son. I was so excited. I never threw up while being pregnant with my second son, but I was nauseous throughout my entire pregnancy. I hoped that not throwing up was a sign that he was not a screamer... ha ha!

After my second son was born, my husband and I waited for the screaming. Hooray! He was just a crier and not a screamer. The second time was a bit easier, but definitely not easy (not that any baby is). We now know why my first son screamed and why my second son did not... my first son had SPD, but we did not know what that was at the time.

After my oldest son was in Pre-K and my youngest son was a bit older, I was able to work on my invention. When my oldest son was six months old, he would throw his sippy cups. He thought it was hilarious! I could not find anything on the market that would fit my table and his high chair. I decided to grab a clamp and drill a hole in it. I attached a cord and wrapped it around his sippy cup. It worked, and I loved it!

I took the clamp and cord device out to restaurants and received so much feedback that I decided to create my own. Well, I had a young son with screaming issues and not long after he turned one, I was pregnant again. I had to put my invention on hold.

After my second son turned six months old, he did the same thing... threw his sippy cups!

I pulled out my invention and it worked. I decided to start creating my own design to make the clamp small enough to fit into a purse or diaper bag, but curved enough to go over a high chair table.

After a couple of years of prototypes, the Sippie Clippie™ was created. As of this writing, the Sippie Clippie™ is on Kickstarter receiving backers. If it is fully funded, it will be ready to ship in March 2017.

When I look back at the moments when I was worried about having kids, I smile because my boys have taught me that everyone is different and that is okay. If I did not have my boys, I would have never learned how tough I can be and I would have never created the Sippie Clippie™. I was always thinking differently than my family and friends and I always felt unpopular. Thinking differently has led me to find the man of my dreams, my wonderful boys, a patent-pending invention, and the courage to just go for it!! God has truly blessed me, and I am so thankful for my husband, boys, and all of the struggles He has helped me through. If you never go through the hard parts of life, then you can never really enjoy the amazing life He has given you!

Author Bio:
Cara Brzezicki is the owner of Jazzie Beans LLC and the creator of the Sippie Clippie™, which is a clamp and cord device that prevents sippy cups from falling to the ground! She loves her husband, two boys, and her sweet dog... Jazzie Beans. Protecting the planet is a very strong passion for Cara. The Sippie Clippie™ is made with recyclable plastic and the packaging is made with recycled cardboard along with hemp ties.

Website: **www.jazziebeans.com**

A Modern-Day Cinderella
by Holly Diederich

I'm just a mom of two—Braelynn, 4, and Kaiden, 2–who had a successful corporate career and knew I was destined for more, who knew I was destined for greatness.

I'm sure you have heard it before, it's the six-figure buzzword. Everyone on a path to financial freedom wants to hit that mark; it's a trophy, it's a badge of honor.

My path was very different from most six-figure earners, but I had a mission to hit $100k before I turned 30. I'm not quite sure how I came up with that goal, but I had it in my mind and I was determined to get there and did it just before the clock struck midnight. It wasn't an easy, out-of-the-gate achievement, but it was a modern-day Cinderella mompreneur story.

I grew up in a home where education was not optional. We had doctors, lawyers, MBAs, a multiple-Emmy-winning writer, a Nobel Prize winner in my bloodline—talk about high expectations. Then there was me. At a young age I understood money and knew that if I wanted something like a new pair of shoes I could get it myself from babysitting, so at 11 I started doing just that. Money gave me freedom, and it gave me control of my life in a household of chaos. I was always taught that education was the key to success, the gateway to money, and even though it was shoved down my throat my whole life, my educational path ended with an associate's degree. Not a proud moment or accomplishment for my parents.

Despite my education, I worked my way up the corporate ladder and was able to shine with my creativity and my out-of-the-box thinking, which is what my clients now call *"The Holly Sparkle,"* but that glittery little lady in my head kept telling me *"go for the gold."*

In February of 2016 I did something spontaneous and crazy and was led by intuition and I launched my coaching business. Becoming a Visibility Business Coach wasn't an instant win, and not my first attempt at entrepreneurship. I had many entrepreneurial struggles and guinea pigs (and was on the hamster wheel feeling stuck and lost) before I found my way into helping women in their businesses. I launched my coaching business with one goal: a mission to help women find their zone of genius to build a business that they are proud of, that makes them feel beautiful, empowered, and puts them on a path to financial freedom. I help women leave a trail of glitter behind them (whatever they want their legacy to become) while teaching them visibility social media strategies, marketing, and how to build a business that compliments their story and their authentic self. I am now living a life that I love.

One of the most powerful lessons I've learned on this journey is to build my business around my schedule, and not the other way around. Being a mom of two kiddos under 5 is not easy. I wanted to create a life for them, but I found myself sacrificing my time with them to get there. Then, I found myself sacrificing myself. Mom guilt x4594656. So one day I had a breakthrough. I told myself I wouldn't sacrifice either myself or my time with my family, and that meant I had to embrace the big O word.

OUTSOURCING. I had to let go of that little voice in my head telling me that I had to be in control of it all, and let go of tasks and things that I didn't love to do and didn't fire me up. Things like graphic design, could I do it? Sure. Do I love to do it and am I good at it? NO! It's not my zone of genius.

The result of setting boundaries and letting go of control was building a 6-figure business in less than a year. I work part-time, 3 days per week, travel with my family, and spend a lot of time with my kiddos. I'm so passionate about helping other moms do the same and build a business where they don't have to give up time with their family. There's been many people who have told me I couldn't have it all. I had to put my kids in daycare full time and work more, but I've cracked the code for work/life balance and proved them wrong.

Website: **www.hollydiederich.com**

The Balancing Act of Business Owner and Single Super Mom
by Shyla Collier

Being a business owner and a forever 24/7 single mom can be a huge challenge. We must factor in the hustle and bustle of meeting deadlines, attending appointments, and making sure clients are satisfied. But the most important thing in my life is always my son.

He longs for special time with his mom, as all children do. I am his sole financial provider, caregiver, protector, comforter, teacher, and his everything. We rely on the love of each other. As a full-time single mom, one must assume the role of mom and dad as well as every other role that is associated with being a mother already. I have a super busy schedule, he has a busy schedule, but we both work together on it.

Even if you are limited on time, find 10 minutes to greet your child with kindness and compliment them as they wake up in the morning. "Good morning honey, you are so special to me, I love you so much, you are very talented, give me a hug and a kiss." This begins your morning with a great start. It even changes the dynamics of the entire day. I have noticed such a big change in my son since I began doing this. Children thrive on words of affirmation. Positivity is key to making it through the tough times.

It is so important for us busy mompreneurs to put aside a portion of the day for our children. Even when working an 18-hour day, as I do at least once a week, I still find time to sit down with him and talk about his day. The rest of the week when I have a lighter workload, we find one fun activity to do together each night. We may go to dinner, have a movie night, play a game, do crafts, or go on a walk to the park.

Most weekends are reserved for him, and we plan at least one big outing. We may go to the zoo, on a trip together, a community event, and the list goes on. He is the primary focus, but I typically do have to sneak in a little work here and there.

Start traditions that will leave a legacy year after year. These can even be passed down from generation to generation. Although we have traditions for every month, we both enjoy December the most. It is my son's birthday and Christmas. Every year we have a party prior to the actual day of his birthday for family and friends. On the day of, him and I go to an indoor amusement park together and to his favorite toy store to choose a toy. He gets small gifts throughout the month to space it out. We watch Christmas movies, drink hot chocolate and eggnog, search neighborhoods for the best Christmas lights, and attend the annual Christmas parade. We make ornaments each year for our family members. My son and I enjoy hosting breakfast on Christmas morning. Lunch is spent with relatives. We have a gift exchange and play games. Make special memories with your children and laugh with them.

When asked what I do for fun, I say that I spend time with my son. You as a mom are the one who makes it an enjoyable experience. It is very rewarding to be a mom. Children grow up far too fast. Time flies; in the blink of an eye they have become an adult. We need to cherish the time we have with them, as we can never turn back time. There will be plenty of time to do things on my own when he is grown.

As the sole provider of my household, money management is crucial to meeting the needs of my son. Friends ask how I can afford to do so many enjoyable activities as a single mom with a child. My answer is being smart with my finances and working hard. We clip coupons, find the kids eat free nights, indulge on free community events, purchase local discount cards, and participate in barter networks. Another good way to cut costs is to purchase secondhand items. You can find great deals on Facebook groups and at yard sales. I save up for large items to pay them in full when purchased. I have never paid interest on a credit card because I pay it prior to the due date. Making a monthly budget will help you a lot. Just remember, it is not all about the money you have but the love that you give.

Remember to pamper yourself as well. Set aside a little bit of time out of your busy day to take a break. I find this one very hard. Once they are in school, this becomes easier. You have more me time. When taking a quiet bubble bath, getting a pedicure, or working on your favorite hobby, you can debrief and escape the stress of the day.

Being single is very hard in itself. Going it alone can be very challenging at times. We all want someone special to spend our lives with on a different level. Dating as a single mom can be tricky. Now that my son is in school, it is easier. Because I choose not to leave him with a sitter while I am on a date, it has worked best for me to go during the hours he is in school. I will only go on evening dates when my family is in town to visit so they get to spend time with my son. I prefer to date single fathers. After multiple dates, we go on play dates and include the children. While around the children we always keep it on a "friends" level. After being single for so long, I know that I am an independent woman and that I can do it on my own. In time, God will bring me "the one." As for now, I focus on my son and cherish the moments that I have with him.

My son, Christian Collier, is now seven years old. He is an aspiring actor/singer/dancer/model. I teach him always to reach for the stars. Children learn by example. I help him to achieve his goals by supporting him and encouraging him with perseverance. If he shows interest in something, I allow him to try it out. Allow your children to try new things and invest in their future. Set aside one or two days a week to bring them to the activity of their choice. We choose a main focus for a certain time period and stick with it. He focuses on acting and choir at the beginning of the school year, typically a sport in the spring, and many camps in the summer. Make every experience a learning tool and a bonding experience. Children can teach us so much—take the time to listen.

There is no greater love than the unconditional love that we get from our children. This is the most important journey that we can take part in. We are strong, independent women and supermoms. Strive to be the best you can be.

Our primary focus should be our children. Find time to give your child the love they need. Wake them up with positivity. Give your children compliments, words of affirmation, and lots of hugs and kisses. It is crucial to spend one-on-one time each day with your children to find out what is going on in their lives. Be smart with your money and remember to pamper yourself, as well as your children. Support and encourage them. Let them try new things and listen to their thoughts. Make every experience a learning tool and a bonding experience. Build traditions to make lasting memories.

Author Bio:
Shyla Collier is the owner of Premiere Social Media, author of Social Media Key to Credibility, compassionate single mother, and a networking and marketing guru. She enjoys helping other business owners thrive. Shyla owns four women's networking groups and empowers women and mompreneurs. Shyla resides in Arizona with her son.

Website: **www.premieresocialmedia.com**
Facebook: **@premieresocialmedia**
Son's Facebook: **@christiantcollier**
Son's Website: **www.christiancollier.com**

Trailer Living
by Joannée DeBruhl

In 2009 my family and I lived in southeast Michigan, near Detroit. The Big 3 Auto company crisis hit everyone hard that year, and in February of 2009 I was laid off. It was my 3rd layoff in 10 years. Although it was a scary time for us financially, rather than going back to a corporate job, I decided to pursue something I loved. My husband and my two sons fully supported my decision.

I attended Michigan State University's Organic Farmer Training Program to learn how to be a farmer. It was amazing! It was a 9-month-long program on their 10-acre organic farm. It was 5 days a week, 45 hours each week of intensive farmer training. At the end of that training I started Stone Coop Farm with 2 business partners.

We leased 2 acres and learned a lot about growing food and running a business. We decided to look for land to purchase and found 30 acres nearby. It was 20 acres of alfalfa for hay and a 10-acre unused meadow. We started building the farm in April 2012. We built a greenhouse, 2 hoop houses, a pavilion, a root cellar, and a home.

My family agreed to live on the property during construction of the farm buildings and the house. We decided to buy and live in a 30-foot travel trailer. We moved into it on July 4th and the house was started the next week. It was supposed to be done before mid-November.

Now let me clarify what this really means to live in a 30-foot travel trailer for 6 months. First, let me share my family dynamics. My husband is 6 feet 6 inches tall. My oldest son had just graduated from high school and was working on the farm with me. He is 6 feet 4 inches tall. My youngest son, a sophomore in high school, is 6 feet

5 inches tall, and I am 5 feet 11 inches tall. We also had 2 dogs, both over 60 lbs. There were a lot of bodies living in this travel trailer! Remember we were living and working on a farm and a construction site, so keeping mud and dirt out of the trailer was impossible.

The trailer was 8 feet wide and 30 feet long on the outside. That means about 220 square feet inside with one 3-foot-wide aisle down the center. Inside, we had 2 pull-out couches for beds for my two sons and there was a queen-size bed in the back of the trailer for my husband and me. The refrigerator was the size of a cooler you might use for a party, but the back half froze all our food. The oven was large enough for an 8-inch square pan, and there were two burners on top. We had one small closet and 1 drawer each for our clothes. Everything else we owned was put into storage.

The most crucial component, however, was the bathroom. First, the ceiling was just over 6 feet tall, so my husband couldn't stand up straight anywhere in the bathroom. The hot-water tank was only 6 gallons. A shower in 6 gallons of hot water means you get in the shower, then turn on the water and try to get it hot enough while you get wet. Next you turn off the water to soap your body and shampoo your hair. Then you turn the water on again and pray there is enough hot water left to get all the soap out of your hair. I didn't even consider shaving my legs due to all the goosebumps!

That summer was great. Our family spent a lot time grilling outside and eating at the picnic table. We didn't have any cable, Internet, or TV, so we played a lot of games, read, star-gazed, and talked to each other. We went to the Laundromat or library to use the Internet. Many of our friends let us stay in their houses when they went away for the weekend so we could take hot showers, wash clothes, and cook real meals.

By October, as the temperatures at night starting dipping below freezing, we started to realize how poorly insulated the trailer was. During November and December we got snow and we had to leave the water running in the kitchen and bathroom sinks at night so the water lines wouldn't freeze. We ran the trailer heater constantly and had to add 2 space heaters to keep us warm. We finally moved into our new home on December 21st.

I asked my sons what they wanted for Christmas, expecting a new video or computer game, since they had not played any of them for 6 months. To my surprise, they both asked to take long hot showers until all 50 gallons of our new home's hot-water tank ran out. We had dragged our kids down to basic needs! None of us will ever underestimate the pleasure of a hot shower again!

A reporter visited the farm a year later and noticed our trailer. I told her our story about living in the trailer for 6 months. My sons were there and she asked them if they would do it again. To my astonishment, they both said they would. They have fond memories of our time in that trailer and we all got a much better appreciation of what it means to have a warm and comfortable place to live. My family all agrees that home is the people you love, not where you live.

Author Website: **www.stonecoopfarm.com**

Motherhood Humbled Me
by Kimberly Bepler

I was one of those girls who grew up with a really devoted stay-at-home mom. Let's call her Betty Crocker. She was the type to greet us with fresh baked goodies after school, the mom that all my friends could talk to, generally the one that sacrificed everything about herself for us, including attending every sporting event, musical lesson, and parent-teacher conference.

Growing up on a ranch and loving animals and babies of all kinds, I had always wanted a BABY really badly. I'm that crazy lady in the grocery store staring at your newborn and the bold stranger in the restaurant that offers to hold your baby. I waited until we had at least one stable job between my husband and I, but I was itching to parent my OWN baby.

Then my baby arrived, red-faced and an eating machine, via a C-section. After the birth I deemed myself a failure for not having the natural delivery I had planned. And breastfeeding hurt—badly. Battered and bleeding, we persevered and successfully breastfed until I went into full-time work at 19 months.

My work was a new career, something I trained for when my firstborn was 6 months. I became a postpartum doula; not a birth-support person but the doulas that care for new mothers AFTER their babies arrive. And I was IN LOVE with this new career.

Quickly I found that I was created for this line of work. It combined all my great loves (babies, breastfeeding, encouraging moms, cooking, tidying, and generally making moms feel like a queen for the day), and it was flexible to work around my mom life. Because that is what

I thought I would be. A stay-at-home mom in particular. Like Betty was. But by then I had a toddler, and he was HARD (I mean bright and curious and adorable and mischievous).

So I went to work for a break from my toddler. And I loved it. I loved it so much we decided the one stable job between us would be mine, and my husband would become the stay-at-home parent.

Surprisingly, this role reversal worked, and within a few years he was doing the laundry, grocery shopping, and even much of the cooking. (Yes, the transition took time.)

By the time he was 5, we had another baby, and I thought, This is it. Finally I get to do things better because I have now worked with 300 babies and I have this DOWN. Wrong. Baby #2 was a feisty noisemaker that rocked our world. She was more independent than her big brother, she screamed instead of grunted, and she learned quickly to keep up with the bigger kids around her. I had clearly met my match. And my doula skills were not holding a candle to this little powerhouse.

I had to return to work when she was 3 months, so daddy took over once again. Off I would go to a new mom who would thank me for every glass of water I brought her, babies who would quickly calm to my soothing touch, and appreciative family members who told me I was the baby whisperer, their guardian angel, their helper. But that was only at work.

The same multi-colored frittata I made at work my kids would turn their nose up to at home. The problem-solving skills I learned to help babies calm and sleep were lost on my little progeny. The laundry I had lovingly sorted and stacked was knocked over instead of greeted with a kid-at-Christmas eyes of relief from my clients.

Even the nonviolent communication I studied at the midwifery college where I taught doula trainings seemed to fall flat at home, in contrast to how beautifully it worked with my clients.

It was almost like I went to work to feel good about myself, and I came back home for a serving of humble pie. Every day I would get a dose of "you are so great and I am so thankful you are here to help me" and another dose of, "you can't make me, you are only my mommy."

I know a lot of men who say their work tears them up and then their family builds them back up again. Not the case with our flip-flopped family life, where dad was the fun one while I was the breadwinner. And the one with all the RULES. In our family, daddy struggled with feeling purpose and satisfaction as he stayed at home raising the kids. I struggled with the guilt that working out of the house brings on. He wins for having the harder job. By far.

But for all my years of parenting I have been dealing with the contrast of glorification at work and smashed expectations at home. Mommy wars aside, I see the desire to be away from your kids to get an ego boost.

My two are now teenagers, and I have reduced my work load enough to be home when they return from school. I don't bake like Betty; my kids prefer candy over baked goods anyway—show me how to make a homemade Skittle and we might be in business. I also don't sew like my mom. Or sell Tupperware. But I can run the kids to events and be there to chat with their friends. I still cook things that clients love and my kids say "looks like poop," but they are maturing and getting more of an appreciation for things homemade.

I still go to work to have my skills shine. I can get tiny babies to breastfeed. I can juggle twins or triplets (OK, I don't really juggle them but I am quite talented with multiple babies). I can make a mean crustless quiche. I can soothe a fussy baby and swaddle in the pitch-black with a 4 lb. preemie. But I am also still regularly humbled by the intensity of the love I have for my kids, and their apparent lack of appreciation for my skills.

This is the part that gets me. My job is a "bonding agent" at work. I help mothers and fathers connect to their babies. I don't need to help them to love and protect them, as they do this naturally. I help them to understand and interpret their baby so they can communicate and feel love coming back from their babies. I know what this looks like. But with my own, I often feel rejected and underappreciated.

This makes my role feel so much more important at work. Knowing that kids rarely show the appreciation for their parents until they are grown (and sometimes not until they have their own kids) makes it even more valuable to start with someone who notices how great you are. I'm so thankful that I get to be a doula in this world of being torn down, judged, and labeled as parents.

Even if my own kids don't see me as the kind of mother I want to be, I can be that sounding board to someone else, possibly someone else who doesn't have another voice of reassurance—or if their inner voice is too quiet to reflect what they know. I want moms to know that they are enough. That they are the right mommy for this kid, at the right time, in the right place.

And even if I have to wait until my kids are grown to hear it from them, I will choose to believe that about myself as well.

Author Bio:
Kimberly is the mother to two lively school-aged kids, a wife of 22 years, and a professional doula, trainer, educator, and lactation consultant. She has been working with postpartum families since she had an infant of her own in 2000, and has a passion for newborns and

their families. She founded her company ABC Doula Service in 2001 and she loves having a team of doulas serving new moms. She also travels and teaches doula trainings all over the US. Kimberly's passion lies in helping new parents and new doulas, so although this is truly her dream profession, she has found motherhood to be the humbling balance that has allowed her to serve mothers with empathy and compassion.

Website: **www.abcdoula.com**

Babies and Business Just Won't Play Nicely
by Stacy Tuschl

I would never have called myself Superwoman. Not even a no-caps, just one of many, super-woman.

I mean, if you have those powers, you don't brag about them, right? And I believed I had them—I so believed I had them.

I was one of the women who could have it all, do it all—and all at the same time. I would read those magazine articles about women struggling with a work/life balance and shake my head, mystified. Just...work harder! Haven't you ever heard of time management? Download some apps! And probably also throw some meditation in there because your chi is definitely blocked.

(Obnoxious, I know. Stick with me here; I'll get my comeuppance.)

If it isn't already patently clear, I felt this way before I had children. I was 100% wife and 100% entrepreneur, all the time. And, bless his heart, my husband actually got it. He was into the crazy little tenacious businesswoman part of me he married.

Which was lucky, since I was working from morning until night. Literally: my husband works second shift, so I'd work from the moment I got up until the moment I went to bed.

And it worked for me. When I say I loved it, I mean I loooooved it. This is not an overwhelm or burnout story. Let's call this a story about getting real.

When my husband and I decided to start a family, I wasn't concerned.

I mean, I was a little concerned, since when you have a human being inside of you, you suddenly find yourself concerned with just about everything. I still can't talk about BPA without getting upset.

But when it came to being a mom and being an entrepreneur? I could do this! Just throw another hat on my head; I could be a full-time stay-at-home mom and a full-time work-from-home entrepreneur.

After all, what better role model for my new daughter than a working mom that's also raising kids at the same time? She'd probably grow up to be an astrophysicist and a Supreme Court Justice—at once!

So, here's the thing about Tanner that I couldn't know until she got here. She is a character; an absolute little cut-up that loves nothing more than having fun. It's adorable and inspiring and, oh, a touch distracting.

Honestly, things were starting to come to a head well before she hit the 18-month mark. Because, have you ever met a baby? I thought I had, but then I started living with one. She is a miracle and a joy... and just a lot to handle.

One day, I was sitting on my sofa working on my laptop while Tanner was sitting in the corner playing. Charming: both of us just sitting there, doing our things. Until, in an instant, Tanner ran over to me and slammed my laptop shut.

She laughed uproariously. All those little toddler brain synapses were connecting "slam laptop shut" to "insane amounts of fun."

And thank you for that brain synapses, because it came to pass that every time I opened my laptop, she was compelled to slam it shut.

"Tell her 'no.'" Well, as it turns out, "no" works when you're in a store, she wants candy, and you then leave the store. "No" works when she insists on wearing a swimsuit in October and you can put the swimsuit away.

"No" is exceedingly less effective when the object of temptation is right there, at all times because, again, Mommy is 100% mommy and also 100% entrepreneur.

And if you want to see a toddler melt down, I mean really and truly lose it, move the thing they want out of reach but still in sight range (because you have to answer emails and still be in sight range of the child).

Moms, let me speak the word of my salvation to you: Daycare.

I started out taking Tanner to daycare one day a week so I could focus solely on work for that one day. And it worked.

As it turned out, separating my business and my parenting made me better at both of them. I was a better mom while I wasn't trying to build a business at the same time, and I was a better business person while I wasn't trying to raise a child at the same time.

Now I take my children to daycare three days a week so I can focus on my business while they're gone, and I can be 100% mom while they're home.

I don't want them to remember childhoods wherein mom was always on the phone or the computer. Yes, it's important to me that they know that I value working, but it's also important that they see me helping people, giving back, and enjoying life.

My new focus is on being 100% present in everything I do. And that's going... pretty well. Not only am I not Superwoman, I'm very much human.

Just the other day, Tanner (who is now three and a half) came over to me and said, "Mom, it's time to stop working now."

Ouch.

But she was right. And I'll take those little reminders when I get them. I told her, "Yes, it is. Let's go play." She beamed, and I took her and her younger sister, Teagan, out to the backyard.

After all, mom time is for being a mom. And work time is for taking over the world.

Author Bio:
Stacy Tuschl is a High-Performance Coach & Business Mentor, Best-Selling Author, Speaker, and the Creator of *She's Building Her Empire Podcast & Community*, where she helps purpose-driven women entrepreneurs and business owners break through their challenges, operate at their highest potential, and create self-sustaining businesses. Stacy is highly passionate about helping women unapologetically be themselves and create a legacy they can be proud of.

Website: **www.shesbuildingherempire.com**

Finding Balance as a Woman and a Mom

Loving Unconditionally
by Chris S.

I inadvertently found a court document sitting on top of my twenty-year-old daughter's closed laptop computer in her bedroom. I had opened her bedroom door and entered specifically to retrieve the antivirus software disk that our family was sharing. As I approached the laptop, I saw a yellow piece of paper that would change my life forever. It was a copy of a court document indicating that the second court date was set, and as best as I could determine in that exact moment, my daughter was changing her name from Alissa to Aaron. Female to male.

My brain started a frantic frenzy. I read it and reread it and began talking out loud to myself. I was crying and becoming hysterical, not knowing what to do or say or think. My youngest daughter was home at the time. She heard me and came into my bedroom, where I lay in disbelief, and she crawled into my bed with me and we talked briefly about the situation. She knew more than I did but didn't know what to make of the situation, being that she was only 12 years old. My youngest daughter told me that Alissa told her recently that she was "trans" and that she would surely see some changes in how she looks. That is it. Nothing more. She didn't know what to make of that concept and said nothing to me about it.

I immediately tried to contact Alissa several times by phone throughout the day with no response. Finally, she walked through the front door and went right up into her bedroom without acknowledging me and closed her door. I walked into her room and said "I have been trying to reach you. What is going on?" I mentioned that I had found the court document and that I was in shock and I needed some answers. I tried to remain strong during our conversation while I tried to get some answers. She said...

"I am changing my body from a woman to a man. I have been wanting to crawl out of my skin since I was five years old. I have been researching why I have felt this way for several years and have connected to people on the Internet that are going through the same things that I am. I have been giving myself injections for four weeks now. Injections in my thigh. I have sought out help by getting downtown Chicago and have gone through all of the doctors and psychiatrists exams. I have met all of the criteria and I will continue to meet with them as my body changes. I am already starting to get more hair growth on my legs. My voice will be changing very soon. I will get facial hair. I consider myself to be a heterosexual male that is attracted to women." Finally. It had come out. I could not imagine the weight that was lifted from his shoulders when he was able to tell his mother what had been a huge daily issue his entire last 15 years, especially when he had not spoken a word about it.

My Instant Reaction.

As soon as he told me that he had driven down to Chicago, by himself no less, many times to go through the entire psychological process and he had been giving himself injections in the thigh for 4 weeks already, I knew for sure that this was very serious and he meant it. I asked him if he was sure and he said absolutely.

"But what if you change your mind?"

"Oh, I won't!" he said.

My reaction was pure support loaded with immediate, unconditional love.

This child of mine has never been all that motivated, and she tended to be reactive in most circumstances. This child found a way to get to the city, two hours away with no traffic. She made appointments and stuck to them. This child does not like needles and was giving herself injections regularly. These are things my kid would not do!

The next day, I called in to work and recall saying to my boss, "I have to deal with something that I have no clue how to deal with. I cannot come in today." He asked if there was anything he could help with. I said no. What I needed was to process this and to pick myself up off the floor. I loved the name Alissa. This was my Alissa. The flashbacks of all of the memories came flooding in. What about all of the firsts and spoiling her to pieces? What about all of the great grades and then it flipping to an almost intolerable child? Where do I go with this information? What do I do? How do I deal with this? I know no one else going through this, and the concept was so new to me. I had plenty of research to do and felt like I had a huge secret and became paranoid and very scared for my child's life. Who do I tell, who do I not tell? The neighbors! The family!

The point is that I am so grateful that my reaction to this circumstance was immediate support and 100% conditional love. I am so thankful for that.

There is much more to this story, but this is the nutshell version. It is six years later and all is still on track with no turning back. I have gotten better about some things. I rarely call him Alissa. I am OK with displaying the photos from his childhood. I only talk to people about the situation if I am very certain that they will be accepting. There are many people I have not told. He looks like a man. He acts like a man. He is a man. I would rather have him be happy with himself in this life than have him not be on this earth with me. I love this child that I nourished in my womb and brought into the world.I truly love this human being of mine unconditionally.

Letting Go and Cherishing
by Elizabeth Wharton

The morning sunlight was dancing on the flowers. Butterflies flitted near our path. The library door was only several yards away, but it would take us a good fifteen minutes to get there. We weren't in a hurry. I pondered the tiny hand that was tucked into mine. It wouldn't be this little for long. How old would she be when she quit needing my hand? Her little fingers would wiggle with each new butterfly she spotted, pulling me so we could get a closer look.

She was amazing, this little three-year-old of mine, delighting in the smallest details. "Ooh, Momma! Smell this one!" she said in awe of each new bunch of flowers we came upon. I watched her bury her face in the flowers, her soft, baby-fine hair adding to the beauty of the landscaping. Simply being near her filled me with indescribable joy and contentment.

My Brynna. Over three years and I was still washed in amazement that she was mine. She was mine... but all at the same time, not mine. This little person, so delicate and intricate, so much a part of me, was her own person, with her own unique purpose in life. And she would only need to hold my hand for such a short time I squeezed that little hand so slightly, wanting to freeze time on that sunlit path to the library. I couldn't bear the thought of this moment fading away in time. I drank in every detail. I poured love over her as I watched her take in the life around her. I imagined that love being a blanket that could wrap around her long after she quit holding my hand.

The next day she would start preschool. It was only part-time, and she was so excited to play with new friends, but it would be the first time I had missed so many hours of her day at a time. A new chapter of life was starting. My heart hurt at the thought of ending the last chapter.

New chapters are inevitable, and necessary in continuing a good story. But, had I cherished enough? Had I made the most of every moment with her? The sadness I was feeling made me think I hadn't. I should have created more moments; I should have felt this level of amazement and gratitude more. She was growing up and I hadn't been enough...

Then that little hand pulled me right next to her sweet little body. "I love you, Momma. You're the best mommy," she said as she wrapped her little arms around me for a quick hug, then spotted another butterfly to chase.

Right then the truth settled over me. Peace unfolded in my heart as I recognized the goodness of the chapter we were ending. The way Brynna was taking in the flowers and the butterflies, that's how I had taken in the past three years. We had created a family culture of purposeful cherishing. Being thankful, being present in the moment, and cherishing are all threads of the same blanket. The truth is, cherishing enough doesn't make the transition void of pain. But it does create a blanket of love that comforts our hearts in the process.

Motherhood is a journey of continually letting go. It starts at birth; this tiny life that has been literally connected to me is now separate from me. And it doesn't stop.

One chapter changes to the next, each with a new level of letting go. Each with a new level of pain in the separation.

My Brynna. We've navigated several new chapters since that sunny morning on the library path. Soon she will start to drive, and conversations of college have begun. When the thoughts start to settle in that it's going too fast, that I haven't done enough, that I'm not ready for another chapter to end—I remind myself of the truth.

I will always remember my three-year-old in her simple floral sundress, smiling, loving, embracing life, holding my hand. Just one of the many cherished moments woven into the blanket of love we have created.

I wrap myself in it, and it comforts me as I prepare for the next chapter of new moments.

Author Bio:
Elizabeth Wharton is deeply passionate about honesty, authentic relationships, and inspiring people to become closer to God and each other. She makes her home in San Marcos, Texas, with her husband and three children. When she is not writing or speaking, you will find her reading or enjoying the company of the people she loves. No matter what she's doing, you will find her with a cup of coffee.

Website: **www.thatbeautifultruth.com**

When I Stopped Singing.. Wisdom from the Journey of a Recovering Burnt-Out 'Momaholic'

by Manisha Ghei

Putting a hand on my shoulder, my ENT surgeon said, "You have vocal cord nodules. Take these steroids and acid-blocking drugs, and, if there is no improvement, we can do surgery." As a doctor, wife, and mother of three, I needed my voice! As a recreational amateur singer, I sang to relax and connect within, but I couldn't anymore. A month later, the diagnosis remained. I agreed to surgical removal. Three months later, post-surgery, post intensive speech therapy and more medications, the nodules were back with a vengeance! I declined repeat surgery, destined instead to continue long-term acid-blocking medications prescribed by my physicians.

Eight years on those drugs led me down a path of total physical, mental, and spiritual decline. In 2010, I was additionally diagnosed with multiple other medical conditions: autoimmune diseases, chronic fatigue syndrome, fibromyalgia and neuropathy were a few. "Fatigue" is an understatement for what it feels like when your cell's energy factories are shot, your nervous system has gone haywire, and your body refuses to function! I lost all function in my left arm, hurt all the time, and could hardly speak more than a few sentences at a time without my voice giving out. No doctor could figure out what to do for me. Helpless and hopeless, I thought I was dying!

Growing up, I was focused, worked hard, and achieved my dream of helping others by becoming a physician. Like most physicians, I was a type-A personality, but, when I became a mother, I was absolutely obsessed with taking care of my children single-handedly, never asking for help from anyone else, including my husband! My primal instinct of caring for my children took precedence over any form of basic self-care.

My second child was born during my medical residency, which entailed 28-36 hour shifts with almost no sleep. Many nights when I could have slept a bit, I utilized that time to pump breast milk for the use of my baby. My husband tried to talk me out of doing that, saying I needed to sleep instead. "You need to relax. It's okay to feed her baby formula." I was physically, mentally, and emotionally exhausted, but hearing "You need to relax" made me frustrated, angry, and isolated. The overbearing sense of duty and obligation was overpowering all other emotions. I internalized my feelings and my fatigue, allowing my own needs to become secondary. The pattern continued two years later with the birth of my third child.

My spirit was dying. Everything became a task, and I wasn't having fun doing it. I refused to recognize the state of severe burnout. It felt wrong to acknowledge, as that would imply I was failing in the job of being a mom. Whatever we resist persists, and it certainly did in my body! My body (and my vocal cords) had to shut down to teach me a lesson in self-care!

In retrospect, my behavior was possibly a consequence of certain early life experiences, starting from infancy, where my subconscious mind had felt, and stored, a sense of abandonment due to an adoption. Disease starts in our energetic body(s) years before it appears in our physical bodies. I had carried forward an unseen and unheard trauma that led me to believe that any time I was not doing everything for my children all by myself, I was abandoning them.

Adding fuel to fire, my first child was born prematurely after a difficult pregnancy and an emergency surgical delivery. She was gravely ill for a length of time. Living in a joint family in India, with its associated socio-cultural pressures, did not help during this traumatic period. I learned to be on guard all the time, like a form of PTSD! I was twenty-three, and dedicated years of my life towards getting my baby better. With significant efforts, she did, but in the process of trying to help her, I did not delve into my own needs at all. Where attention goes, energy flows, but I gave my body the message that "I" was not important. Inattentive to my own self, the vital life force energy, or "praana," stopped flowing. Illness took hold.

Now back to the year 2010, it truly felt as if someone had pulled the rug from underneath me. I was very ill. If I would get through this, something had to drastically change. At this low point in my life, I was forced out of denial into an acknowledgement that there was a problem deeper than what drugs could help with. I needed to detach and move to that place of pure joy that had always been within me, but had somehow gotten buried beneath this pile of responsibilities, and possibly even a twisted sense of guilt towards my first child. I needed to learn how to let go. Having moved away from clearly expressing my own truths (most moms are guilty of this!), I had suppressed saying what I really wanted to, even to myself.

During my training at The Chopra Center, I learned that we have multiple Chakras or energy wheels in our body. The fifth Chakra governs the thyroid and vocal cords, and how we clearly express our own truths. Was it a surprise then that I experienced vocal cord issues? This realization was magical! Suddenly the fog had lifted, and my purpose in life, my "dharma," was clear. I learned to let go of the fear of rejection and abandonment. The importance of self-care and rejuvenation was to be my legacy to my kids. They needed to learn from this in-recovery mom that self-care is not selfish, that self-care is essential for lifelong health and happiness, that self-love and compassion is essential before you can authentically share that love with others.

Now I lead my life—and especially carry out my duty and responsibility as a mother—from a place of abundance and knowingness that as long as I am truly present in the moment I am with my children, they will be OK. I do not have the need to live in this addictive fight-or-flight mode, filled with fear. I have the realization that letting somebody else care for them sometimes is NOT abandoning them, and I can vocalize and actively recruit help from others without guilt.

I'm on an ongoing journey of recovery from my addiction to my kids (what I call "Momaholism"). There have been many unexpected detours on the way. I find gratitude in each one, as they have been learning experiences in how to love and forgive both myself and others from a heart-centered space. I'm trying to stay present without judgment or self-criticism, and most of all, without any expectation or attachment to the outcome(s), whether positive or negative. Now, when I feel angry, disappointed, sad, or frustrated while being a mom, wife, daughter, daughter-in-law, doctor, small business owner, I don't try to hide it, especially not from myself. I acknowledge the emotion; I own that truth.

To heal, it is important to acknowledge and respect how one feels, because if we ourselves don't, others won't! The moment I give myself permission to acknowledge what I am truly feeling in my different roles, without analysis, it connects me with my inner self and brings me into that place where only peace exists. There is no need for a façade any more, there is no fear.

As this life shift happened, spiritual teachers and many healers miraculously appeared. I am grateful for their guidance. I trained and board-certified in Integrative and Holistic medicine and Functional Medicine. Though I was already a doctor, now I was a healer too. I applied what I learned, first on myself, slowly healed emotionally and recovered physically. We live our lives based on our prior experiences, but can, with our intent and mindfulness, change the perception of those experiences.

Breath is an easy way to connect with your inner self. Mindfulness can happen here and now, when we pause and focus on breathing. There is enough medical research showing health benefits of meditation, yoga, breathing, and mindfulness. These should be taught in childhood, but most certainly before embarking on the journey of pregnancy and motherhood, which though very personal and spiritual, can sometimes also be traumatic.

As mothers, if we don't ground and center ourselves on a daily basis, the pressures can lead to stagnation and demise of who we truly are. Even twenty minutes of daily mindfulness practice(s), whatever that may be for you, is enough to restore hormonal and neuroendocrine balance and prevent disease. With attention to wholesome nourishing diet, rejuvenating sleep, conscious breathing, self-care and self-compassion, we stimulate the crucial relaxation response. There isn't one mindfulness or self-care practice that works for everyone. Find what anchors you into that place of calm.

While I'm trying to learn to sing again, I invite you other "momaholics" like myself to join me in creating a global consciousness-based and mindful mother's community.

Let us set and hold the following mutual intentions:

"There is no chaos, only a sense of control in every situation, no matter what it is; during this beautiful journey of motherhood, we should discover our true selves; we have the strength and support we need for being healthy; and we pass on this enlightened energy and wisdom to our children and to the world."

Namaste!

Author Bio:

Dr. Manisha Ghei, MD, ABIM, ABOIM, ABIHM, IFMCP, is the Founder and Medical Director of Praana Integrative Medicine & Holistic Health Center, PLLC, in Sugar Land, Texas, USA. She is multiple Board Certified in Internal Medicine and Integrative Holistic Medicine and a pioneer in the field of Functional Medicine, being certified in the first ever cohort of practitioners from all over the world to become an IFMCP (Institute for Functional Medicine Certified Practitioner).

Website: **www.praanaim.com**

The Present of Being Present
by Emma Porter

If you were asked on an average day what percent of your time is not mentally present, would you be satisfied with your answer?

Why is this question of value to contemplate? Because being present is a present to oneself and those around us, which includes our children. Another term to describe being present is mindful; simply this means paying attention to the moment without judging it and not wishing things were different. Sounds hard, though practice reaps wonderful side effects.

From the moment we become a mother, our roles seem to increase. We may already be someone's partner, daughter, sister, a colleague, an entrepreneur, and without a doubt the person a child looks to for basic needs, including security and love.

Being present is a significant part of my daily practice that allows me to live without a sense of feeling overwhelmed, fosters a sense of peace, and in turn cultivates joy.

In 2015 I found myself experiencing some depressed and disheartening feelings. Divorce proceedings had begun, and I was struggling with the health of one of my children and my own chronic pain. I returned to an old habit of mentally zoning out when I felt overwhelming emotions jumping in my mind.

I felt like I was a juggler of challenges in a circus that only I and my children were invited to. The state of my home became a symbol of my overwhelmed struggles, and a house that was once open doors to all to enter, I started to close up. Instead I made other projects I could not put off as priorities and I became exceptionally judgmental of myself as a mother.

"You do not deserve to be a mother" and "if they only knew," they being people who regarded me as a "good" mother. Then it dawned on me through listening to some comments from friends and a mentor that I had a lot going on to address, so no wonder I had slowly dropped some of my practices when it came to taking care of myself.

I started to encourage myself to drop labels and bring awareness of how I felt and where I felt it, and most importantly, what does that experience require to nurture feelings of what I preferred. In my case I had to ask for help and be open in regards to my house and the health of one child. To thrive vs survive required holding up fears and stepping through them, and I promise you, the reader, it was not as scary or embarrassing as my imagination had created; it was a relief, and I was met with nonjudgmental support and encouragement.

Our response to the external situations around us as mothers can help or hinder our well-being; being present, if practiced, can turn our storms into calm water, dissatisfaction into gratitude, and fears into adventure. The more being present in a moment is practiced, a new uplifting habit is formed.

How does one practice being present, though?

The breath and the five senses are little yet significant examples of keys to helping me, and I wish to share.

The breath is always there to utilize and requires no extra props, such as relaxing music, hot bath, glass or wine. Deep, slow breaths have been proven to relieve anxiety and promote relaxation. It is possible to do without anyone being aware, so an added bonus if you tend to feel self-conscious.

Bringing one's attention to the five senses helps with a focus for the moment. For example, a child having a lengthy tantrum.

Sight – I notice the colors around me, the shapes and objects, I see a child expressing theirself.

Hear – I notice the sounds around me, without judging any noises as "good" or "bad." What else can I hear, one or more noises, is there anything new that I can hear?

Smell – What can I smell? Indoor or outdoor smells. Strong or faint.

Taste – Is my mouth dry? Where does my tongue rest in the mouth? Any tastes to observe?

Touch – What does my body feel like? Tense, agitated, tired? The feeling of standing or sitting down, body unsupported or supported?

More often than not when I work through my breath and senses, gratitude starts to flood within me, which helps shift my well-being to a place that helps my interactions with others.

Thich Nhat Hanh wrote in *The Miracle of Mindfulness: An Introduction to the Practice of Meditation* "Don't do any task to get it over with. Resolve to do each job in a relaxed way, with all your attention. Enjoy and be one with your work." I became open to seeing my challenges once again as opportunities, with the approach that I am a work in progress regarding the discipline to become more present in life.

With my own children I believe that when I am present they receive a mother who is calmer, far more content, laughs more, is ready to face their concerns rather than sweep them away, supportive, kinder, nonjudgmental, is ready to try new experiences, and most noticeably feels more productive in all areas of her life. Fears diminish and peace is experienced. Being present was the present to myself that initially felt scary, as it showed me my preferences in life, but led to so much more. Go ahead, you and your children deserve and are worthy of the Present!

Author Bio:
Emma Porter is a mother and works with Montessori Preschoolers. Her passion is in finding practical ways to encourage people to believe that their emotional and spiritual well-being matter. For example, she is a Dunisha™ Master and a Facilitator of Chakradance™. She resides in Arizona and can be contacted and connected through the:

Website: **www.earthspiritcenter.org**

Hide... And Go Seek
by Jen Vandermaar

I'm an expert hider and a closet seeker.

My hiding skills were developed prenatally. Did you know that we pick up influence and energy from our mother and her environment as we develop? Hers was fear—and hiding.

My father was the total package. He was every kind of abusive and mentally ill. I only spent 2 of my 36 years of life with him, but the first 2 years of a child's life sets the tone for the rest of their days.

Hide. Stay safe and out of his radar. If he can't find you, he can't hurt you. I remember figuring this out as a toddler. These old survival skills are my everyday, subconscious skill set. And they are making me miserable.

Hide. Stay under the radar. If no one can see or hear me, then no one can care. What if they find out what he did to me? I'm hiding so deep inside myself that I don't know who I really am.

Except there is a knowing that wants to surface. Somewhere inside, all my ambitions, dreams and light have held on despite being denied and hidden for decades. Denying myself of myself has manifested in a depression that I can't shake. I'm captive in my own custom prison.

I didn't even realize I had depression until I had our two children. Then it was amplified to a level that I couldn't ignore.

I'm taking a leap of faith by writing this because it exposes me. I have decided that you, reading this, is worth my coming out of hiding. I feel safe telling you because I have a sneaky suspicion that some can relate.

Can you relate to feeling that there is a part of you missing out on life, but you carry on anyway? Do you feel exhausted from taking care of needs that don't belong to you? Are you pissed off that no one will give you what you want, without asking? If you can't shake the feeling that you are meant or capable of amazing life experiences, then I want to give you the encouragement to start.

It's so hard. The starting is so hard. I've started with big breaths and baby steps. Why did I decide to start now? Because I fucking decided. I made the choice. I realized that this is my life. My life. Your life. What the hell are we waiting for?

For me, this is a moment-to-moment process. Changing my inner dialogue to positive things I would encourage or praise my daughters for. Making choices that will make me happy in the moment. There is a ton of laundry to fold right now, but I choose to write to you, because this makes me happy. Big breaths and baby steps. When I first chose to start seeking, rather than hiding, my choices were very small. Like choosing to have a shower, small

You can absolutely do this. I have so much faith in you and love for you. It is safe to come out now.

I am doing this for me. You do it for yourself. It would break my heart to learn that one of my daughters were choosing to live the way I did. I am setting an example for them that I am proud of. I am setting an example for myself that I wanted when I was small.

Because I choose to.

I am getting better at making choices for my happiness. It takes practice, and sometimes I go back into hiding, but for shorter periods. I can't turn back now after the relief I feel after making happy choices. That's what I wish for you. The relief of happiness. You are not alone because I choose to be with you in spirit, excited for you and your new journey. Let's be seekers, together.

Author Bio:
Jen describes herself as the *"Worlds Most Below Average Housewife"* - with pride When she's home not making supper, she's thinking about becoming a photographer, a real estate investor, a children's book author and a gold digger. Hailing from picturesque Prince Edward Island, Canada.

Instagram: **@jenvandermaar**

Letting Go of Perfect
by Micah Klug

I have the problem of always feeling there isn't enough time in the day. There seems to never be enough time to make sure the children's needs are met, or my husband's, or the house-work—and this doesn't include my business adventures!

If we are not careful, this list can grow to be endless. We will find ourselves starting to become trapped in a never-ending cycle of frustration and fear. And to me, I somehow think if I can't get everything done, then this is a reflection of who I am... and I'm a perfectionist at heart.

Being a perfectionist can be good (and also bad) depending on where you find and decide where your value comes from. Do you find your value coming from the possibility of crossing everything off your list? What if you don't get anything on your list done? Do you give yourself grace?

I remember a prayer that one of my parents gave when I was a child. They prayed that we could "do all the things that Thou (God) would have us do." I struggled with this prayer primarily because in Matthew 5:48, Christ tells his disciples, "Be ye therefore perfect, even as your Father which is in heaven is perfect."

I thought, Now I have to be perfect all the time, get all the things I want done, and now get all the things God wants done! My candle was burning out at both ends. I became overwhelmed, anxious, and constantly tired.

Throughout my teenage and young adult years, I came across a talk by President Russell M. Nelson in my personal studies. He relates a personal experience in relation to his scripture study of Matthew 5:48: "The term perfect was translated from the Greek teleios, which means 'complete'. Teleios is an adjective derived from the noun telos, which means 'end'.

The infinitive form of the verb is teleiono, which means to reach a distant end, to be fully developed, or to finish."

Please note that the word does not imply "freedom from error"; it implies "achieving a distant objective."

Weight lifted off my shoulders when I read this. I didn't have to be perfect in the sense as I understood it to be (being without error). Christ doesn't expect you or I to be "perfect" in the sense of never making a mistake in our lives. Christ asks us to do our best, come to Him so we can be molded and developed by Him. This is a lifelong process!

There are things we can do our best to be perfect in, such as paying our tithes, personal prayers, reading the scriptures by ourselves and with our children. The rest the Lord will help us as we draw closer to him. Being perfected by Him will take our entire lifetime, but rest assured, you're in great company. If you're willing to pay the price, He can make so much more out of you than you can by yourself. He can make more out of you than your fondest dreams.

Let go of perfect.

Let go and give yourself permission to partake of the Savior's grace. He suffered for you and knows your deepest and most tenderhearted feelings. It's okay to make mistakes, it's okay to seek forgiveness and heavenly help. We all need it in our lives. Remember that the Lord loves you and desires greatly for you to return to live in His presence after your mortal journey. All we can do is our best. His grace takes care of the rest.

Author Bio:
Micah Klug is a Christian, wife, mother, author of a cookbook, and blogger. She runs a lifestyle blog to help people strengthen their faith, home, and family by living simple without losing quality or sanity.

Website: **www.HomeFaithFamily.com**

One Mother's Story of Struggle, Survival, and Triumph
by Leilani Manako

Motherhood has been a journey. A lot of my struggles have been staying home with them. It did not come naturally for me and it still doesn't.

At a young age I knew I was going to be a mother. I knew I was going to breastfeed. I knew I was going to have a natural birth and I knew I was going to be a stay at home mom. It was as if it were in my DNA and apart of my destiny to do so. The funny thing is, I didn't even like kids. They made me uncomfortable.

At 20, I had my first daughter. I researched the pregnancy and what was happening with my body. I researched the sizes of the baby, did the ultrasounds, and never missed an appointment. I had done all the research of what was happening before the baby came and nothing really about raising a child.

I had relied on a lot of what other people told me. "Oh, don't hold the baby too much, you'll spoil her," "make sure you put her on a feeding schedule." I was oblivious. I had relied on a lot of my motherly intuition to kick in, but having no practical application I was completely clueless of what to do. I tried the cry-it-out method. That was probably one of the hardest things I've ever had to do. I had developed depression, extreme fatigue, and tried to cope with comfort food. I had gained a considerable amount of weight that continued to make feel miserable, inadequate, and wanting to give up.

6 months later I find out I'm pregnant with baby number two. It's another beautiful little girl. These two hooligans are 17 months

apart and rambunctious! They really gave me a run for my money. I would find cherry cheesecake spread all over my feet and sheets. The bathroom sink flooded with toilet paper, water overflowing onto the carpet, toilet, and shower, and two little girls covered head to toe in think creamy lotion.

Overweight, miserable, exhausted, tired and depressed God definitely had something for me to learn. 5 years later, baby number 3 was born.

From the beginning, I had a really rough seven years of marriage. I had lost myself. I had lost my confidence. I felt like I was there to only serve my children and husband and I didn't know who I was anymore. I had become someone else, someone completely different. My confidence was down the drain and I completely lost my sense of individuality. At the time I didn't know I was highly empathic and constantly an empty vessel.

Any mother knows that you cannot be a mother if you don't take care of yourself. I had developed a lot of fear and anxiety.

In 2013 I ended up homeless and divorced. I tried to go back to my hometown, but the children were court ordered to stay in Arizona. I lived out of a hotel, missed my daughter's birthday, eventually I found an apartment and spent Christmas day moving. I spent the eve of New Year's sobbing in an empty room curled up on a mattress on the floor. I didn't know anybody or have any friends. I was alone. These traumatic events led me developing post-traumatic stress disorder PTSD.

I had spent the next few years doing all sorts of odd jobs to make ends meet, sometimes working two or three jobs at a time. Shifts would start from early in the morning to late into the evening. By the time I got off work, I would sleep 3-4 hours, get the kids 5:00 am, off to school for my oldest two and the littlest one off to the babysitter.

Within this time frame, my anxiety and depression continued to spiral and eventually developed extreme adrenal fatigue.

At this time I worked as a server and a bartender and lost both jobs simultaneously gone under. The businesses had gone under and I was left with unpaid wages and still trying to balance motherhood.

At this point I had completely lost my faith and spirituality. I found a job doing cabinet refinishing. I was still suffering with high levels of anxiety, PTSD that seemed to continue spiraling downwards.

I can remember driving to a job and almost not being able to make it. In my car I would think, "What if I just let the car run into the median? Is this really the only thing I'm meant to live for?"

I remember sobbing and cried out for anybody, any God, anything to help me. I literally felt like my spirit was about to leave my body.

But I fought. I remember driving straight to the gym, putting my headphones on, and getting on the stair-master. I told myself if I don't climb until I can't climb anymore I was not going to get through this alive.

Desperate, I started my healing journey late 2015. I enrolled in yoga teacher training with specialty studies in energy healing. The journey to healing myself had been nothing short of a miracle. As I found a way to heal, love, and forgive myself I found God again.

By way of the Universe, I've ended up back with my husband, back to my children, back to my Home and more Whole than I've ever been before.

Author Bio:

A native to the beautiful state of Utah, Leilani Manako left the Rocky Mountains for the painted desert of Arizona in early 2005. Leilani has accepted motherhood as her greatest challenge and most rewarding moment. She's learned humility, surrender, peace, grace, and unconditional love amidst struggle, survival, and hard-learned life lessons. Leilani has a passion for transformation and helping others on their journey. She's serves as a Reiki Master, intuitive energy healer, and actively lives a peaceful Yogic lifestyle.

Email: **leilanisoulwellness@gmail.com**

Red Crayons
by Valencia V. Gibson

Mom! My underwear is pink, music to a laundering mother's ears. Oh, to walk into my home and not step on a tiny metal race car, sit on a plastic doll, or trip over the laundry basket, filled with soiled clothes times three.

What would I give? Absolutely nothing! No matter how clean I kept my very first apartment, or how much easier it was to study for exams in pure silence. I wouldn't trade the fussing, and bickering of kids and creative differences for anything. Can it be overwhelming at times? Unquestionably! Especially when your husband can be an even bigger kid at times (No offense to his ego, or the men alike). I never like to toot my own horn, but I'm sure many women who have stayed home for more than eight hours even once in their lives can agree that a mother's job trumps a 9–5 and the commute in rush-hour traffic combined.

From that first flutter in our wombs, call from the adoption agency, or the first time we bring our precious child(ren) home, the clock of parenting starts ticking. We obsess over our qualifications before children, our best features as we are raising them, and what our kids will feel about their childhood after they are all grown up. We wonder if we will raise successful children, or will they stray from our teachings. We strive to give our children everything we either had growing up, or never had at all. We constantly pick up extra assignments, and frustrate when the Libra scale of motherhood tips a little too much in one direction. However, it seems that many of us rarely find time for ourselves. I wouldn't know what a break looked like if it packed my bags and gave me an all-expenses-paid vacation. And don't even get me started on that four-letter word some refer to as rest—I'm trying not to say that too loud in my mind, I might wake my children.

In all honesty, motherhood is a theme park filled with a variety of roller coasters. Some fun, and some that give us enough butterflies in our bellies, to fly around the whole earth in a day. My son was my firstborn, and he taught me how to listen while I slept. I could never look away for more than two seconds when he was a toddling free with no other sibling(s). If I thought for a minute I was going to place him in a crib, and close my eyes, I was only fooling myself. Trying to get a little shut-eye while he slept never worked after two years of age. Naps always resulted in a crib fugitive, an overflowing toilet, or a crayon mural on my walls, etc. Boy, I'd sure like to meet the smart person who thought of crayons, and thank him/her for their many contributions to my clothes, shoes, tables, walls, and how they melt so beautifully in the backseat of the family car.

However, my son could not top his crayon-eating sister, born three years later with her eyes wide open. The minute she learned how to walk, she dominated everything, and big brother was not happy about that at all. Now let's fast-forward. I don't know what tomorrow may hold, but I hope the best for my children, as any mother would. We are now in the elementary stages. That place where they are no longer babies, and are semi-independent. But they're not yet pre-teens either, and somehow have all the snappy attitudes of a pubescent. So most of the time I forget that they are still children, and often find myself saying "You should know better" when they make childish mistakes.

News flash! They are still children, hence the term childish applies. It is my earnest prayer that someday I will understand why I push my children so early, and hard. I haven't a clue if whether I am trying to mold them to the expectations of the schools they attend. Schools that expect a wiggly six-year-old, and a curious nine-year-old to sit still for six and a half hours a day, with a thirty-minute visit to the play area, 5 days a week. Or if I am truly the one to blame, for lacking the resources necessary to place them in schools that are more challenging and conducive to their success.

Oops! There goes that dreadful word, blame. How easy is it as a mother to blame ourselves for the quirks and behaviors of our children when we can't even take credit for all forty-six chromosomes that make our children who they are? We can point the finger at dad, but for every one finger a mom points, there are eight pointing right back at us! Dad can spend a week with the children in our absence, feed them junk and fast food and NOT comb hair, make them take baths daily, or go to bed on time. And he would only be given a pat on the back, and met with compassion. While mom is crucified for being absent in the first place. Not to male bash, because dads have a lot of great qualities when they apply themselves, but that's just it. This moment is not about dads. Yet it is just like a mother whose life is consumed by her family to take the attention from herself, and focus it on the qualities of another. We have tons of great qualities, and we should never blame ourselves for doing the best we can to be great mothers.

I am reminded of a time where it all became very overwhelming for me. For the sake of working to provide, I found myself having a nervous breakdown. For starters, my husband had been laid off from his employer of several years, and the children were feeling the adverse effects and not responding well to their change of schools and our move from one side of town to the other. I was getting calls every day from my son's teacher about his behavior, and I could not be the PTA parent who frequented the halls of my children's schools staying abreast, or reinforcing instruction given. Neither did I have the support of family members who could visit in my place, seeing as how dad had lost his vehicle. I wanted him to fill in the gap so badly, but he was too distraught to see what he still had, as opposed to what he'd just lost. And with technology ever evolving in communication, I did not want my son's record to be saturated with behavioral issues. So I did what I think any mother would do, I stretched myself far and very thin. Wounded emotionally, I still managed to make up for everything and everyone else's shortcomings as a wife, mother, daughter, granddaughter, employee, friend, etc. I landed myself a two-star stay in a city hospital with chest pains and anxiety. As a high point of my admittance, I received a visit from a residence priest. He asked me what was my reason for being there. After I told him what my beliefs were, he, expressing his exhaustion for my busy schedule, responded in the most charismatic way possible: "I am so concerned that you want so desperately for your kids to have a father, that they don't have a mother." Talk about a wake-up call. That was it for me, because he was undeniably right!

I was discharged with a purpose, upholding a vow: to make time for myself even if all I can think about at times are my children, and what I want to do better. Simply because now I understand that if I do not take care of myself, my children will be motherless. I encourage all mothers to find their happy place, drop the supermom persona, and accept the help that is offered. Many of us live by the "I got it" law, feeling like we must do it all, especially when we do not have a lot of support. And there is no single way to define what taking care of yourself means. Nonetheless, let us take a moment of mindfulness to recall what we did for fun before we had children. Or what makes us feel good when we do get a moment to enjoy ourselves, and how can we rearrange our schedules to get more of it. One method that works for me is blocking an hour out of my day while the kids sleep, play, or are at school (if I'm off work). I take time away from the to-do list and everything else calling for my attention. Whatever your place of serenity is, find it, and make time for yourself.

Empowering Caregivers with Mindfulness
by Seema Kapur

I am a mother of 17-year-old daughter, who has autism; she is nonverbal. My clinical background is from the field of occupational therapy. I am also a Reiki and meditation teacher. I will address an important piece of this puzzle called autism which is gradually consuming families, and that is the stressors that caregivers, parents, go through in day-to-day lives and how mindfulness can play an important part in overcoming them. This is based on my experience of working with numerous behavior coaches, therapists, doctors, psychologists, and then coming back home to my most wonderful and effective teacher, my daughter.

Mindfulness comes from the word *mind*. This mind cannot be touched by meds or therapy. Why? Because our mind is often chained to habits that we have formed due to our upbringing, society, fears, worry, anger, preconceived ideas, etc. To touch this mind, a change is needed. This change is really about a way of living. It is about our state of mind. Only then we can see our kids and our lives in an open, spacious manner so we are not limited to what works, what does not work, and not be afraid to challenge our fears.

Often we are so oblivious to daily day-to-day stressors and overlook or neglect, especially when we are parenting and caring for a special-needs child. By practicing mindfulness, we ourselves can learn from our kids as well as support ourselves and them in this maze of life. One major and important aspect that is overlooked and not taken care of is how to remain in the presence of the pain and suffering that we see in day-to-day lives without becoming overwhelmed.

My daughter is nonverbal, and although she has no physical deficits, she is dependent for her needs due to learning deficits. I embraced mindfulness and meditation several years after her birth; during that time I was struggling with depression.

As I progressed and moved forward in my practice, life with my daughter started to become more fluid and fruitful. With all of the challenges presented with my daughter, I can honestly say that this practice has been my saving grace. I've had periods of anger and deep frustration, but never to the point of sheer depression or hopelessness. Every time I felt like I was at a point of no return, it always pulled me forward with new direction, hope, and perspective.

That is why I am writing this today and why my mission and vision is to show parents like myself, who have kids on the autism spectrum, with learning disabilities, with emotional or other physical challenges, how amazingly important and altering this practice can be.

I am listing below how mindfulness and compassion practice can help them and kids in day to day life:
- Letting go of labeling and judging
- Acceptance
- Clarity
- Releasing guilt and self-compassion
- Being Present
- Patience and setting boundaries
- Be a mindful teacher within by learning from your kids
- Flexibility
- Letting go of fear and distress
- Letting go of control, be open
- Clear, mindful communication
- Inner calmness through self-awareness
- Increase sensitivity to self and others
- Roundedness
- Compassion

A simple practice which only takes as little as a minute can help to remind you of your inner strength. Place a hand on your chest and one under your belly button as a gentle reminder that you have everything you need within. Take deep breath, count till 10. Close eyes if that helps. It's a quick pick-me-up simple technique to remember you are loved.

It's okay to ask for help. If you are someone who has to do everything and you struggle to let people help you, practice asking for help and accepting that your way is not the only way. Openness helps to see others' view point and help in learning new ways. Why I want to teach mindfulness? When I first started practicing and decided to teach, my teacher said to me that teaching comes from your own direct experience. We can repeat what is written in the books, repeat the words of our teachers, but the true teachings come from your own experience, as that's when they become alive. What I am sharing here is my own direct experience of accumulative experience as a mother, therapist, and a Reiki/Meditation teacher. It's what I teach. It's what I practice. And every time I do, it never fails to amaze me.

Practice and learning is ongoing and no way complete, as it's lifelong and I want to teach parents and caregivers what I have experienced and learned all these years and show them how to help their kids connect to their breath, their body, their feelings, the earth, and each other. As caregivers, parents, teachers, family members, we are connected to kids. Kids with autism are like any other kids; to grow they need the freedom yet they also need the discipline, patience, and guidance to bring them back gently to groundedness of earth so they feel safe and secure.

It is hard sometimes for us because we can't seem to understand the perspective of children with autism and what they see, feel, and experience. We don't know what it's like to see the world in this way, and we watch them struggle to make sense of why they move and behave in the way they do. Same way kids don't know how to connect and reconnect, as they have a very thin grounded connection and their growth and development depends on who is holding and how someone is holding their hands in this maze, puzzle of life journey.

This is why we as adults first need to look at ourselves and do some self-care. I can tell from my experience as well as what I hear from teachers and therapists that children reflect back our energy to us, our state of mind and how we are feeling. So if we've had a bad day, feeling tired, anxious, children act like mirrors and reflect it back. The more we can do to stay centered, calm, and grounded using simple mindful meditation techniques, the better it is for them.

To summarize, I found over the years that every time I calmed my mind, my daughter would become just as calm. I realized we were linked, bonded, energetically, and that on some level my daughter could sense and feel everything that I was feeling. This served as motivation to keep up my practice.

The most important way this has helped my daughter and me is that it gave me the ability to look at her more deeply and to look beyond her tantrums, the struggles she was experiencing, and into what was behind her fear or anger. It taught me to take the time to center myself, breathe deeply, and to ask myself what it was that I could not see that she could see or feel. It taught me compassion, equanimity, and patience. If we step back, we might see what this teaches us about our life and our choices. If we practice moments of mindful attention to those precious minutes when we are with children, centering our energy so we can allow them to do what they need to do to cope in this world, yet showing them they can trust us to guide them into a calmer state, then there is no final solution. Just a moment of peace.

Mindfulness and meditation is a practice, a way of life, resting on the time-tested three pillars for anything we want to do: patience, persistence, and perseverance. This is about empowerment for ourselves so we no longer will say to ourselves that I cannot do this because I don't have this. This in turn will empower our kids. Because we cannot give others something that we do not have. Empowerment ignites empowerment.

Author Bio:

Seema is an occupational therapist, Reiki and meditation teacher, and author. Originally from India, she is now settled in Arizona, US. She has two teenage kids, one girl with nonverbal Autism, who is an inspiration and drive to help find her inner strength. She teaches families, practitioners, and children mindfulness and meditation. Seema's vision is to help families with special-needs kids in coping with everyday stresses to be more grounded so they can find their innate strength themselves and set up programs in special schools about meditation and mindfulness.

Email: **thehealingvalley@gmail.com**
Facebook: **@LotusReikiReborn**

Pondering Apron String and Umbilical Cords
by Lori Jill Isenstadt

Many of us worry about being the good-enough mother. We are constantly asking ourselves if we did enough. Did we do the right thing in a situation, or is our child now going to be scarred for the rest of their life? Did we protect our child when they needed protection? Are they going to be in long-term therapy as adults because of how we raised them?

There was that time period that I questioned so much and finally let it get the best of me. Other people said I was hovering too much, *overprotective* they called it. She will never learn how to do things on her own if I am always right by her side. Overseeing things. In earshot.

What did that kid on the playground say to her before she was pushed headfirst in the sandbox? My two friends held me back as we sat on the bench about 20 feet away. I stood up and pushed them away. Was this the right thing to do? I tried to run to her and they both stood in front of me. I let them block me from going to her. Was this the right thing to do? Was 5-year-old Alisha ready to take on the sandbox bully all on her own? Is there a bucket tall enough to capture my tears when I went home and cried about it later that night?

I buckled under the pressure, as I was tired of being criticized for not being able to cut the umbilical cord. At the same time, my stomach was in knots in how I handled the situation that day. What did I do wrong? I know exactly what I did wrong. It came to me in the middle of the night as I nursed my 6-month-old as she lay next to me in bed. Yes, that is exactly right. My 6-month-old daughter was sleeping in bed with me. Another thing the proverbial "they" warned me I should not be doing. Eff them, I said!

As Carly nursed and made all her noises that melted my heart, I kept going back to the sandbox incident. Nothing about it felt right, and of course, I battered myself emotionally. What did I do wrong? The answer popped into my head at that exact moment. I swear it was like someone was talking directly to me. What did you do wrong, Lori?

Well, for gosh's sake. I could see it so clearly now. I had been hanging out with these moms for over a year. We learned about each other, what makes us tick, our likes and dislikes. Our kids spent a lot of time playing with each other as we got to know each other better.

In some ways, I was the outsider. That didn't bother me so much. I realized early in my mothering career that I was the outsider, the weird one who did things differently with her kids. The one the others made fun of.

After all, I was the mom who "had to be different." Those were their words, not mine. I homebirthed. My family was vegetarian, we co-slept, did not vaccinate, chose alternative healthcare, did not send my kids to nursery school and kept them close to me. No sleepovers at friends' house or grandparents' house.

Yes, of course, I was annoyed at all the comments. What if there is an emergency during the birth? Aren't you afraid your midwife might not make it to you in time? They say that babies who sleep with their parents can suffocate to death when you accidentally roll on top of them. Your kids are going to be so sick from not eating meat and getting all their protein and vitamins.

Now just so you know, I was not a total pushover. I had my opinions and had no problem sharing them with this group of mothers. What do you mean my midwife might not make it? What about your husband having to drive you to the hospital during bad weather and being a nervous wreck and having to take his attention away from you during the throes of active labor? Babies suffocating in bed with their parents? How about babies dying, from SIDS, all alone in their cribs? Why aren't you appalled about the chemicals you are exposing your kids to from the meat and dairy you serve them?

Now comes the time when you might ask. Friends. These were your friends? Well, in a very sick and twisted way, yes, these were my friends. I could talk to them about many common feelings of motherhood and parenting. How our husbands were as fathers. What stupid things they did and said. How helpful or not helpful they were to us. We would complain about why on earth our husbands just did not see the pile of clothes on the couch or the toys all over the floor or the mess in the kitchen. Why did we have to act like their mothers and tell them to clean up? Why couldn't they take the initiative? We loved talking about our sex lives, or for many of us, the lack of a sex life. I had a sounding board during the times I was so tired that I could not see straight. Or when my mother-in-law was driving me crazy. These other moms, they didn't have such quick answers for the same things they were suffering with. We could commiserate with each other. Talk things to death, upside down and inside out. And we would all feel better by the time we were done. My mommy friends are the reason I survived the early years of motherhood.

I definitely got many of my needs met as a mother. So I stayed with this group of mothers that I had met at a mothers' group several years ago. We met on a regular basis and they fulfilled many of my needs. Not all my needs, and in fact, had a knack for making me feel bad or questions some of my decisions.

Especially all the comments about cutting those apron strings. And yet, I stayed. I stayed because this group of mothers met more of my needs than they made me feel bad. Does that make sense to you?

Now, I did find my peer group a few years later, and if truth be told,

I was the least of the weird ones in this new peer group made up of what others would say were really, really weird mothers. They did all these out-of-the-mainstream stuff that I did, and on top of that they home-schooled their kids the one thing that I was not doing and the one thing that really separated the kind of weird to the really, really weird label they were given. I should say that this was in very conservative Long Island, NY, and it was in the early 1980s. Now, much of what I was into then would not really be considered so weird now.

Let's get back to that night, though. When I was breastfeeding Carly. In the quiet and stillness of the night, I realized what I did wrong in the playground that day. When my daughter was bullied by that kid in the playground, I was also being bullied. I let the bullies bully me. That is what I did. My friends were bullying me. Trying to get me to mother my child the way they felt was best. I let them override what I knew to be in the best interests of my child. If I did not know this for sure before that day in the playground, I really knew this now. No one knows my kids like I know my kids. No one is going to care and love my kids like I do. No one has to deal with the fallout from life's events with my kids like I do. From that day forth, I did my best to not let their label of "overprotective mother" get in the way of doing what I felt best. Sticks and stones may break my bones, but your names will never harm me.

Lessons learned in my life as a mother are never ones to be kept to myself. When you feel strongly enough about something, stick with your convictions.

Do not let the bullies bully you. Twenty-eight years after the sandbox incident, I can confidently say to myself that I have done a good job. I did what I felt was best. I am the good-enough mother.

Author Bio:

Lori Jill Isenstadt, IBCLC, brought up in New York and now living in Arizona. She has had a good marriage to Alan for the last 36 years. Together they have raised 3 human beings who are now 32, 29, and 27 years old. Lori has a private practice and is the host of the popular iTunes podcast called All About Breastfeeding, the place where the girls hang out. She spends her days supporting, educating, and advocating for the breastfeeding family and enjoys helping mothers who are experiencing breastfeeding challenges.

Website: **www.allaboutbreastfeeding.biz**
Email: **abreastfeeding@hotmail.com**

Going the Distance: A Love That Wins
by Roz Barrett

Momma, do you need a word of encouragement today? My prayer is that, as you read this, your heart will have a moment to exhale with the relief from the inner torment good mommas seem to struggle with endlessly. If my words resonate within one person's heart and she feels grace filling the crevices of her own hurting soul, in her journey toward personal wholeness, then please know, dear one, it was worth all the struggle to string these sentences together. You, my dear, are worth it!

My message is simple. You do not have to do everything right as a momma to raise your kids well. Let me introduce you to a love that goes the distance in raising your children's hearts from toddlerhood to adulthood and in tandem heals your own heart's insecurities as well. Love so forgiving and merciful that you don't have to be an "expert" when you begin this job of parenting young lives. God is love. His love is the arrow in our journey. Faith in His love is our road map, and transparency will be the key or legend on our map. Remember this truth: all arrows point home. Right to God's gracious Daddy's heart.

The Prophet Isaiah said, "He will feed His flock like a shepherd; He will gather the lambs with His arm, and carry them in His bosom, and gently lead those who are with young." God is highly invested in those hearts who give him access. He is committed to getting us to safe pasture as we raise our little ones. Invite Him in to your messy, moody, momma struggles.

Love is tangible. Our children can feel it. We love down pillows and big fluffy blankets and we love comfort food. Love is a feast for the senses. We can touch it, taste it, and smell it. Love weaves comfort, and more importantly, security and healthy self-worth into the fibers of our children's lives. This is a foundation they can both build their lives on, and one you can launch them to distant shores from as well.

Love is transparent. Our children can see it, and even when we've failed in our words or actions, believe that we still love them. They possess the sweet gift of simple faith. Faith simply means to believe the good in someone. Our children have the ability to forgive quickly. It's a God-given gift.

Sincere apologies help your children identify their value and worth as an individual. Their tender hearts respond quickly to the restoration that we initiate through our brave communication of making things right. As we lead by example in how to repair breaks, cracks, holes, and tears in our relationships, we are giving them tools for success in life. As Winnie the Pooh says, "Be brave, little Piglet." Our children need encouragement to be brave and do the right thing, even when it's hard. "Be brave, mommas of littles," you have what it takes to be lovingly transparent.

Love is truthful. Our children can trust it. We tell our littles, "Yes, the shot hurts" at their doctor's visits, but explain that the shot will protect them.

Love is honest, not condemning. Honest love reveals the truth about our own motives, needs, wants, and other issues of the heart. One of the best gifts we can give a child is a love for the truth. My five-year-old grandson was excited that his Nana was going to spend the night at his home. He and his big brother helped me take my bags up to their guest bedroom.

You know how there is a moment when you can nearly read their precious little minds? This gift of perception causes all the momma alarms to go off in our heart. My grandson proceeded to ask me simultaneously as he climbed on top of the dresser, "Nana, want to see me jump on the bed." He already calculated he could clear the ceiling fan; he didn't, however, consider the wood bed frame which jutted out inches from the mattress. As he was making final deliberations or gathering last-minute courage, I engaged his heart. "Declan, no, it's not a good idea to do that." He looked at me then looked at the situation, again recalculating and reassuring me he was indeed capable. Two more times I cautioned him as I moved toward him, "No, this isn't a good idea." When I was in close proximity, you know the moment, I was nearly close enough to grab him, but not quite, he jumped. He landed safely. The next part is priceless to my heart. I said, "Declan, I am very disappointed that you chose to not listen to me. You chose to jump after I said no." I then left the room. My grandson felt the break, the tear he had caused between us. He ran after me into the hall and grabbed my leg and said, "Nana, I'm sorry." I bent down and told him the truth: the reason I told him no was because I not only loved him, but I saw there was something he didn't see, something that he could have hurt himself on if he missed the bed. Then I forgave him. We repaired the connection of the heart of our relationship.

Not many of us have completely rich childhood memories. Most of our parents did the best they could with what skills they had been taught. Forgiving our parents is a significant key to raising our own children well. I have been on this forgiveness journey most of my adult life. I would have disqualified myself at the start of my children's lives because I was a mess.

My Heavenly Daddy saw me differently. I was a candidate for His grace. His love went the distance in my heart, and healed the many broken places gradually. Then He began to reweave the tapestry of my life into one that reflected His goodness at Christ's expense. As my son was leaving home at the age of twenty-three, we stood in the kitchen saying our goodbyes.

He had graduated from college, and was engaged to a lovely young woman. I was sobbing as I told him I loved him. My words surprised me as I heard myself say, "Nick, you're leaving now? I finally understand how to be a parent."

Healing takes time. God's love doesn't give up on us. His love will be enough to keep us on track and cross our finish line. God's love is a great sign post, a most dependable arrow. Just invite Him in.

Author Bio:
Roz Barrett was born and raised in Michigan, where she lives with her husband, Rick. They have two married children and three grandchildren. Being a Nana has provided the joy and treasure of passing on her love for reading, cooking, and all things that twinkle (Christmas Lights - Downtown Rochester) and sparkle (July 4th Fireworks - St. Clair). Investing her heart in women to see them come to wholeness in Christ and fulfill their destinies is her passion.

Email: **eagleswings@cfaith.com**

How to Balance Work and Kids and Thrive
by Wanda Krause

Tracy (name changed) invited me over for dinner. She had something to tell me. Her husband had informed me the day before, so I was prepared. After dinner, she suggested we go to another room to chat alone, and there she broke it to me. She was diagnosed with cancer, and also hyperthyroidism. Tracy has significant accomplishments in sports, and although it was apparent she was physically and emotionally exhausted, she did look strong. Just like I used to, she could pull all-nighters, night after night with work and continue work and be there for her kids during the day, easy. Mothers who care so passionately about their work and so selflessly for their children tend to stretch themselves to extremes, heedless to the fact that they can hit rock-bottom.

In a sense, that week Tracy admitted defeat. I fully know the psychological and physical toll balancing work and kids can all of a sudden take when all along you've done a superb job at juggling it all by stealing all hours of the day and night, only to find out you, too, are human. She would embark on a steep learning curve in visioning, planning—for life, and reflecting, in fact, on her whole purpose. Her wake-up call wasn't one to stop her from functioning in life. Rather, it was to show her how to create greater impact, fulfillment, and love in family and work. She hit rock-bottom; she was willing to make all the changes needed. Her defeat would open her up to new ways of being as a mother and change-maker. We set a date to get out the markers and 3'x4' sheets to plan it. The journey began.

On my own journey, I have learned four absolutely critical principles to thrive while balancing work and kids. The first two few people think of and the last two few people really practice. The first of the four is to evaluate what is energizing and what is energy-depriving. If you're not sure where to begin your journey, take a step back from everything. You need a bird's-eye view of where you are spending your time and energy. If you don't understand why you are stretched and stressed, you can't make the necessary changes to thrive as a mother making a difference.

Simply ask, "Is this fulfilling to me?" When anything is unfulfilling, one outcome is failing to be truly present and patient with your kids. You're also less likely to be kind to yourself. Do you feel excitement, creativity, expansion, peace, and fulfillment through your activities? Or exhaustion and stress? This may sound like a no-brainer, but really do set aside some quiet time to ask yourself the question with these qualifications and actually write down what comes to mind. I guarantee this exercise will help you become so much clearer on how you are managing your energy. What has been critical for me is to eliminate what sucks the energy out of me and incorporate more of what creates joy—hobbies and work-related. There is no equation for how many activities to dump. It isn't easy, but this can't be a half-assed attempt. You actually have to sacrifice some things in your life where you really are removing things that are not serving you from your daily routine—things that you once thought you couldn't. This principle was literally life-saving for Tracy.

To know whether or not something serves you, you will rely on the second principle, purpose. Same goes here, if you're not clear on what it is you really want to see happen in your life and what you want to do with it, you won't be clear on what daily activities will help you thrive or not. You will get caught up in other people's visions, goals, and demands. When you are clear on your own purpose, it will become so much easier for you to say the word No, and free yourself for things that really do light you up and help you feel and be productive, and in less time.

Tracy recognized that what she was working so hard to achieve wasn't truly in alignment with her bigger dreams. They were aligned with her dreams, but not the big ones! To get the difference will be crucial. She allowed herself for the first time to dream really big about what her most amazing life could look like. She could now admit the consequences of pulling all-nighters to her health, mental clarity, and ability to be present with her family. From the perspective of alignment to her true and higher calling, she could choose what lights her up. The latter is what I call the larger version. We get caught up in trying to fulfill the desires of the smaller version at the expense of the larger version. Start saying more No's to things that are not in alignment with your massive dreams and larger version of who you are and begin doing things that support your greater purposes. If you are not clear on your purpose, a mentor can help.

The third is delegate. Not all things related to your purpose or life, in general, will be joyful, yet, they need to be done. For example, doing the laundry, car maintenance, and some aspects of marketing are not what I absolutely love doing. These activities might not only frustrate me, they take me way more time to do than they could someone else. When you delegate, you are more efficient with your time and energy.

What will it require of you to start delegating? For Tracy, it meant accepting that not everything has to be perfect. That perspective changed everything. She handed over more of the cleaning up after dinner responsibilities to her husband, even though she knew the kitchen might end up far from perfectly clean. For her, much more was at stake, and so she decided to let go of the controls. The principle of delegating is critical to all great mothers who aspire to greatness in their work.

The fourth is self-care. From my first year in university, I knew that this would be the cornerstone to juggling the most demanding things in life, and so I have stayed true to this principle as best as I understood it. Especially during exam time, even if I slept a few hours a night to study (which I'll circle back to), I would be extra vigilant about jogging or hitting the gym. From when I was very young, I would go into a quiet space and practice mindfulness before I even knew it had a name. Mindfulness, such as through meditation or walking in the forest in appreciation, will ground you.

They help you to remember your inner strength and being and align with that greater and limitless power. I have achieved a lot on my journey before having children and with children, and I absolutely know I could not have done all I have and raised beautiful children without exercising and practicing mindfulness.

Stress is the number-one reason behind disease. Mindfulness and exercise serve to reduce the stress hormone cortisol in the bloodstream. Cortisol leads to increased risk of depression, mental illness, decreased resiliency, and numerous diseases.

Through mindfulness and exercise you can dramatically lower the stress hormone and increase the capacity mentally, emotionally, spiritually, and physically to perform at high levels. Tracy completely revamped her diet and sleep habits and made exercise an absolute. Her energy levels soared in the face of battling the two diseases.

I admit I didn't fully appreciate the critical place of sleep in productivity and well-being until after a period of extreme stress coupled with sparse sleep when I was also diagnosed with hyperthyroidism. I eliminated the disease entirely by a year later through diet, exercise, reintroducing mindfulness practices, and respecting sleep. According to Arianna Huffington, every disease, whether it's heart disease, diabetes, or cancer, is connected to sleep deprivation.

If you are not making well-being a priority through daily ritual and practice, you cannot hope to balance work and kids and thrive. My wake-up call at that time was largely due to my kids. I decided that I had to be a healthy mom to be there for them fully, hence, the loop back to purpose. My purpose is to be a healthy mom to raise healthy, abundant, beautiful, successful children and contribute to leadership development. Many of us wait until we get a wake-up call before we choose to embrace the principles for balance and success. Obviously, it needn't be so. But, as Dr. Dyer reminds us, too, it is critical to realize that we are the ones who must choose balance; no one will create it for us: "The single most important tool to being in balance is knowing that you and you alone are responsible for the imbalance between what you dream your life is meant to be, and the daily habits that drain life from that dream" (Dr. Wayne W. Dyer).

Author Bio:
Wanda Krause, Ph.D., mother, ski enthusiast, change strategist, CEO of Krause Consulting, is assistant professor in the School of Leadership Studies, Royal Roads University, and an award-winning author and editor of four books. She works with purpose-driven people to get out of reaction mode and playing mediocre to smash their glass ceilings and build a thriving life doing what they love. Her mission is to create political change through leadership development.

Website: **www.wandakrause.com**

The Greatest
Teacher-
Motherhood!

The Best Lessons in Life Are Learned from Our Children
by Anya Bruder

I became a mom fairly late in life, after I had basically made my peace with a life without children. I'd guessed that it just wasn't in the plans for me.

When I went to the doctor to confirm the pregnancy, he said, "Congratulations, your life will never be the same." And even though he had said it in a kind of almost malicious way with a negative undertone (he was a really old, grumpy doctor), little did I know how right he would be.

My life did change forever in an unbelievably beautiful way.

Were and are there struggles? You bet. In fact, basically every day.

In the very beginning they were more of a physical nature. From cracked, bleeding nipples, infected episiotomy, to breast infection. I had a tough go in the beginning.

But I don't remember much of how I felt then. Yes, glimpses. I did remember the pain of contractions and giving birth and what came after. What I remember way more vividly, however, is how I felt about my little boy. The wonders of holding him, of him breastfeeding, were elating. It was pure bliss. Then came the little changes, him getting more alert, rolling over, starting to crawl. Every step such a wonder.

I loved breastfeeding. For me it was all about bonding time with my baby. I never read or watched TV during breastfeeding; that was Luke's and my time to just be together.

Almost every day and certainly every new stage in the development brings new challenges. It never stops. But I grew with it. My son pushes me to the limits almost daily. It brings forth the worst in me but also the best. I want to be a better person and a better parent, for myself and for him. Every day, I get a new chance to handle situations better, to grow and to become that better version of myself.

Some days I yell way too much, I am too angry, to impatient, too...you fill in the blanks. But it doesn't last for long because there are two things for certain: the love that my son and I have for each other is beyond any doubt, any question, and not based on any condition, and children have an immense capacity to forgive.

Watching my son reminds me of what counts in life, when he is just being a child: the happiness, the joy, the wonders of new things, the sometimes brutal honesty of children, the inquisitiveness. His first and foremost goal is to have fun.

Somewhere along the way to adulthood, we lost most of this. Watching him reminds me that we need to remember to reclaim some of the "child" within us, to have fun, to laugh and just be.

I try to find a balance between letting him just have fun and teaching him about responsibilities. I try to prepare him to see that life is not only about having fun, but that it is a big part of it.

My biggest challenge for me as a mother so far was when I finally made the decision to leave my husband after years of suffering. My first concern is and will continue to be for my child. No child wants to see his or her parents separate, and so much emotion comes up around this topic. I support him through this difficult time as best as I can. Children are amazingly resilient, and as long as they know beyond a doubt that they are loved and their basic needs are met, they are extremely adaptable.

Children are amazing and teach us so much about ourselves if we are open enough to let them. Finally, for the first time in my life, do I truly understand what it means to love unconditionally.

What a gift it has been.

Bless all the children, for they are pure love.

Author Bio:
Anya Bruder is a certified Stress Management Coach who has overcome her autoimmune condition by changing deeply engrained emotional patterns. She helps other women to assess their current lifestyle and supports them in finding more beneficial ways to manage stressful events. Her focus is on a holistic approach that addresses all four planes: physical, mental, emotional, and spiritual. She encourages women to find their true self again, which is an essential part of the healing journey. Working through life's daily challenges and teaching them to live a holistic and ethical lifestyle, she honors the individual spirit of every woman she has the privilege to work with in a kind and compassionate manner.

Raising a Mother
by Ruchika Behal

"Children are our greatest teachers. They give us the perfect opportunity to change and to grow"

A little over fourteen years ago, my first born made me a mother. What I believed would follow next would be "raising kids."

I could not have been further from the truth. What I have learnt from my experience - at every step it has been more about raising myself as a human, elevating my consciousness, becoming more aware from within so I can become a mindful parent.

I have overcome many hurdles and had many insights in the process of raising myself. The first challenge was an eye opener. I has imagined, the minute my baby would be born, I would feel the unconditional boundless love, have the willingness to endlessly give and sacrifice my being. But it did not happen.

The first couple of weeks rather months, left me exhausted beyond belief from lack of sleep and self-care, constantly nursing and just wanting to be who I used to be.

Seeing my spouse assume the role of the father with rather ease was a wonderful surprise, but dare I say, it made me a tad bit resentful.... resentful because he could go back to "his life" during the day and return home to be the hands-on loving father in the evenings, and I had to be the mother all the time. I felt unsupported, alone, could not go back to my old life and there was no accolades or parent of the year award at the end of this. I was resentful because the maternal feelings I thought I should be feeling were not coming to me naturally.

Don't get me wrong... I had always wanted to be mother, I loved my baby, and I enjoyed nursing, gazing and being with him..... But not all the time.

I had presumed nine months would be long enough to grow into a mother, feel like a mother. But I was in transition. I soon realized it was not the change I was resentful of, it was the place in-between, where I had nothing to hold on to–the transition from the old to the new. I began embracing that even positive changes such as the birth of a child have to go through a transition. And the transition begins after the change... in fact which is the right order. I had to give myself time and patience. As we transition we learn, we grow and evolve.

One of the other reasons I felt the resentment was because I was struggling to live up to society's image of a mother. An image that I had been fed. And that was my second learning. I had always said I want to raise little humans with a strong gut (intuitively and digestively). But here if I was not living a very important phase of my life, following my own gut, not doing what I believed was right for me or my kids . How would I hope to ever teach them to listen to their own gut? I had to walk my talk. I began by learning to trust my instincts, shutting the outside noise or trying to overcome the temptation to compare my children to others and drag them through everyone else's agenda . I put aside my guilt to be constantly doing something "stimulating with my babies." I did not shut down my life, rather I made them a part life, my chores, my idea of fun and got rid of the attempts of trying to get everything thing done while they were napping. Instead I began to create me time and make it known it was ok- it was ok for me to want to be by myself and have a purpose beyond raising kids.

And that lead to the next awareness that Self-Love should not be confused with being a narcissist. I learnt Self Love is not about being self-absorbed or self-centered; it is about getting in touch with ourselves, our well-being and our happiness. I had always known in an airplane when the oxygen masks descends the first rule is to put on your own oxygen mask before you assist anyone else. It was now time to put into practice. I accepted that doses of self-love were important for me- because as a tired or bored mummy I was no good. I could only love them unconditionally once I understood how to love myself, I could only be "present" when I felt stimulated and fulfilled. I started making time to cook for myself, volunteer, and allowed myself to do things that fulfilled me. As a become more patient with myself, the more patience I have for my children. As I let my inner over-critic self, I am becoming more realistic. And allowing myself to be human.

Practicing self-love bolstered "letting-go" of habits that no longer served me. I learnt the discipline of letting-go, especially when it came to raising kids. We all have certain expectations and they do influence the way we are and how we raise our kids. But believing kids are their own people and will be who they are meant to be- it was necessary for me to learn to step aside. Let go of the control of how things or the outcome should be. As my children were growing up, one of them began getting interested in cooking. I am a passionate cook and it was natural for me to be very controlling in the kitchen in the name of safety. I had to step away (physically) to realize it was not that I was being over protective rather it was my desire to control the outcome, and the fear of failure or mess. When stepped aside, I let her creative-self flow, not instill my fear of not getting the recipe right (failure) and as a result our family got to enjoy the deliciousness. I am constantly letting go of perfectionism, the desire to only do the best or be the perfect parent. It's a habit I'm trying to break, with some success and learning there will be disappointments along the way.

And it is ok! As a mother it is my natural tendency to not let my kids feel pain or disappointment. I have the innate desire to make everything ok for my kids. Certainly, disappointment is not a pleasant emotion and surely not perceived to be a positive experience. I have had to understand it is not a bad emotion and something that should not be avoided. There have been moments when my kids have disappointed me. And I know there have been equal if not more times when I have had to say no or disappoint them. But knowing there is love and best intention at the end is the most important thing. For me it has been a learning to see disappointments as an opportunity and help my kids see it in the same light.

While we try to teach our children all about life, our children teach us what life is all about. Having kids is a huge part of human experience; it is our opportunity to watch ourselves like never before as they provide us with the perfect mirror. Children remind us to watch our intentions and actions because you never know who is innocently watching. It is in this way that our children are our gurus, teaching us to become aware of ourselves like few others can. I think about the gift my children continue to give – the gift of self-discovery. I nourish them, and in turn they nourish me. Together we grow and bloom. And my journey to raising my awareness continues....

Author Bio:
Ruchika Behal, is a mother to two, a wife and a certified health coach. She has lived the life of a global nomad and has truly embraced "bloom where planted." She is extremely passionate about nourishing lives with every thought and every bite. It is her endeavor to empower her world find healthier choices. Over the last decade and a half her focus has been to raise her little humans with strong set of values and an equally strong gut (digestive and intuitive).

Website: **www.ruchikabehal.com/about-health-coach-ruchika**

This Blended Life
by K L Young

The Oxford dictionary defines "blended" as a mix of different types of things and together they make a product of the desired quality. Blended means to merge with one another so that one is not clearly distinguishable from the other, to form a harmonious combination or harmonious by being similar in appearance or behavior. This is an accurate depiction of my blended life and my pursuit to become the best blended mom I know how to be... a creator of harmony, that's me!

Being a mother of seven children was never a part of my Barbie dream house fantasy! If you were to ask any of the main people that have influenced my life, such as my grand parents, parents, bonus parents, and several mentors, they definitely would have never guessed this life for me. However, somehow God saw fit to give me the most incredible seven gifts that I would dare not ever exchange. You see, I "inherited" three of those incredible gifts when I married my husband eleven years ago. One of his children was from a previous marriage, and since he did not know his father, my husband became the only father he knew.

The other two children were under the age of eleven when I met them, so needless to say that blending this ready-made family was challenging. So in essence, with my child from a previous relationship, we became a blended/blended family. With the four children I mentioned, later in our marriage we had three more to add to this blended party life, and boy has it been a party. It has been a roller coaster journey of ups and downs, but it has made me a better person, wife, daughter, sister, friend, and most importantly mother. Being a mother of so many different personalities, attitudes, beliefs and value-minded little beings has been my favorite part of living this blended life. I am a better person filled with better dreams, better aspirations, and better relations with other people besides my children. Who knew being a mother would grow me and help to create a harmonious unit, a family. My most memorable moment was being out in public with all of the kids and everyone calling me mom and the general audience thinking that I was the biological mom to all of them. Also, seeing the look on their face when we explained otherwise was priceless. You see, to be seen as one big happy family on the outside is one thing, but to mirror that same ideal on the inside is a whole new ball game. This is the holy grail of "this blended life"! Every blended family I know wants this type of unity. Achieving this happy ending has not been easy and most definitely started somewhere. Well, my humble beginnings had to start with the elements that brought me into being. It leads to the extraordinary seeds that were planted in me long ago without me knowing it. Now introducing the sun and the water to my seeds... the women in my life.

The women in my life prepared me for this gregarious task, and I'm ever so grateful for it. From all of my grandmothers and their sage advice, tremendous affection, and constant engagement, this gave me the tools to be patient, loving, and available at any time and available anywhere. I remember times when I would visit them, go to various places with them, watch television, and just share a meal with them.

Countless memories invade my mind of how I was being prepared even then. My mother is and was a generous caregiver to all the neighborhood kids, her nieces and nephews, and any child she ever met. I marveled at how she could get other children to listen and obey better than the parents themselves. To me, she was the fun, hip, and best all-around mom, and this showed me how to have joy in any situation. She also is very confident and assured and would move heaven and earth for any of her children. I definitely inherited these traits. My stepmother is and was a shining example of how to love a child that is not your own. She never treated me any different, never criticized or complained about anything or any situation.

She only concentrated on loving me and meeting my needs. I'm sure you can guess what kind of stepmother (blended mom) I turned out to be.

So in summation, here's what I have learned from these women and in my own travels...

- Be their light. Children need a true and clear path to follow. They need to know that there is hope and how to navigate the world. We are their example.
- Be engaged in what they like to do. From video games, mall runs, or movie night at home, children need to know that you are there for them. If you never support them, they will never support you or your authority.
- Give them a voice. You have to know what they are thinking and how they are feeling about things in order to solve problems, mend fences, and advocate for them when they cannot.
- Acknowledge who they are. With having seven of my own, this was important for me to learn. You have to treat them as individuals and reward them for that individuality. This goes a long way for them and for you the caregiver.
- Love them unconditionally, not with conditions. Love is something they know and will always count on. We say it repetitively and so matter-of-factly that it is engrained within their spirit. But in order to grow them into effective members of society, you must adhere to any lessons and any revelations about who they are, and that will aid you along the way. I may not always agree with them, but I embrace it and them as well. This shows them love and lets them know that it will always be there and will never fade.

This motherhood thing is an ever-evolving essence that I embrace and shine light on along the way in order to leave a growing legacy for generations to come. And hopefully create a great and thoughtful human being in the process that feels the same and shares it with their growing world.

Author Bio:
K L Young aka Kayla Lucas Young is a free spirit that loves life, her family and meeting strangers because they all have the ability to change her being into something higher and more beautiful. K L is a blended mother of 7 with ages ranging from 30 to 1 years old. She is a writer, poet, relationship life coach, lay biblical counselor and co-founder of D' Young Experience (DYE). DYE is an organization geared toward helping couples and families, especially blended families live healthy and fruitful lives in harmony.

Website: **www.dyounglife.org**

Bringing up Family: In Good and Bad
by Shalini Tyagi

The opportunity to write for this book came at a time when we were battling with quite a few health issues in the family, issues that made us rethink about what is important in life. At this time I was asked to share my feelings on motherhood: the one topic that is close to every mother's heart and about which every mom will have something to contribute. So, despite all the struggles, I just could not pass up this opportunity to put in my thoughts.

For me, being a mother is so, so, SO many different things. If I begin with one thing I would just keep stumbling upon 30 other issues, topics, and most of all my insecurities. After trying to choose one particular topic from the broad spectrum of motherhood, I decided to talk about what I feel about this journey in general. What I have experienced so far.

The one thing that many of us agree with is that before having kids, we were perfect moms. We might not have known the type of mothers we wanted to be, but we were so sure about the type of mothers we were NOT going to be. The pushing, nagging, and annoying type of moms. The exact kind of mothers we are turning out to be. How easy it was to chart a route map to perfect motherhood, and many of us had it all marked to perfection.

Then along comes the first baby and it is nothing like we are made to believe it will be. Yes, you do love that sweet, sleeping, angelic face to pieces. A love so fierce it could just consume your whole being. Yet no one warned you about the screaming-for-no-reason, never-sleeping baby. Those initial years when your mind, body, soul are so full of being a mommy. Each waking and sleeping moment is just about this tiny being. Those days of learning, discovering and constant self-doubt. *"Am I doing it right?"*

After a few years, two kids, and a lot of good and bad days, I would say that I have got some semblance of control and order back in my life. With a 9-year-old and a 4-year-old, this point in a mother's life is no less challenging. As many of you would agree, the struggles at this point are again very real. Now your kids are out venturing into the world. Meeting new kids and adults, discovering the world from their own perspective. Getting influenced and influencing others.

Now is when the conflicts begin. You scream, you shout, and most of all you say NO. Here are kids who go to school and their world expands, they start evaluating you on a scale of other moms and my mom.

You limit TV time, you take away iPads after the designated time slot, you demand completed homework, you insist on healthy meals, and the list goes on. This all leads to confrontations that can be really energy draining.

There are times when you start questioning your own actions. The constant feeling of losing control. Not knowing how to balance my heart telling me to let kids get their own way and my mind instructing me to just make them do what is right, to draw the line.

After one such session of "no more TV and games," I decided to take a feedback from my 9-year-old son, as many times I feel maybe I need to be a bit more laid back. What better than looking at motherhood from a kid's eyes. I asked him, "What type of a mother am I?"

Me getting all mushy and waiting for the reply, was informed, "OK kind."

This was so not what I wanted to hear. I continue, "Please explain."

The answer was so unexpected: "See, some moms are good, some not so good. Nobody has a bad mom because all moms just want to win."

Now I was confused. I ask further, "Win?"

And very innocently my son hands me the last piece of this puzzle, informing me, "Yes, winning for a mom is making her children good people. Don't you always say it is very important to be a good person? All moms must want that? That is why they are not so good sometimes."

When I sit and ponder on this conversation, I actually understand that most of my focus as a parent is, in one way or the other, on this. It is true I have time and again pressed on my children the importance of being good human beings, before anything else. Being the type of people who can see right from wrong and have the good sense to choose what is right. People who can be compassionate and respect others despite their social standing.

Despite all my efforts, at this stage when I want to focus on bringing up good people, I'm often plagued by self-doubt. In a world where you see less and less of good people around, how do I stop the world from taking advantage of my kids' goodness and innocence?

In this nasty world, kids' safety is every mothers' concern. How do you teach them to stay safe and protect themselves? What I see as a solution is to tell them about the evil lurking in the corners. Telling about the bad intentions behind a stranger's kind and friendly smile. To keep eyes open when a teacher is over-helping or a relation is too attentive. Trying to teach them to be good and kind and being smart about it all.

Still, what breaks my heart is my four-year-old baby girl's wide-eyed amazement when I gently tell her about good touch and bad touch. The unspoken question, that why should she not trust the beautiful world she just started discovering. Despite what I WANT to tell her and what I HAVE to tell her, I try every day to raise my daughter to be a strong and smart person. Repeating to her to always remember she is strong, smart, kind, and beautiful. To know when to slap the stupid off anybody's face who try to tell her otherwise.

Another challenge that I feel we face is raising kids with a strong sense of family. As we all will agree, as kids grow, family dynamics change; our relationship with them evolves on a daily basis. There are days when I'm the center of my kids' universe and other days when I'm not even a good enough mom. Being part of a family and caring for each other brings out the best in kids. Allotting small responsibilities gives them a sense of being in control of their lives. The older ones watching out for the younger ones and vice versa. Siblings forming bonds so strong that can withstand the ups and downs that most certainly await them.

In this journey of motherhood, if my kids look back at their childhood with fond memories and want to relive it, I would say it was not a journey wasted. A family that remembers its good times with a smile is a family that has evolved together, grown together.

In bringing up our children, we raise a family, in good times and in bad, in sickness and in health. Along with kids, I try to become a better person each day, teaching some, learning some.

My mother always says, "If you want to instill good in your kids, first the parents need to find the good in themselves. Don't expect your kids to become something that you are not ready to be."

With this thought I try to change in myself something for the better.

As I try to do this and much, much more every day, I can just assure all you amazing mothers that you are doing beautifully.

I love and cherish each and every beautiful, annoying, and not-so-easy moments of this unique journey that only a mom can share with her kids.

Having kids might at times not be all it is hyped up to be. But for me, having kids mean a brighter sun, longer periods of happiness, and shorter spells of sadness (really, they don't give you a moment of peace, even to be sad). Kids mean trips are more fun and you can get out of many sticky situations by informing people you have small kids. You become more or less embarrassment-proof.

I will leave you all with these thoughts from my journey so far. As I continue to run (bad hair no makeup and all) towards my "winning," I wish you all the same victory run.

Author Bio:
Shalini Tyagi is a mother of two school-going kids. Her son is nine years old and daughter is five. She decided to be a full-time mother after her son was born. She is an amateur writer whose writing is simple and inspired by her own life experiences and thoughts. To further pursue her love of writing, she started her own blog.

Website: **www.tyagishalinid.com**

You Said She Was Mine
by Prabita Rajesh

My little Advaith is a piece of my heart. To me, he is the most intelligent and spontaneous child there can ever be. He made friends easily, spoke my native Indian language, Malayalam, so fluently and clearly, that most times we forgot we were talking to a 2-year-old. He was my whole world when suddenly, one day we found out that I was pregnant again... Surprise! Surprise! Especially considering that my first pregnancy came after several months of infertility treatment, the fact that I was still breastfeeding Advaith, and still had my cysts for friends. They say that you don't conceive during breastfeeding, but I guess when the time is right, the stork just decides to fly your way.

When I told him the good news, Advaith was the happiest. I prepped him up saying he would help look after the baby, bathe and feed and play with his new playmate. He was excited. He always wanted a baby sister when most little boys his age wanted little boys to play with. He accompanied me to my doctor visits so he could see his baby on the screen. He loved feeling my tummy as the baby blobbed around and spoke to "her."

I was really worried as the delivery date came close, since he had never stayed away from me—not even for a day. I was more stressed about how he was going to manage without me and me without him than even the arrival of the new baby.

The day the pain arrived, after a whole 24 hours in the hospital labor ward and a C-section later, they handed me my beautiful little girl. In Indian families, the birth of a boy is highly celebrated and brings immense respect and acceptance to the mother, especially in her husband's household. Advaith had brought me all that and much more, especially since we had to go through a lot of heartache before he came along. But giving birth to this little princess had made my childhood dreams come true: that of being a little girl's mommy. My own doll to play with! We were going to name her Anashwara: it means "Forever, eternal."

Advaith took one look at his little sister and then at me in the hospital gown, bound to the bed with IVs and monitors, and then ran right out of the room. My poor baby just couldn't bear to come back in and look at me again. He left without even saying goodbye, though once he reached home, he wept the night away saying he wanted to be with me. Early next morning, though in intense pain, I dragged myself out of bed, walked around a bit to convince the doctor to remove the urine bag, and changed into my own clothes from the scary hospital garb so that when he arrived he would see me back to normal. He felt much better upon seeing me on my feet and wouldn't let go of me that day. He thought we would go home the same day.

Once we reached home a couple of days later, he wanted to give Anashwara a bath right away! When I told him he couldn't bathe her right now, he said, "But you said I could!" Then he wanted to feed her, play with her, sleep next to her...all my carefully constructed refusal was met with, " But you promised!," "You said she was mine." "You agreed...." All my conversations from the previous several months of preparing him for the new baby's arrival were starting to pop right back at me. Sigh!

He couldn't understand why everyone was coming to see her. Couldn't understand why there were only gift bags for her. They asked him questions only about her. It was always about her! In fact, one day it got him so upset that he went and took it all out on my new beautiful beaded curtains, hopelessly tangling them beyond salvage. Ever since, whenever I go to see a newborn, I make sure I get little gift packs for the siblings as well and spend more time with the older children.

On our part, my husband and I did everything we could to make him feel OK. We let him do "important" things like hold her on a pillow, get her towel, hold her bottles, pour water when I did bathe her. Except when I was actually feeding her, I spent all my time with him reading, painting, and playing with him and letting my daughter be. I figured she was too small to understand that I was focusing on her big brother. I enrolled him in a playschool so that new friends and activities kept him active and occupied. I talked a lot to him about his little sister and how when she was a bit more grown up he could play just like he wanted to. But more often than not, he was still so upset.

Initially it was only the furniture and his toys that took the brunt of his emotions. But slowly, to my horror, it started getting directed at the baby too! Once he threw such a hard toy at her head that my poor baby couldn't even cry. Though I was angry myself, I tried to make him understand that this was not the right thing to do and that he needed to apologize and give her a hug, which he did readily.

Onam is our biggest festival. Anashwara was around 3 months then. My mom had dressed her up and Advaith in new clothes. She had used the customary kohl to deck up her granddaughter, and tiny red bangles adorned her little hands. In the evening after I got back from work, I was feeding her and I saw a black round mark on her hand, and looking at it closely saw that it was a ring of 8 small teeth! Advaith just could not bear to see the attention she was getting and the fact that she looked so pretty and dolled up that he had actually bitten her!

I have never been that upset and angry with him before. I couldn't bring myself to speak to Advaith. I felt I had failed as a mother. I couldn't get through to him. I was extremely worried and so full of concern for how both of them were going to turn out as the days went by. Should I quit my job? Should I keep him in school the whole day and get him back only late in the evening? Should I send him away for a few months till the baby was slightly older? Or should I send the baby away? Restless thoughts. And I had no peace of mind. How could I handle the situation better?

That night, sensing my mood, for the first time he slept away at his grandmom's place and came back next day, all of the previous day's activities forgotten. But I still wasn't in the mood to talk to him, and after many apologies and attempts to soften me, he started to go into a panic tantrum mode, and that's when I had to break out of my own shell and pick him up again and comfort him too—he was just 3 and a baby too. I had to understand that there would be many moments like this in life when I may not be able to get through to either of them, and they still went on and did whatever they chose to do, but I had to still stand by them and reassure them with my hug and presence. He's never bitten her after that incident. For many months after that, every single day, I made sure Anashwara was dressed and dolled up so he would get used to seeing her like this.

Anashwara, from the time she was a few months old, had eyes and ears only for her big brother. She followed him everywhere with her eyes, and when she was able to move, she was his shadow. Now he is 7 and she 4 years old. If we got angry with him, she would say, "He is my brother, don't talk to him like that!" She would refuse a piece of her favorite chocolate or a pack of crisps if there wasn't one for him as well. Her biggest joy is wearing his hand-me-downs and picking him from the bus stop after his school day.

He is smothered with several hugs and kisses all day long. They are inseparable and the best of friends. Of course I still have to referee at times, but most of the time, they are able to sort things out on their own. He is her big brother and her hero. And I guess like most men, he loves all the attention and treats her like a little princess.

My heart fills with warmth when they sit snuggled together in the cozy chair watching their favorite cartoon, and I unconsciously say a prayer that they always remain like this... Forever.

Author Bio:

Prabita Rajesh is an Indian but based in the UAE. She is a full-time working mom with 2 kids aged 4 and 7. She is an architect by profession and also loves reading, painting, and traveling to new places and trying out new things. Though stressful, she loves her job, but is also constantly guilty for not giving enough time and attention to her kids, their education, their health, their extracurricular activities... about everything! Then she looks at her own mom, who just retired after more than 30 years of a full-time career as a healthcare personnel, and sees how independent and "not-so-bad" her kids have turned out eventually—and prays that things will be OK for her too.

Email: **prabitarajesh@gmail.com**

I Am Because We Are
by Niti Garg

My daughters, 3 and 1, are growing fast, but at the same time I feel that I am also evolving consistently as a person along with them. Sometimes I look in the mirror and wonder who is this woman standing on the other side? I have changed so much since I had kids. Very few changes are apparent (as in extra kilos), but mostly it's deep, internal, core-shaking changes in my personality.

Let me begin my story by mentioning the phrase that may sound cliché but is completely true in my case: Being a mother is indeed the best feeling in the world. And there is no better achievement in life than to see your kids growing from tiny little babies to mature individuals. There is nothing more rewarding but to witness the progress of your own kid.

Trust me, I have seen lot of other kinds of academic and professional success in life, but they stand nowhere close to what motherhood feels to me. I had kids in my early thirties, which is considered a bit late in the culture I grew up. When I was in my late twenties, I was struggling hard with relationship trouble, career failures, and lot of social pressures. I had several of those hopeless moments where I felt that I may never have a family of my own. I had almost convinced myself that I would live as a single woman forever, but then the world changed for me. Here, I am, happily married, in a stable career and with two beautiful healthy kids roaming around me (literally—I mean as I am typing).

Motherhood has done wonders for me! I don't think I can explain that in its entirety here, but I will try my best. I have become so much more patient, calm, kind, disciplined, mature, hopeful and a more positive person, to say the least. My never-ending confusion is gone, my dilemmas don't exist anymore. I don't lose my mind over simple things. The most amazing change in me is my enhanced capability to love and be loved. Honestly, I can't think of any negative side of motherhood. But all the positive developments in my personality have come across gradually, and the journey has its ups and downs.

With my firstborn, I was extremely apprehensive about everything. I tended to be overprotective of her (which ended up hurting her more than saving her), got too worried over her natural cries or illnesses. I doubted my own abilities to care for her and even considered at one point sending her away to India to be taken care of by my mom so that I could focus on my job better. Thankfully, I didn't take that decision, and instead decided to take a partial break from my job. It turned out to be the best decision for me and my little one (also became the reason for bringing our second daughter in this world).

In my path of motherhood, the most valuable lesson that I have learned so far is that the most precious gift we can give to our kids is our LOVE! Unbiased, unlimited, uncontaminated, unprecedented love. Alongside, we need to continuously find and create newer ways for the expression of love. We have to keep kids as our topmost priority and take pride in it. In a more practical sense, we need to give them our time and energy as much as we can. In the present world, it's very hard for full-time working professionals not to compromise those key values with the desire to seek job promotions with the sacred goal to secure the best resources for our kids. For most of us, it's unavoidable to do full-time job in order to provide for our kids, but we should do our best to find time for them.

We need to find a job that don't keep us too preoccupied (mentally or physically), even if it pays a bit less. Let's face the reality: the corporate world is harsh, and people out there are judgmental about gaps in your resume. This current system needs to be changed; in fact, some companies like mine have taken positive measures in that direction, like providing paid bonding leave. Always remember we are not just the providers to our kids but also a source of inspiration (intentionally or unintentionally).

Lastly, we as women deserve to enjoy motherhood! It is the most fundamental joy of life. So all my fellow mothers, let's be strong, tell our stories, set good examples for our kids, get stronger together, and build a loving, nurturing environment to raise our next generation.

Have a happy motherhood!

Author Bio:
Niti Garg is a full-time professional in semiconductor industry and a PhD in nanochemistry. She is the mother of two little girls, who keep her on her toes all day long. She is highly spiritual person and practice yoga routinely to keep her my mind and body in sync. Besides, She likes to experience innovative kind of therapies to attain better understanding of human mind and it's control. She is the founding member of an NPO called 'foundation SEED' that works for the improvement of life conditions in rural India by generating sustainable employment and educational empowerment. Writing is her new found love. While, She is still learning the art, she enjoys sharing her life changing experiences with utmost honesty. She loves to compose poetry (in Hindi) in her free time.
Her composition can be checked

Facebook: **www.facebook.com/filhaalzindagi**
Website: **www.foundationseed.org**

Maa, Mom, Mother
by Yogini Thakkar Arora

"Maa, Mom, Mother"… A word that each mother waits to hear ever since she knows she is expecting. But on a fine Sunday morning when you are about to savor you hot cup of tea and you hear "Maa, " your instinct instantly knows that this hot cup of tea is not in your destiny for the day. To give you the history of it, on a fine Sunday morning I wake up all energetic to take on the world (I mean my children), decide to be the best mom, and not to lose my temper. I take all three for a shower; the eldest and the youngest are quickest, while the middle one loves to do splish splash for a long time even after he is done. So while he is still in the bathroom singing his nursery rhymes, I pick up my tea, assuming it is going to be at least twenty minutes before he is out.

Barely had I picked up the cup I hear "Maa" from the bathroom. I asked my maid to check. I really did not want to give up on the cup of tea, as it would be at least another fifteen minutes to get him out and dressed. But she was shooed away and I hear it again, "Maa," and this time louder and stronger than before. I suspected something fishy, and I rushed to the bathroom to see him in a pool of bubbles. I wonder when and how did this happen? I look around and see the brand new baby bath bottle is all empty now. It was one of the best brands which my husband picked up on one of his travels. Oh, and more importantly this was the second time he has done this. I could almost feel my face turn red.

I look at him in anger and he screams, "Maa, soap went in my eyes" in his cutest tones, washing away all the anger. I look at him and smile wash his eyes and ask, "Why did you do this?" He simply replies, "But I was doing body wash only. " I did not know what to do, smile or cry or get angry. So I sat and wondered, was I really angry at him? Does he even understand what he just did? He just mimicked us putting the tiny bottles of shower gel in the tub to make a bubble bath. Or was I scared of answering to my husband about what happened to the new bottle of body wash? I had assured him that I would keep it away from the kids and be careful, unlike last time. It was just the fear within me that was getting angry. I was angry at myself for not being careful, but the ego in me did not let me accept it, but a beautiful smile sure did make me realize it. I wished to be a kid and play in all those bubbles, and I sure did a bit.

I realized that most of the time that we are annoyed at our children it is some fear or expectations within us. We expect our children to behave in a certain way or have envisioned them to grow up a certain way. But what we tend to overlook is that neither of us is a total replica of our parents, nor have we lived up to our parents' expectation 100 percent. Now every time my child does something wrong, I think before I react, whether it is something that needs to be handled with stern words or simply by making them understand.

Anger is simply a reaction of inner thoughts or simply lack of food and energy. Similarly, all the tantrums that the kids do are also a reaction of their emotions. Once we become aware of it, most of the issues get solved. The other day my kids chipped the thermocol into small pieces and made snow out of it. I opened the door and all the pieces flew right in, the house was a mess. I looked at them and they sweetly said, "Mommy, it's snowing and we are having so much fun, come mommy, play with us."

Kids are smart enough to judge our expressions and become even cuter when they sense danger. But this time I decided to take the other route—I decided to let them be children, and even better I let the child in me free and enjoyed the snowfall. The smiles, the moments were priceless.

Just this awareness has changed so many things between me and the kids. They treat me as a part of their gang rather than always worrying about my reactions. I have started enjoying my time with the kids much more. I cherish their smiles. I realize that these moments will not last a lifetime, nor will these naughty acts. They will never be this small again. Why not let them live those moments where they can do all that they want? As they grow, they will be bound by many rules, so why start now? The best part is that now, when I say things calmly and explain, they understand better and we have a fruitful discussion.

Most often we are so occupied with our thoughts and chores that we forget to enjoy the small moments of our life. Before, when I did the bed and the kids would want to come and play in the sheets, make tents, I would be stern and say, "Please let me finish my work. I have a thousand other things to do." But with the strong intent to enjoy the small moments, I let them play, and trust me, those smiles are definitely more precious than the five minutes that I would save by not letting them play. The cherry on the cake is to hear "You are the best Mom in the world." That makes me smile. It is truly these simple pleasures that make their childhood beautiful.

Children have a very selective memory. They never remember our instructions, and neither do they remember our stern words. All they remember is the love and the lovely moments we have with them. As they grow up and they think of their childhood, I want all these moments to flash in their heads. We being stern may help them a bit to learn things quicker, but definitely will not help build memories.

Author Bio:
Yogini Arora is a certified Clinical Hypnotherapist. She has done her diploma in hypnotherapy from Hypnosis Motivation Institute, California. Her desire to help people using the power of mind made her take up hypnotherapy as her career. Yogini has worked with various local and international clients to help resolve various issues,

including weight loss, anger management, public speaking, past-life healing, life purpose, sleep issues, addictions, and self-worth to name a few. She now runs a complete Mind, Body and Soul Detox program, to Reawaken the mind, revitalize the body, and rejuvenate the soul.

Website: **www.yovanathemindcoach.com**

Lessons and Blessings
by Deborah De' Brown

I've learned that life is filled with lessons and/or blessings. No matter how hard we resist, we will ultimately experience one or the other or both simultaneously. Being a parent is one such example. To me there's no job on Earth as challenging or compatible as being a parent. It is the most honorable thing a person can give to mankind. The early threshold of motherhood is not for the faint of heart. Motherhood is a spiritual calling. It's also one of the most exciting and thankless job that I've experienced on this planet. Before I go any further, here's my acronym for

Mother:
M Master
O Officer
T Teacher, Trainer
H Helper, Human
E Educator, Excellent
R Relief, Ready

To sum it up, moms have to be a master at what they do, sometimes having the stamina of an officer, be able to teach all kinds of subject matter, train our children for various life skills, help when it's needed, cry because we're human, educate the world about our wonderful offspring, be excellent at everything ???, and most of all be relief and ready in crises and crunch times.

What a resume!!

It seems I inherited the task of motherhood from an early age; I had to learn to take care of my siblings because I was the eldest. I vowed to myself (in my teen years) that I wouldn't have children. I figured the world had enough issues without me adding to it. Somehow destiny intervened and I became pregnant at sixteen years old. I gave birth to a beautiful son who somehow would end up becoming my Master Teacher. We grew up together, and the lessons that I learned were patience, tolerance, compassion, understanding, entrepreneurship, and most of all how to give and receive love. By choice, ten years later I added another son to my family unit because I didn't want my first son to be without a sibling. My second son's gift to me was learning how to navigate the legal system, and learning a sense of fair play. Both of my children came as a result of conscious and unconscious choice. One choice was super apparent to me: I was to remain a single parent until they became adults.

The very first time I laid eyes on my sons, I fell in love. My hopes and dreams were higher than the ones I had for myself. I wanted them to become productive and outstanding men in the world. I wanted them to be able to navigate their worlds without undue hindrances. Hindrances that could possible cripple them, such as racism, prejudices, sexism, poverty, illiteracy, hopelessness, homeless, and any other possible isms that could possibly trip them up in this world. I wanted them to be the best fathers and husbands. I wanted them to be culturally sensitive and aware, to be polite, but assertive. Most of all I tried to instill in them a sense of reverence for God.

Now that my sons are adults, I can look back and see where I wasn't perfect with all my hopes, dreams, and intentions. I can see the hits and misses of my love. Some of my intentions were fruitful and some of my intentions fell by the wayside. No matter what, I never, ever gave up on my children. On most days my energy gave out before my heart gave up.

Watching them become men gave me plenty of food for thought. Periodically, there were days when I asked myself "Could I have done better?" "Would I change some things if I could?" Within the recess of my spirit a small voice said: "No! If you would have made a change, you wouldn't be you, and they would not be them." This makes sense because neither of us would have learned the valuable lessons that have sustained us as a family unit. We wouldn't have experienced the divine love of God and each other.

Now I have grandchildren, and my wishes, hopes, and dreams have taken on a new dimension. A dimension of trust and wisdom. Trusting that things will work out, and having the wisdom to carry out the task of the ultimate motherhood... being a grandparent!!

Author Bio:
Deborah Brown known as (De') is the Owner/Operator of PaRicDe Enterprise & Ministry, LLC PaRicDe Enterprise is an Interfaith Ministry and Spiritual Center that specializes in Integrative Health & Wellness Education. De' who has been in Ministry for over fourteen years is a certified Life, Health, and Spiritual Coach, whose services are tailor made for her prospective client health interests. The company focus is to help facilitate a spiritual and natural transformation for the client depending on their need for natural health, wellness education, spiritual development, or holistic products. The Ministry also offers many tailor-made clergy services, workshops, seminars, community resources, professional referrals, and natural products. One of De' passions and gifts is doing 'Toe Readings' which is ancient Soul Reading modality.

Website: **www.deministry.com**
Email: **rebuildtemple08@yahoo.com**

Mom's Place in a Child's Heart: The Journey
by Anjali Shah

"Mom/Mother." Even when we say this word, our hearts are filled with joy and love. This love-filled word only tells us about the spirit of a mother.

Who is a mom, who is a mother? A mother is the foundation of a family, who takes care of each and every chore with a smile on her face. From cooking your favorite dishes to helping with your homework, from organizing parties to solving your personal problems, she is the master of all trades. No one knows how she handles everything so easily, but she just does!!

I want to express the journey of a child's emotions for his mother in the course of their lives. I have penned down these thoughts based on my own experiences and some heard and seen incidents.

Every woman in the world would wants to experience a motherhood that gives her life meaning, definition, and a reason to spread more love. Bringing another life to this world makes her own life complete.

While she is taking care of this huge responsibility of raising her kids, the journey of emotions that her children feel for her is quite notable, and in my opinion, it takes a course of its own, and I would like to define it with the help of the letter *U* in our alphabet.

I know you will be curious to know how. My experiences might be able to answer your questions and doubts.

In their childhood, mom is everything for the kids. She is the solution to every problem, every question, and every curiosity. Their motto is

My Mom Is The Best during that period. A mother's place in their life is on the topmost position of the U.

When they grow up a little, and they start going to school, a stranger enters their lives as a role model. That person is a teacher. The teacher is their idol now. A mom can be very educated but can never compete with the teacher. The Teacher Is Always Right is the new motto. It's very normal for a mom to hear "Mom, you don't know anything" during that stage. Mom's place goes downhill from the top of the U now.

As they grow up more, it gets worse, especially in the teenage years. That's when it goes to the bottommost point of the U. A mom is a mom, she never changes, but the behavior of a child changes rapidly. Their priorities change. Now they feel that their mom is orthodox or "uncool"; she doesn't understand how modern gadgets work, has a dated fashion sense, and doesn't even know how to use a smartphone. Children sometimes don't like the way a mom expresses her love and care because it embarrasses them in front of their friends. They will frequently say "I am not a child anymore." Well, that hurts!

The next stage is higher education, when they need to leave the house and take up their own responsibilities. This is when the journey up to the other side of the U starts. They start to realize how their moms would do each and every chore without complaining. They start to appreciate everything a mother does, be it cleaning, washing, budgeting, or cooking. The food plays a main role, actually. No food can beat a mom's home-cooked meal for any person in this world. The child starts missing the mother, and the respect and appreciation just increases from here on.

The last leg is work! Now a mother's pampered child has to take up every responsibility alone. Household chores, work stress, future planning, everything. The frequency of calling mom increases, to ask for recipes, her opinions, or sometimes just to hear her voice to relieve the stress. This is when the mom's place bounces back to the topmost point on the U. Kids now have the maturity to understand, value, and respect a mother and everything she did/does for them. The motto is back to My Mom Is The Best.

And when they become a parent themselves, they know how to raise their kids perfectly, just like their mom raised them. And they are always relieved to know that their parents are there to help them in every stage of parenthood.

This is the journey of a mom's place in a child's heart, in my opinion. All the moms reading this, think about it, you must have experienced some of it, if not all, at some point in your lives.

NO OTHER LOVE IS LIKE A MOTHER'S LOVE.

The Law of Opposites with My Warriors
by Savitha Avish

The only similarity between my two sons is their liking for cucumber and milk. That's it! Everything else is in the Opposite theory. And this really fascinates me day in and day out, as a mother of eight years, because it proves to myself the fact that every child is unique.

Eight-years-old Aromal and Four-year-old, Arjun, my two warriors... Well, neither really live up to the names they have been christened with—if you need to find them, you need to look under the table, as my husband sarcastically states. But of course I, as a mother, would like to proudly say that they are "warriors" in their own ways. Aromal means beloved and is also the name of a legendary hero who lived in northern Kerala, India, during the 16th century. Arjun means white or clear and is also the name of a legendary hero, Arjuna, who was an archer, an important character of the Indian Hindu epic Mahabharata.

Ever since my second son Arjun, was conceived, my exposure to this "Law of Opposites" began and holds good till this moment. Aromal's pregnancy and my first experiences of motherhood will always be memorable, a wonderful 9 months that I would always cherish in my lifetime. The best part was getting to eat anything and everything without having to bother about weight loss or gain. Arjun's 9 months were depressing—just the opposite!

Ha! so there it all started... The Law of Opposites with my two god-sent precious gems...

Everything in both these warriors, right from the way they sleep, their taste buds, to their everyday body language, it is all divergent! Just yesterday, I gave them both vegetable pasta and Aromal came back with a colorful plate because he ate all the pasta except the veggies in it and Arjun came back with a bland-looking plate because he ate all the veggies in it except the pasta.

And so with likewise situations, my everyday story revolves around these two lil interesting, demanding men... oh and along with my main man.

Have you ever wondered if, once you become a parent, every decision in your life that you make till your grave shall be children-centric? That's why I always tell soon-to-be parents that once you become a parent, that feeling is forever...

But having said all of the above and knowing that my approach to both my boys shall be adaptive depending on their different temperaments, as a mother, I am clear about one thing that I will teach them both the same, no matter what, when, where and how: to be a good human being! Seeing, reading and hearing about all the ghastly things women go through, especially in India, I shall always make my boys understand that they need to respect and empathize with women and their feelings in every walk of life. I am sure, if I succeed in doing that, my role as a mother of two boys shall be fulfilling. (Disclaimer: No, I am not talking of any gender equality here and I dare not walk into that sensitive area!)

We always knowingly or unknowingly end up advising our girls but we hardly take the effort to make our boys understand likewise except for clichéd things like "boys don't cry." We just end up bringing them up as boys and that sums up everything, doesn't it? And I realized that if I have to bring about that kind of an effort, it can only happen when it starts right from home, by making my boys understand and realize the importance of pitching in for small chores for their mother, grandmothers, aunts and cousin. For example, I have already started explaining to Aromal that he needs to tinkle with the toilet seat up so mamma can use it cleanly too when it's her turn to use the bathroom.

It also set me thinking recently that I should soon start off and try to make them as independent as possible. Yes, *self-sufficient* is the word. They should be able to handle themselves mentally and physically because we are all progressing in a world where tolerance levels are smaller for both genders than before and still diminishing (men hardly had any tolerance levels anyways, haha...). I shudder when I think of how relationships will turn out to be 10 to 15 years down the line.

I hope and pray that my warrior princes grow up to be responsible, independent, capable and down-to-earth men by being the support and guide in the right direction to the females they cross paths with in their lives. I thank God every day for blessing me and Avish with our two lovely precious gems, our life!

Just a while ago, the following lines popped up on my Facebook newsfeed. I am a big fan of Mark Zuckerberg and his wife Priscilla Chan for all the good thoughts and actions that they do and convey to the people around by making use of their capacities and power! This is what came up:

"For those whom I have hurt, I ask forgiveness. For those whom I could have helped more, I ask for understanding. For all the ways I could have served the world better, I ask for strength to be better this coming year. May you all be inscribed in the book of life. May we all be better this coming year than the last." Did it set you thinking like it did for me?

God Bless your lovely world too.

Author Bio:
Savitha Avish is an Indian home-maker based in Dubai. Being a proud

mother of two little overenergetic boys (8 and 4), she barely manages to listen to silence in her otherwise "house of noise"! It's in these rare moments of silence that her thoughts get penned. Born and brought up in Dubai, Savitha holds an Engineering degree in Production and has a Masters in Marketing. On a sabbatical now, she was contributing to Alstom success before motherhood beckoned and is a learned an avid Indian Classical dancer, with various performances under her belt.

Email: **savisavvy@gmail.com**

My Life as a Parent
by Carolyn Murray

My parenting career began in 1977 at age eighteen, and if I learned anything after having five children and 40 years of raising children, it's that parenting never ends.

The reason that I refer to my parenting as a career is because it was work and I valued my job and worked hard to be the best that I could possibly be at it with hopes of one day becoming exceptional at it. I know that none of us have mastered parenting, but I do feel that I have achieved a level of comfort in mothering, and have earned my mother title. I learned many years ago that many people will have children, but not all are mothers.

At eighteen, I didn't put much thought into fears of the world, such as sex predators, gangs, drugs, bullying, or racism (we're a biracial couple). Admittedly, I had a false sense of security in my world (Tucson, AZ) that I had grown up in, but it was also a different time. My children played in the front yard, baseball and football in the street, and had the freedom to ride bikes around the neighborhood without any thought of them being approached and taken. It's not that I didn't keep a watchful eye, because I did. I always knew where they were; boundaries were always in place. It was just a relaxing time to be a parent and a child then, although, I did have some fear of cults since Charles Manson, Son of Sam, and Jonestown Massacre were big news back then. I was afraid that someone would come along and sell my children a sack of lies, snatch them up, and initiate them into a cult. This fear led me to introduce them to religion so that they would have the education and knowledge to know what was truth and not go searching for some spiritual answers. I worked hard on them being confident and secure within themselves so they didn't feel the need to go looking for something to make them feel loved or whole. I had a fear of them drinking poisoned punch more than the fear of them being approached by a sex offender and abducted.

In 1989 we left Tucson with our three children and moved to Phoenix, AZ. In 1990 and 1991 we added two more children to our family. We had children ranging from newborn to high school age, and I was beginning to see a shift in our environment that was beginning to expose my children to drugs, gangs, and bullying. These were things that I hadn't put any thought into, so I had been unafraid, but these things were now slowly working their way into our world, and it shook me enough to make me wake up and take notice. We experienced the mean girls, gangs, and drugs. Some of these experiences were a little easier to conquer, but each of them left some battle scars. As a parent, you don't want anything hurtful to come their way, but that unfortunately isn't realistic. Life sends you in a direction at times that you wonder if there will ever be a break in the storm, or at least a pause. But either way you must hang on and continue to fight a good fight. I had to build an army and establish unity within my family. I wanted them strong mentally and for them to understand the importance of uniting as a family because they were going to need to be an army of strength for each other at one time or another in their lifetime. I also taught them to have a voice; they would need to be heard because life would challenge them one day because that's just life—it isn't always easy, and it's never perfect. I had to think of the possibility that a day would come for each of them that would challenge them and shake their world a bit, and they would need strength and perhaps each other to get through the cracks of life.

I raised strong, kind, and compassionate children, both male and female, because I felt that's the one thing that I had to offer them. I wanted them to grow up to stand up for what they believed in and to always remember that there was an entire world of hurting people. I'm happy to say that I have succeeded, but you don't have five children without some bring-you-to-your-knees moments, and it is in those moments that I'm reminded that I'm powerless and can't control certain situations based on their choices. I learned and accepted many years ago that their choices may not be what I would have chosen, but as a mother my job is about celebrating the children that I have, not the children that I thought they would be. I leaned on my faith to remind myself that we are all flawed, but if your heart is pure and the love that you give is real, that's what is important. I stand strong in my faith with the belief that we'll get through whatever comes our way and continue to forgive and love each other. It's a difficult thing to do, love unconditionally, because we tend to place unreasonable expectations on those that we love. My expectations were for them to be good, kind people that would create a life that gives them peace in their soul and happiness in their heart. I pray that each of them have that today.

I'm thankful for the women in my life that helped to create positive memories and watched over my family when I couldn't be there. My mother helped with my older ones while I worked, and dear friends and my older children helped with the younger ones. I am a firm believer in it taking a village to raise a child, because I needed the people that helped me along the way. I admire and respect the strength and support of the women in my life that helped me when I needed it. I try to do the same today for my children with my grandchildren. The best advice that I could give to parents today is don't be afraid to ask for help.

All my children are adults now, and I can say that one of my favorite feelings is the joy that it brings me from enjoying our relationship as adults. The respect continues, but a lifetime friendship has blossomed, and that makes my soul happy.

The Ups & Downs
by Kimber Bowers

There are those moments that never change. Moments where that certain gentle touch of a finger on the palm of your hand or across your cheek, that certain look or that certain nuzzle up against your side in just the right way bring back the recollection of the first time you ever held them and all of the emotions come flooding back... Feelings of wholeness, of peace, of gratitude, of all of the senseless struggles finally making sense in this one cumulative moment... Feelings of everything you ever doubted finally falling into perfect place, everything just right, just as it belongs... No matter how old my children get, I still carry these feelings with me. They are my purpose. They are my pride. And perhaps, sometimes, that's a little too much...

Parenting... it's a bit of a roller coaster. There are moments of ecstasy. There are moments of pure terror. And there are moments of everything in between. You will be frazzled. You will be exhausted. You will have moments where your plate is so heavy that it feels like the weight of the world is on your shoulders and no matter what you do, no matter how much you give, no matter how hard you try, somehow it doesn't seem like quite enough. But those moments will pass, and when they do, they give way to that gratitude, that lovely sense of peaceful alignment with the universe where all is right.

The trick is remembering that peace in the moments of frenzy and allowing them to pass. We all reach moments that feel like the breaking point. We get puked on, we get yelled at, things get thrown at us, we go days without sleep, our minds are overwhelmed with lists, and in the crux of it we tend to ignore our own needs. The miracle of motherhood is this: just when you think you've hit the end of your rope, somehow, you always find a bit more wiggle room. We learn, as mothers, how much more there is compared to what we thought there was. We learn, how much more we are. We learn that things have a way of turning around and that moments do pass. We learn that it may not ever be quite how we expect it, but somehow we can all get what we need.

We all know that children are impressionable. And I can't tell you how many times something minuscule has come back to haunt me.

"Where did you get those?" My three-year-old asked the other day.

"Grammy bought them for me," I answered.

"Why?" She asked.

And I could have said because I needed them or because she knew I would like them, but instead I said without a thought, "Because she loves me."

Twenty minutes later I found my daughter crying and asked her what was wrong. "I can't find a present to give you!" she exploded.

"I don't need a present!" I assured her.

"But how will you know that I love you?" she quivered. And my heart sank. I knew immediately where this idea had come from, and in hindsight saw the error of my response. It is hard to explain to a three-year-old that presents don't equal love when they've already put that together in their head, but I scooped her up and held her and did my best to show her that the love was there.

I wonder how many little messages like this are sent without us ever noticing. I wonder how many random statements are misinterpreted and internalized into beliefs about the world that we never intended to instill in any way. It is impossible to know what meanings kids assign to the words we say and, because we are speaking above their heads and not always giving full thought to what we say, it is often not the meaning we intend. But I can do my best to correct these issues when they show themselves. And I can set an example in how I live my life and hope that actions speak louder than anything I may have haphazardly said.

Most of the time I think of it as though I am teaching them, but in reality, quite often, it is the other way around. "I don't know what I am supposed to do," I said to my husband this morning in regard to a business acquisition, and my 8-year-old overhearing from the other room piped in, "You can do anything you want to do, Mom." And I sighed, a deep, knowing sigh. Because although he may not understand the gravity of the situation, ultimately, I know he is right. These children are in my life for a reason. We are on this journey together, finding our purpose together, and inspiring one another to do the same.

I do the best that I can. Sometimes my emotions get the best of me and I wonder if I've made a mistake. Sometimes I yell. Sometimes things get messy. Sometimes I am not sure I am communicating the example I would like to set. In all honesty, sometimes I question what kind of mother I am. Be assured, no mother is perfect! I have learned to accept these moments, or more accurately, to embrace them. I take them as an opportunity to admit to my children that I don't always know. I apologize. I make it evident that I am fallible, but that at the end of the day, I love them, more than anything, no matter what, and that I will continue to always do the best that I can. I ask them to help me do better. I hope that this teaches them to approach their own lives with the same willingness to learn. I hope that it also instills in them compassion for another's learning curve. The results aren't in on this yet, but they seem to be pretty great little people so far, and I'd like to think that perhaps I have in some way contributed.

Motherhood for me is a journey. A journey that allows me to discover and rediscover myself and my roles in this world. I am constantly brought to face and accept my own emotions and my own powerlessness. I am constantly brought to the realization that I am defining my experience and that it is up to me to bring purpose to my life and to support these children as they find their own place in the world. There is a lot of balance required by this gig. I have learned over the years that while I love my children and they do bring meaning to my life, it is not up to them to be my "purpose." I have learned that in order to inspire them to live their own purposeful lives, I must first passionately explore my own. I do my best to involve them in my exploration, to share the experience, and to encourage them in any exploration of their own.

One day not too long ago, I asked myself what kind of messages I wanted to send and what kind of example I wanted to offer them. I seek to build my dreams so that one day my children will have the courage and the faith to build theirs. I seek to create the life I want so that one day they, too, will create their visions. I seek to care for myself so that my children will learn that it is okay to put themselves first sometimes. I seek to be authentic with them even if at times it feels that I may be presenting a weakness of sorts, so that they may learn that it is okay to make mistakes and that one can learn from them. I seek to live from gratitude and compassion and I hope that they will learn to honor these traits as well. It's not fair to expect my children to break the mold if I haven't even begun to chisel at it. Rather than allowing them to be my purpose, I will instead inspire them to become their own!

I know that this all sounds rather lofty, and perhaps it is. I learn more as a mother every day and my perspective is constantly evolving. What I have come to embrace and know is true is that all things exist within love. All of those frazzled moments and exhausted on-the-verge-of-breaking meltdowns, always give way to peace again. Anger, confusion, sadness, doubt, all dissolve into love. And I have learned to trust in that. Even in the midst of chaos, I can recall that love, and trust in its return. If there is anything you take from this, I hope it is an inclination to trust in that—to trust that you are doing the best you can, that love IS, that peace comes back around, and that whatever happens, we will grow through it; and if you are having any doubt, just go hug one of your kids.

Author Bio:

Kimber Bowers lives with her family in Dallastown, PA, where she seeks to offer support and assistance to other families in the community. Like many of us, she has come from a long and winding past that required release and growth to navigate purposefully. After years of clinical depression, low self-esteem, grief, anxiety, and learning to cope with chronic autoimmune disease, she is now living content with gratitude and ease. All of these experiences have led her to NOW, where she can be of service helping others to discover and forge their own purposeful paths. Through her business Loving Light Holistic Wellness LLC, Kimber offers compassion, love, and acceptance openly and freely, encouraging others to discover and embrace their own power to create and navigate change while facilitating growth through that process.

Website: **www.lovinglighthw.com**

The Most Valuable Lessons I Learned From My Kids, Not From Kindergarten
by Theresa Nicassio, PhD.

Most of us have heard of the popular book All I Really Need to Know I Learned in Kindergarten by Robert Fulghum (2004). I'm going to take a big risk and let it go on record here by saying that I have not found this to be the case. In fact, in my experience, the most valuable lessons I learned were from my kids, not from kindergarten.

Nothing could have prepared me for motherhood. Seriously... nothing! No books, no advice, not even spending time with kids could have shown me any semblance of a map of the journey that I had decided to embark on, one that would change the very fabric of my being. While we all hear about the joys and the tribulations of parenthood, the opportunity for inner growth and discovery is often overlooked. As a therapist of 30 years, and as a mother of two beloved daughters, the soul journey has forever transformed my life and has created a deep sense of meaning and purpose that I never could have learned from even Mrs. Susie Bentley (my dear kindergarten teacher).

Contrary to popular belief, I've come to believe that motherhood is really about service. I found this service began for me from the moment I became pregnant. Overnight, the world shifted from "me" to "we" in a way far more potent than the similar shift of choosing to be with a life partner. Suddenly every aspect of my life, including everything I ate, drank, breathed, or even put on my skin and hair would impact the little unknown being that resided within my body. Everything changed because I knew another's life literally depended on me making healthy choices in a way that I had never experienced. We're talking accountability in the truest sense of the word.

The truth is, had I known how challenging the experience was going to be, I may have chosen not to venture down the path of motherhood. On the other hand, had I known how much my heart would open and transform me, exposing me to the potential within me to love in a way I never would have known, nothing would have held me back. Choosing to become a mom, both via giving birth as well as via adoption, was the most profound, humbling, and sacred decision I have ever made in my life. I love being a mom.

When our first daughter (Alex) was born—actually, even while she was being born, a part of me died: my pride. A Kuhnian shift was immediately felt. I fought to do everything I could do to ensure that she came out of my body safely, even though there were complications that suggested she may have been at risk. In that moment, literally nothing else mattered. I didn't notice or care how many doctors and nurses were swarming around me during that vulnerable time—instead, my whole world became centered around the little baby inside of me and her safety and well-being. When she came out safely, no words could describe my relief, my joy, and the love in my heart for this new being that I had been hanging out with for 9 months, but had never before been able to meet face to face. It was a moment that no words can describe.

Amazingly, I had a similar emotional experience the first time I met our second daughter (Angeline), even though she had never resided in my body. Somehow, this beautiful and vulnerable little 14-month-old toddler and I seemed to already know each other at what I would describe as a soul level, with no apparent reason for such an immediate bond. The how and why of this will probably always remain a mystery.

With both of my daughters, while I felt a deep connection, I had no idea who they were, how they would touch my life, and how their life journeys would unfold (nor mine, for that matter). I simply said "YES" to entering the journey, even though the path and the struggles to follow would sometimes feel like too much to bear. As I think most mothers experience at some point or another, there were times when I would ask myself why I had "signed up" for the job and whether I could tolerate some of the biggest storms of it, such as the dreaded teenage years. During those times, I knew those doubts would eventually pass, but I'd be lying if I said that motherhood was always easy—because it certainly is not.

For me, the absolute hardest part of my journey as a mother was living with the uncertainties around my own debilitated health condition and my associated fears about whether I would be able to be around for my girls and not leave them motherless. This aspect of my motherhood experience has led to my own transformation into not only a new life as a mother, but professionally as well, leading me down a path of embracing aspects of living that I had never believed to be relevant to me and my life path. And yes, I'll explain...

After my daughter Alex was born, I became very sick and couldn't seem to get better. Every infection possible seemed to find its way to me. The most obvious of the many symptoms I had was the assault on my respiratory system. Basically, my immune system went on strike—and not for days or weeks or even months, but for years.

It was horrible. My fantasies of being able to energetically and joyfully play with and care for my daughter in the ways that I had so looked forward to were overshadowed by my desperate struggle to breathe. My little baby and growing child only knew a mother who could barely waddle around, perpetually coughing and wheezing, needing to spend large amounts of time in bed. This was not at all what I had imagined motherhood would be like, nor how I wanted my daughter (and later, both daughters) to know me. However, given the seriousness of my condition, I realized that the most important thing was that I do whatever I could to stay alive and not leave my daughter motherless—at least not before she graduated high school.

Many times I would lay in bed weeping, fearing that I would be taken under before then, sometimes sharing these fears with my partner, who was also scared. Miraculously, I never gave up, even though the challenge before me to stay alive felt Herculean.

This carried on for over a decade, until I finally discovered that a primary underlying cause of my debilitation and immune challenges had to do with food sensitivities. Strange as it may sound, this was one of the greatest blessings of my life, because it meant that there was something that I could do to turn my health around, enabling me to be the mom that I had so longed to be.

Powerful and inspiring, my experiences created a fierce passion in me to help others. If I could help at least one other person from having to suffer as I did, then it would give meaning to my experience. Following this calling, I have become an author of an internationally acclaimed book (YUM) that is changing the lives of others around the globe. How amazing that the lemons of my life are now providing a lemonade elixir of hope and healing for others. This outcome of motherhood had certainly never been on my radar—since kindergarten or any time since!

Motherhood has been my greatest teacher... I don't think there is anything in my life that has been more influential than the privilege of the experience. In addition to being humbling, motherhood is downright hard. It's fun and it's terrifying.

Most of all, I have found motherhood to be rewarding in the most indescribable and transformative ways. Before becoming a mom, I loved people and I loved life. However, since becoming a mom, I have learned a whole different paradigm of what love can be—a love that is bigger than life itself.

Author Bio:

Dr. Theresa Nicassio, PhD is the author of *YUM: Plant-Based Recipes for a Gluten-Free Diet*, a psychologist, mother, gourmet raw food chef, and nutrition educator. She's won numerous awards, including the 2015 Gourmand World Cookbook Award as the Best Diet Book in Canada and a prestigious 2016 Best in the World Award for the same category. Passionate about public awareness and empowerment, Theresa also offers her expertise as a wellness specialist to the community as a magazine columnist, public speaker, radio and TV guest, as well as contributing through social media and her website.

Website: **www.theresanicassio.com**

Heart-to-Heart, Tete-a-Tete

84 Slices of Motherly Pie
by Christine Summers

I did it singlehandedly. I wish that I would have had the support of a husband and father during the child-rearing years, but that was not the case for me. Now that I am 50 and my kids are 27 and 22, I write with the utmost confidence from the heart, soul, and from personal experience. I am a believer that life is school.

1. Get on the floor and play with your children. Play throughout life.
2. Give. Give more. Expect nothing in return. See what happens.
3. Take photos often. Include yourself in photos with your kids.
4. Teach your children about self-care and essentials in life by showing them how to take care of the basics like: hygiene, nails, shaving, bathing, our bodies, makeup, balancing a cheque-book, sexual education, consequences, discipline, compassion, etc.
5. Take care of yourself first. Take care of others next.
6. Get your hair cut on a regular basis. You feeling and looking your best is so important to our overall daily functioning.
7. Feel the emotions as situations arise and find positive and healthy ways of coping with life's challenges and opportunities. All emotions are valid. Coping is the tricky part.
8. The cup can be either half empty or half full. Your choice. If you don't like the way something is going, you have the power to change it. Really.
9. What goes around does come around.
10. Fully receive and give compliments and gifts. You deserve them!
11. Love unconditionally.
12. You will experience loss and heartbreak throughout life. Think about what you learned from the experience and move forward.
13. We all make mistakes and we all are in the "school of life." Remember to forgive yourself and others.

14. The classic look is always best. Think pearls. Think what would "X" (the person that inspires me the most) wear or say or do in this situation. It works!
15. Simplify. Less really is more.
16. Life really is about the moments. The sweet split second smiles and giggles. Colors. The breeze. Rainbows. The ocean. Sunshine. The moon. Trees. Birds flying in a V formation. Honey that bees produce. A touch. A hug. A spectacular kiss. Doing things just because you want to help someone else. These are THE things.
17. Don't ever lose sight of your family and your friends. Hold on to your identity.
18. Be objective and open-minded.
19. Judging others will come back to you. Karma is really a thing.
20. Don't make fun of other people. It's not nice or kind. What if you were that person?
21. How can you make someone else's day? Take action.
22. Clean up trash when you see it on the side of the road. Don't litter.
23. Expect nothing in return. See what happens.
24. Read something inspirational every day.
25. Find the inner peace that comes from your heart.
26. Stretch your body. Your body thanks you.
27. Upon waking, be grateful. Upon sleeping, be grateful.
28. Read and read more. Teach your children the joy of reading; it will stay with them their whole lives.
29. Communication is the key to life. For all relationships.
30. Praise. Praise more.
31. Children really do learn by following your lead. Lead by example.
32. Nurture your friendships. The connections are important.
33. If you want to be successful and fit, you need to be around people that are successful and fit.
34. You will make mistakes in life. Accept it. Learn from it. Pull up your big girl britches and move forward.
35. This is not a dress rehearsal. Enjoy the moments.
36. Release all fears to the universe. It is fear that holds you back.

Live.

37. Listen to your parents. They have more experience than you do.
38. Set boundaries. Some things are NOT okay.
39. Listen to your inner voice. It's always right.
40. Junk food catches up with you.
41. Don't sweat the small stuff. Really. Let it go.
42. Ask for help when you need or want it. Live fearlessly.
43. Be the best that you can be. Always. There is only one YOU.
44. Control impulse spending. You don't need it. I promise.
45. Stay active. Your body thanks you.
46. Plan for your future. No one else is. YOU are the first bill that needs to be paid.
47. Don't smoke or use drugs. Think about it.
48. Pursue your passion. Period.
49. Stressed? Breathe deeply.
50. For the most part, TV is a waste of time. You could be doing so many other positive and productive things.
51. Kids really do grow up fast. You don't realize how fast until you look back and go "Wow! where did the time go."
52. Goals. Write them down and review them often. Always have something to look forward to.
53. Always be considerate of others. Be on time. Be dependable. It goes a long way.
54. Take care of your teeth. You will be very glad that you did.
55. The person that broke your heart, you WILL get over them.
56. Parents are human too.
57. Credit cards are for emergencies only. If you can't pay them off in 30 days you cannot afford it.
58. You are not cool if you are the one wasted at a party.
59. Take care of your car (body) and it will take care of you.
60. No tanning beds. Ever.
61. Be spontaneous. It's the only way to LIVE.
62. Remove negative people in your life.
63. Nap. Nuff said.

64. Be confident. Always. No one is better than you.
65. Realize the effects of food.
66. Be generous. Always.
67. Be an attentive driver.
68. Listen. Repeat.
69. Say "thank you" and mean it.
70. Stop being "too busy" for others.
71. Surround yourself with people that are more like what you want to be. Watch what happens.
72. Respect your body inside and out ALL of the time.
73. If you don't understand something, ask enough questions until you do.
74. Spending "time" really is what is most important. Think about it.
75. Teachers aren't responsible for disciplining your children, teaching your children about balancing checking accounts, managing money, or teaching your children about sex education. It really is supposed to come from home.
76. There are many paths in life. Yours is not better than anyone else's. Some have tougher roads than others.
77. Looking back at photos, you will realize "those were the good old days."
78. Breathe. Meditate. Take a class. Journal. Talk. Exercise. Breathe more.
79. Be very proud of your Freedom and thank soldiers for their service when you are around them.
80. Every single thing that you put into your body or onto your body absorbs through every organ and system that you have and either nourishes or causes inflammation and disease. Read labels, research, and be your own advocate.
81. Health really is number one. Without it you don't have much.
82. Learn something new every day.
83. Give hugs freely and often.
84. Respect your elders. Period.

Author Bio:

Christine Summers is a mother of two adult children, ages 22 & 27. She currently lives outside of Phoenix, Arizona and previously lived most of her life in both Wisconsin and Illinois, which are Midwest states in the United States. Chris is a realtor/office manager for a property management & real estate firm. Chris enjoys sharing her wisdom, passion, and words of inspiration.

Consistency Is the Foundational Powerhouse
by Sandy O' Neal

Being a mother is what I was born to be, and I literally felt that in my soul after having my first child. The Universe and I finally aligned in a beautiful way when I became a mother.

After my daughter was born and I held her close in the quietness of my room, I thanked God for this miracle that would change my life forever, and I made a vow to God that I would raise this gift he had given to me with the very best of my being. Five years later, I gave this same vow to God when he blessed our family again with the birth of my son.

What an incredible time I have had raising these precious beings who have come to share my earthly experience, enhancing my daily existence beyond anything I could have dreamt. These little beings have brought such color to my life, and my world became brilliantly brighter and more alive once they arrived. And I believe they have taught me as much as I have taught to them throughout the years of being their mother.

Now, several decades later, I can vividly see the fruits of my steadfastness and the effort that I poured into my children many years ago as I created an environment full of love and respect for them where they could thrive and become the best versions of themselves.

When looking back on the early developmental years with my children, the greatest takeaway that I can share with you is the value of consistency during those early formative years of their lives. This is that precious time when it is often just the two of you sharing your day together before the schooling years start and the play dates have to be scheduled because they are so plentiful.

Being consistent with your children when the easiest thing to do would be to give in—give in to the will of your child because you're too tired, too rushed, too overwhelmed, too busy. All the toos that come after your day has been filled with everyday routines that often include household chores, driving to and from school or to the grocery store, doctor visits, and the many other activities that can crowd your day. When the easy thing would be to grab food through that drive-thru window out of its convenience because the thought of going home and making a fresh meal sounds like more work than you wish to exude. Being consistent with nightly reading or bedtime routines. Whatever the convenient route would be for you, making the choice to stay consistent with your child will have a rewarding payoff down the road.

Pulling the "too much work" card can derail your vision and erode your family values if played too often and can erode the foundation you want to build for your children. Find what you value most and stay consistent with those values and boundaries and you will be looking back at the work you put into your children's lives and knowing that you did your best. Pull back from activities when you are feeling overwhelmed or too busy. Keep your schedule suitable for you and your child.

Being consistent through the early formative years has proved to build a solid foundation for my children to grow FROM. Having this consistency gave them boundaries where they thrived and grew into incredible beings who are kind and respectful of others.

Our babies grow up so fast, so take time carving out your values and staying consistent with your children.

There will be time to rest in your future!

Author Bio:

Sandy O'Neal is a mother of two, a Life Coach, and a Certified Hypnotherapist. Sandy helps remove limiting beliefs and negative behavior by promoting personal growth and development. Think HAPPY—Hypnotherapy, Anxiety reduction, Pain & Performance management, Yearly goals.

Website: **www.sandyoneal.com**
Email: **atransformedlife.sandy@gmail.com**

Raising Children In Today's World
by Thembi Bheka

Imagine the culture shock of moving to a country with $5 in your pocket as a single mother after a failed marriage. Imagine finding out the country and especially the city you chose has another language you do not speak and let alone understand. Imagine beating all those odds, getting an education and building a business, raising a child as a single mother all within 10 years?

That is the power of us women. We are blessed abundantly and beyond what we can imagine. Despite the challenges we encounter, we rise stronger and better. Able to do anything for our children and provide them with the best resources within our reach.

Is it easy? No. Is it doable? Absolutely—I am proof that this can be done over and over again. My mother did it, I did it, and I have seen many more women raise children with or without the support from their spouses in an environment that does not seem to be conducive for any living human. I see it in the news, the refugee camps and abusive environments, and I know the future generations will continue to be strong and raise great children. However, it is up to us current mothers to lay the groundwork for the future generations.

How do they do it in such a changing world? A world which is filling with more negativity and sadness than joy? A world where your child is surrounded by more fear than courage? Having grown up a few decades ago where a child was raised by a village, you can imagine the shock and difficulty I encountered when I had to raise a child alone in a foreign continent, let alone country. A world where a neighbor cannot discipline your child for fear of being too nosy.

Needless to say, things have changed drastically. It probably has to do with the modernization—whatever that means to you. Everything and everyone is now so modernized. There is a lot of child trafficking, abuse, and you can't trust anyone with your child anymore.

This for me was the reason I decided to become self-employed. I did not want strangers bringing up my child. As a nurse who worked 12 hours, that would have meant seeing my child only at bedtime. I decided I was going to decide when my child needed to interact with others and my boss would have no control of it. I would decide when I wanted to stay at home and cuddle with my babies. It truly has been a blessing and a big learning curve for me.

However, not everyone has that opportunity. Even if you did, your children still has to go to school and interact with the outside world. How do you then bring up your child in a noisy, cruel, and seemingly cold world? Well, you make it warm for them. No matter the cruelty everyone is showing out there, create a positive environment at home.

One day, my daughter came home and told me about a friend who was always blaming everything on her skin color. This friend had decided she would not go to university because her chances of getting a job were slim due to her skin color. How sad is that? My daughter asked me for an opinion and I said if skin color determined who hired you, I would not be who I am. I would not be a successful real estate investor coaching many to be financially free. Oprah would not be the most powerful woman in media. Skin color does not chose who you become. Your background does not define you. Your history is not your destiny. You choose and decide your destiny, and you can be anything you want to be.

That is the message we should teach our children. As Michelle Obama once said, "When they go low, we go high." When everyone is negative, you become positive, when they see the glass half empty, show them the glass half full. In my household, we do not talk about the challenges that might block our success; we talk about how we can overcome those challenges, and be what we were destined to be. As I set higher standards for myself, my children mirror that. They see that their mother is not defined by her marital status, her mishaps, or even the car she drives. I am defined by the impact I make in this world, an impact to make the world a better place, the philosophy to positively impact many people's lives every day, and as Gandhi said, "To be the change they want to see in the world."

"Tell me and I forget, teach me and I remember, involve me and I learn." —Benjamin Franklin.

There is no greater gift we can give to our kids than involve them in the good things we want them to mirror. Involve them in our reading, in our businesses, in our lives, and in the volunteering and giving we do. Recently my 15-year-old daughter started a YouTube channel because she got inspired shooting my videos for my coaching program. You want your child to grow up and help the world, start volunteering with them. Chances are they will follow suit. That is why take your child to work program is successful. Involvement is the best teacher.

Let us build a better world for our future generation simply by involving them.

Author Bio:
Thembi Bheka is a real estate investor, coach, and a member of the prestigious REIN. She is the founder of Real Estate Real Riches, an online educational company that teaches others how to invest in real estate. Her passion lies in giving back to the community through charity work, and conducting free real estate seminars to immigrants.

Website: **www.realestaterealriches.com**

Delay the Gratification
by Sarita Talwai

Some kinds of gratification have to be deferred. Other kinds have to be denied. That is the mantra we grew up with. New clothes only on birthdays and important festivals. New uniforms only when the seams could not be let down any further. Text books to be used with utmost care because they had to be passed on. The empty leaves in the old notebooks taken to the book binders, to be used as rough books for the next academic year. Library books passed on from friend to friend so we could read four books for the price of one. Unbeknownst to them, our parents instilled in us habits that have stood us in good stead through life.

The stories about the "urban poor" doing the rounds is alarming. The twenty-somethings running out of cash in the middle of the month, and then nearly starving themselves till they are paid again, makes sensational copy. It extracts a grim satisfaction from readers with frugal habits, but it also sends frissons of fear in parents of young adults. In a world of relative plenty, the youth has stopped using money as a security blanket. It is now the sable cloak which announces their arrival. The deceptive power to purchase at a swipe of a card or a click on an icon clouds all good sense.

Our children deserve to experience the joy of waiting. As doting parents, we sometimes presume their needs, thus erasing all the pleasures of prospect. Anticipation is an enjoyable journey, and we owe it to them.

Instant indulgence has far-reaching consequences. The child develops an illegitimate sense of entitlement. His patience is dulled. His pleasure is momentary and he is constantly seeking new stimulations.

The value of the gift is in direct proportion to the delay in receiving it. The more appeasement, the more dissatisfaction. The more they wait, the more they will cherish.

The fallout of instant gratification is perceptible. Our young people are angry, disgruntled, and restive. They want instant promotions and increments. The smartest brands and latest gadgets. Bank loans and credit cards lull them into a distorted sense of well-being, and they are unable to cope with reality. This reflects in their relationships and in their academic careers.

Waiting is a pleasurable activity. It sharpens the imagination and opens new worlds. It may lead to the invention of a new board game, or the rereading of a favorite book. The creation of a fantastic Lego structure or the composition of a silly limerick or the planting of a seed. How can we deny our children such wonderful presents?

Author Bio:
Sarita Talwai is a freelance counselor, and a facilitator at Bangalore Writers Workshop's creative writing course for children. In her free time she is an avid reader and traveller, reserving a special interest in writing about South Asian geopolitics. She is a regular contributor to the newsletter published by Banjara Academy, a premier counseling center in Bangalore. She strives to solve a minimum of three crosswords per day.

Email: **talwai_s@yahoo.co.in**

Finding a Loving Way With a Bad Case of Rudeness
by Rachel Peachey

"I'm not playing anymore!" said my 3-year-old in a huff. The words were exactly what I might expect to hear coming out of his older cousins' mouths. I was taken aback, and was tempted to laugh more than anything else. But it got worse.

"You're stupid," was the next attack. It was then that I knew that we had a bad case of rudeness. My sweet little boy was becoming corrupted and influenced by others. It was something I knew he would have to face, but I wasn't prepared for it at such a young age. Or, perhaps I had assumed he would always ignore poor examples from others—I mean, wouldn't my little angel automatically discard rude language and attitudes?

The rudeness made me angry. A fury arose in me that I had only known to appear with tantrums. All mothers know that speaking rationally from a place of anger is nearly impossible. It's when the yelling monster comes out. Sometimes irrational consequences began spilling out of my mouth, making my son angry and only causing me guilt.

We battled back and forth, and at times, I admit, his rudeness was matched by mine. Other times I judged his words, saying, "That's not nice." But to no avail. The rudeness stuck.

Then I had an epiphany. It's amazing how quickly in your anger you can forget the reasonable, helpful things you should be saying to your child. In a flash of saneness, I remembered my life as a preschool teacher.

I was constantly pulled and tugged by little ones who wanted to tell me the mean things their classmates had said. My response was always, "Tell him/her you don't like that. If he/she doesn't stop, then come tell me." Surely I could do as I had asked my preschoolers to do.

So my new response to rude comments from my little one was, "I don't like that." I was amazed at his response. It wasn't immediate, but he did seem to care about how I felt. He looked at me, his eyes grew wide. I could tell he was thinking. And slowly, he gave up the rudeness.

The best part about it is that I'm providing an example I can be proud of. If my son struggles with a classmate or cousin who says something rude or mean to him, that's exactly how I'd like him to respond. It's a way for him to stand up for himself without lowering to the level of rude comments and attacks.

The other surprise is that now, should I need to say, "I don't like that," he almost invariably responds quickly with, "Sorry, mama." I'm not sure if he picked that up because I'm fairly quick to apologize to him or because he's been watching more Peppa (who is very polite by the way) lately, but it's a nice change from "You're stupid."

Young children are quite the challenge and responsibility. I've always believed firmly that a positive adult example is the best way to teach. However, it's much easier said than done.

Under fives have a way of awakening such frustration and anger that we parents lose our self-control. Any parent who's experienced a tantrum or rude child knows this is the truth—which, let's face it, is every parent.

Now, if the rude monster appears, most of the time I can hold it together and find that one phrase, "I don't like that," to help set me, and my little one, back on track.

Author Bio:

Rachel is a mama, wife, blogger, Montessori teacher, and freelance writer. She lives in Guatemala, the land of eternal Spring, where she wakes up to homegrown coffee and a stunning panorama of volcanoes. When not working or playing with her kids, she can be found volunteering at a local library she helped begin, or baking. Follow her adventures on her blog, Volcano Mama, where she writes about Montessori homeschooling, parenting, and the Montessori philosophy.

Website: **www.rachelpeachey.com**

Actions Speak Louder Than Words
by Valerie Langley

As a mom of four small children, I absolutely adore my daily meditation time. The only time our house is quiet is when everyone is sleeping. So when I am able to just get still and quiet and relax, it's like heaven has come to earth for a few minutes. When I take time for myself with my meditation I get very protective of this small window of time that is just for me. What I have realized is that my actions with this are speaking volumes compared to my words.

It was a Sunday afternoon. I had been with our three kids a lot over the weekend and was 7 months pregnant with baby number four. So my husband agreed to watch the kids so I could have some quiet time for me. I was so excited because there was a talk I had been wanting to listen to by Gabby Bernstein. I was just enjoying the solitude of no one asking for my attention and listening to the talk. At the end she did an amazing powerful meditation. So I was doing the meditation sitting on my bed in the zone, visualizing, focusing, just zoning out in my Zen mode. About halfway through the meditation I heard the bedroom door open. My husband, who was watching the kids, was also watching football and lost sight of what the children were up to.

So I think to myself if I just ignore them they will go away and let me finish. Well, I'm sure I looked like a statue of Buddha with my pregnant belly sitting Indian style and my hands on my knees. The children realized I was meditating, as they had seen me do it many times before, but they didn't leave and they didn't try to talk to me or bother me. I could feel them climbing on the bed, and now I was thinking they were trying to see what was playing on the computer. There was beautiful meditation music on, and they seemed to be mesmerized. I could hear the whispers among them and feel them getting settled on the bed. So here I was really trying to stay in the zone not being distracted, to hold my focus and vision, and then all of a sudden I can feel tiny little hands in my hands. I didn't fully open my eyes because I didn't want this to end. I glanced out of the tiny slits in my eyes just to get a glimpse of what was going on and saw that they were sitting just like me, Indian style, palms up on their knees in a circle with me and overlapping our hands. They had closed their eyes to meditate with me. My heart melted. My actions were what led them to this, not my words. It showed me how important my actions are not only to our children but to all those around me. The saying a picture is worth a thousand words comes to mind and reminds me to continue to be the example I want to see in my children and in the world.

Author Bio:
Valerie is a wife and mother to 4 precious children She is also an RN and Strategic Success Coach for moms. She has found the amazing tool of meditation to have changed her life and that of her clients lives. Valerie helps moms connect to their soul purpose and find happiness and fulfillment in life without feeling stressed and overwhelmed. Valerie also hosts holistic wellness retreats for women and meditation workshops.

Website: **www.valerielangley.com**

Mum's the Word
by Nina Birgitte Price

Shit... and then some. Yes, that is what you heard, the first word from me is a curse word. A curse word that was exhaled in a loud growl to the suitcase that is still in our hallway, unpacked, eight days since my husband came home from a business trip. It is opened, and its contents have been thoroughly explored by our two blue-eyed sweethearts (devils), and I can trace my husband's laundry all the way to the playroom. I take a photo of it and WhatsApp it to my dear hubby, threatening to use it as firewood if it is not removed immediately after homecoming. I send the same picture to my dear girlfriends, but this time with a pledge of them sympathizing with me, of how my life has become.

I am Nina, mother of two girls born 21 months apart, living in Texas but Norwegian at heart. Adam, my Irish other half, works for a company that moves us around, and I am the parasite on his back.

Together we have lived in Norway, Ghana, Netherlands, and now in Texas. We have a six-year-old cat that has now lived in 4 countries and 10 houses, and our darling daughters that came while we lived in Holland. I am a chiropractor and work 25 hours a week while I am doing my specialization within pediatric and prenatals.

I am trying to be Hollywood healthy and direct my children around sugar, processed food, carbohydrates, and give my kids enough exercise. In practice this often results in me saying yes to that enormously expensive organic, yet unhealthy, ice cream in the fridge as long as they leave me alone in the kitchen while I am preparing their incredibly healthy snack and lunch for tomorrow. So... I am the mom who contacts the school about their unhealthy sugary and salty meal plan, which might have been very Hollywood wonder mama at the time, but then send my kids with a ready meal to school the next day. The word *hypocrite* sneaks into my mind...

Every day I am trying my best to be a part of the white shirt, clear skin, well-exercised and calm supermoms out there that I see on "pinstagram." And every day I fail... I still blame my two-year-old pregnancy for my growing (!) belly and waistband. I swear, I keep explaining to people that I must have the world's worst metabolism, considering that I have not sat down for a meal in years and therefore should be as slim as I feel like I deserve. Everyone knows that food that you inhale while packing backpacks or chocolate that you munch in the corner of the pantry while kids are screaming due to the carrots on their plates is not allowed to be added around your waist! But I guess the amount of calories I eat in the form of leftover bread crust is over 'the recommended daily amount' and turns out to be enough to increase my belly to the point where my daughter announces that mommy has a baby in her belly (I have not).

I keep thinking that I have met my low point of snacking or binge eating, until I do something even more unthinkable and have to lower the standard of myself again. Yesterday while I was cleaning out my car—our car is my storage place—I found five drinking bottles with various content, enough raisins to fill my biggest Tupperware, socks in fifteen different varieties (not one pair), some notes from school that I never read, and some nachos under my daughter's car seat that I ATE. I mean... I saw it, I shoved it into my mouth, and a split second later I realized what I had done and thought... a new low point. But do you think I spat out the soggy nacho?? God no... I swallowed it!! I mean, I clearly have no pride!

Anyway... my day goes on and I forget to feed my cat and have to rewash my laundry as it has developed its own particular scent after drying in the washing machine. I negotiate with my kids regarding their clothing choices, I lose, and I bring in two children with shorts, raincoats, ballet shoes, and sleep hair to daycare again. I then realize that I have forgotten show and tell for the third time in a row, so I try to tell them that instead of bringing a bunny that starts with a B, we brought a bankcard. Not very well received, and apparently against school policy. "Walk of shame" has now gotten a whole new meaning, and I drag my feet down the corridor feeling like the worse mom ever before running off to work, relieved (something you will never hear me admit) to have a break from my sweet (exhausting) children. Hours later I literally run out of my office door again because I miss my kids so much, to then discover that the smiling sweet kids that I remembered have become cranky and tired and want more ice cream while I am prepping dinner and healthy lunch for the following day.

I try to not say no to my kids—Facebook told me that was wrong—but to redirect their attention to the playroom or outside area. This works... if I am the horse they can ride on all around the house or if I chase them around the garden or play hide-and-seek. So here you have their disciplinarian and house authority crawling around on all fours, making horse noises, while they tell me where to go by pulling my hair or kicking my side. I don't know... it does not feel like I am doing this right!

Last week my car broke down and I had to entertain my kids waiting for the tow truck. As I was under the car trying to Facetime my husband while having him show me which wire I needed to wiggle to get the car to start, I let the kids run free inside the car, secured, of course, and I did not think anything more about it. As the tow car arrived, he needed to get into the car to put it in neutral, only to find a car decorated with sanitary pads (and I shop at Costco, there were MANY) all over the front seat, steering wheel, and dashboard. They were all opened and stuck to every available spot in the car... the embarrassment!!

Many times I have asked myself why I am so determined to make absolutely everything so hard for myself. Is the solution to good parenting really to never push them away and tell them to do something on their own? Will my kids be confident in their environment if mommy is limiting herself to be perfect in every way (clearly without succeeding) or to break her back to do it all? Only to probably have a breakdown and have to set aside time to be sick and learn how to live again.

I have always believed that in this tough world I need to give my kids a strong start and be a good role model. Give them confidence to be themselves, make good choices, know what they stand for and go for what they want. Don't stress them by trying to be perfect, but let them take their time and find themselves. Cheer for them when they make it, encourage them when they try, and comfort them when they fail... but not do it for them.

So, why do I fail in this? Why do I let everyone tell me that I need to be a ninja mom that destroys herself in doing everything, and even be perfect while doing it? Work, nutrition, child raising, exercise, body sculpting, juicing, fermenting, and child care. A mom is suppose to do it all these days. It used to be a village to raise a child, but these days it seems to me that parenting is my husband and me trying to make it in the world where laws are made by social media. Have we forgotten the importance of teaching them to take in life? To teach our kids that more is not necessarily better?

That success is not measured in "likes" and how neat your house is. Having a mum that binge eats leftover dinners at the counter while gulping down the third coffee to stay awake, reading research papers while waiting for the green traffic light, and forgetting to wash out the conditioner from her hair surely cannot be sending a good signal to them?!

Women of Pinterest, I don't know how you do it. Consider me impressed! I don't know how your house can look like it has never been entered but still be a playpen for your kids while you only serve home-cooked meals. Never say no to your kids, your boss, or your PTA. But I am changing tactics... I need to show my girls that a mommy doesn't have to strive for perfect, but it is OK to just be "good enough." That she can be happy even though she does not have a house that looks like an interior magazine or a career that is blooming, but that she loves herself, her time is precious, and she values her body, mind and spirit. Only by example can I create little people that respect not only everyone else, but most of all themselves. Not for being perfect, but for being happy.

Author Bio:
My name is Dr. Nina and I am from Norway and live in Houston, USA, with my Northern Irish husband and two beautiful daughters. I have always had restless legs and I have lived in Germany before moving to Bournemouth, England to study chiropractic. In 2011 my husband and I moved to Takoradi, Ghana, for two amazing years and then we lived in Holland for two years. After being a stay-at-home mom I am finally back at work and I love it. But as many other mamas, I struggle to find the right balance in life. I hope my contribution in this book gives you an insight in a working expat mama's life and her struggles to live up to her potential.

The Art of
Parenting

Mom, Can I Have an Instagram Account?
by Renee Tarantowski Baude

Those dreaded words.

As a mom, kids are guaranteed to say certain things to you: "Mom, I love you." Your heart bursts with love.

"Mom, I hate you." Your heart is pierced in that moment. "Mom, can I have 5 dollars?"

"Mom, can I go downtown?"

"Mom, can I have an Instagram account?"

My philosophy on parenting is best summed up by prompts from Shefali Tsabary's book *The Conscious Parent*. "Am I able to perceive my relationship with my children as a sacred relationship?" translated to a simple mantra that I can remember in an instant: I am love and light. I see the sacred love and light of the Divine in you. And, "How can I rise above my own fear of change and transform myself to meet the requirements of my child's spirit?" I also translate this into my own quick mantra: My past should not determine their future.

With these two mantras I can tackle any issue, at any time. My goal is to create an environment of compassion and love independent of physical location. If I'm in the aisle of the supermarket and my child decides to lay down and have a fit... I become love and light and see the light of his spirit—not a screaming child lying on a dirty floor.

When my children were smaller is was much easier to create a sacred container for us to dwell. I like to compare kids growing to repotting a plant. The first pot is tiny and filled with the roots of pure love. As our children grow, we need to get bigger pots to contain not just the physical size but all the new thoughts, ideas, and emotions that are offshoots of the roots of pure love. At some point, it seems to be different for each child, the pot begins to be filled from sources other than us. Social media can take over the pot if we aren't paying attention.

Fast-forward a few years, I read the text, "Mom, can I have an Instagram account." My response was yes with the suggestion that we set it up together. Evidently, he only read the yes part. Within minutes I had several likes from him on my own account and a direct message.

UGGGHHHH! This is NOT the way I wanted to introduce my teen to Instagram. I met this challenge how I meet all of my parenting challenges, I used my mantra. My past should not determine their future. My parents did not protect me or educate me on the what could happen to a young naive girl. I had experiences that I do not want ANYONE to go through, but especially my children that I have tried so hard to protect. Leaving the ghost of my past behind, it is now my turn to respond to them as their own person—separate from me.

Setting the Boundaries:

I was determined to have my children use electronics in a very specific way. I didn't want their youth being sucked up with screen time. Even as very small children they were only allowed to watch 30 minutes of videos a day. I chose videos so that I could control what they watched. I never used the TV as a babysitter; I wanted them to understand that screen time had a beginning and an end. This house rule served me well once we were exposed to iPods, phones, and chrome books for school. They have an understanding that electronics are a tool.

Intention, Awareness and Expectations:

The kids and I have many conversations about our intentions and expectations. I create an awareness of what could happen, what might happen, and I have a file of newspaper articles about what HAS happened. I find the file is very powerful. When they hold a photo of a girl and her cyber bully victim, they get a quick clear picture of what can happen when things go wrong.

Setting an intention with your kids is very important. Wayne Dyer has a quote, "Our intention creates our reality." It is what you will go back to again and again. My son doesn't plan to post photos, but he wants to look and see what everyone else is posting. That makes it super easy for me to monitor what he posts, but his account is NOT private. That means that anyone can comment or follow him. On Instagram he chooses who he will follow. This has been my biggest challenge. Young girls practically bare all ON PURPOSE. It is my job as a mother to protect my son from looking at other women's breasts. I ask point-blank, why do you want to look at a girl's breasts? I answer for him because it is a bit awkward. "Because you are a young man and that is what men do." I go on to explain that men are to be respectful and honor women. I follow that up with some women don't realize their value and when they don't, often they reveal too much. It becomes his responsibility to be respectful of women, no matter what they wear. I often ask, "How is she adding value to your life?" "Do you honor and respect her?" Ultimately, I make the decisions, but I haven't had to do that yet. We have revisited this conversation time after time.

I ask my son what are his expectations from his Instagram account. He expects that he will keep up with his friends during the summer through their posts and keep up with a few on direct messaging because he doesn't have a phone. I admired how he was thoughtful in his process. We discussed what language he would NOT be using while messaging and we agreed that I would be checking his account periodically. Of course I can't manage the language of his friends, BUT when they come over I let them know the expectations of what is allowed in my home. When the boys are disrespectful, and it does happen, I call them on it instantly. Only one kid hasn't come back to the house because of my expectations.

My daughter's account is a different story. She does want to post, message, like, and keep up with everyone! We have a different set of boundaries. First of all, her account is private. I check her photos every day. We established her intention and her expectations. This entire process created an awareness that an Instagram account is more than just posting a photo of a cute kitten. I had to meet the spirit of my daughter in a different space than the spirit of my son while remaining in the environment of love and compassion.

Final thoughts:

- Pick a parenting mantra. I am love and light. I am the person I want my child to become
- Set boundaries
- Establish an agreed-upon intention
- Develop awareness
- Discuss expectations and outcomes

Author Bio:
I live my life as a prayer. The titles of what I do include Mom, Writer, Jewelry Designer; the common thread is being a guide for those seeking a sacred way of living. I take the wisdom traditions and apply them to our collective experience in this 21st century. The malas, prayer chords, and intentional jewelry are spiritual tools for women connecting to their soul's purpose.

A Letter to My Curious Teen – #PeriodPride
by Vasantha Vivek

My Love,

This letter is what I usually share with you during our chit chats. But the need as a letter—a piece of paper filled with love—is to be referred at times when your manhood rises to its peak. This letter will help you to be rooted to the ground.

My boy, the first thing I want to tell you is that in no way are you superior to the other gender. You too have your best and worst. So be gentle in your relationships with the other gender as son, brother, friend, husband, father, and father-in-law.

At the age of 10, one day you asked me, "Why Amma you have not done pooja today?" I replied that I was tired. You accepted this with no further queries.

And another day, you enquired about a sanitary napkin advertisement on TV. I told you that it's a kind of diaper used only by women. I don't need to mention that the discussion extended more than 15 minutes with a series of questions and answers.

Now you have grown up and entered into your teens. Last week, you asked me with concern, "Amma, why are you so tired today? Do you need any help?" And I'm proud that I have raised my son as a loving guy who respects womanhood. So this letter, my dear.

My curious teen, this is the right time to tell you that RED is not danger, but Red is divine. RED is not shame, but RED is fame. RED is not pity, but RED is pride. RED is not weakness, but RED is the power.

RED is not waste, but RED is life. So celebrate RED.

Kanna, it's my duty as a mom to teach you the values of womanhood, how to respect women, how to encourage and support them, grow with them and excel with them. I want to emphasize 5 important things to you:

- A woman is not the weaker sex. She doesn't need your pity; she needs only your understanding.
- A woman has her mood swings. Don't judge her, but try to be with her at those tough times.
- Women have different kinds of hormonal problems. So don't ever compare one woman with another.
- Man is always a part of Woman. So don't ever try to exclude her by your words, actions and treatments. Your inclusion makes her stronger than you expect.

Try to remember the above advice when you feel some pressure in your marriage. And when your ego as a male emerges, take a deep breath, pause, relax, and read this letter. Then you will calm down for sure, since this is a letter filled with love and love only.

Stay Humble;

Stay Positive;

Stay Loved;

Stay Happy;

With loads and loads of love, Amma

Author Bio:

I am Vasantha Vivek. I am a happy woman, daughter, sister, wife, mother, teacher, friend, mentor, seeker, lover. I am from Kovilpatti, a small town of Southern Tamilnadu in India. I am a teacher by profession. I was a professor at an engineering college for nearly 15 years. I learned a lot as a teacher. Hope I have inspired some hearts during this period. Teaching is my passion. Reading is my love. Cooking is my heart. I enjoy reading and writing very much. I start & end my days with reading. Now I started writing also. So come, My Sweet Nothings. I am happy to write articles for other blogs too.

Website: **www.mysweetnothings.in**

The Art of Raising Teens
by Christine E. Goodner

Parenting teenagers always scared me. I enjoyed every stage my kids went through, from floppy, cuddly newborn to inquisitive preschooler, and on through grade school. But I was always worried about parenting teens. Maybe it's because I gave my parents a bit of a hard time in my own teen years, or because I always see teens portrayed as angry rebellious kids on TV and in movies. Whatever caused my anxiety about it, I dreaded it any time I thought about my girls becoming teens.

I won't lie to you—sometimes those teen years weren't easy. But now, with a senior in high school and one in college, I can say that this is one of my favorite stages of all. Sure, there are tough moments. I can't accurately describe the fear I felt when each of my children drove off by themselves for the first time. Or how I can't sleep until I know they are safely home at night. I worry about the decisions they make and the friends they make. But overall what I've found is that my teenagers and their friends are amazing people. It seems funny now that I was so worried about my kids turning into one.

This is what I had to learn as a parent of teens: there is a ton of pressure on them about what they do. There is tremendous pressure to keep up grades, volunteer, be involved in extracurricular activities, stay active with friends, and have concrete plans for after high school and on and on. As a mom, I feel like my biggest job was to buffer against that and help my kids focus on who they are and who they want to be.

What do they love? What makes them excited to get up in the morning and be an active participant in their own lives? What drives them to want to do well and be involved? I would find myself saying to them a lot "you are a hard worker, you will be just fine" or "it's OK to be different, this is what makes our family successful after high school."

It is important to me as a mom that they know that I see and value who they are. Yes, I expect them to do their best, but I also expect them to be true to themselves.

Should they strive to get the best grades they reasonably can? Yes, because it teaches them to put their full effort into something and develop discipline and perseverance. Should they get involved in the community and volunteer? Yes, not to pad their pre-college resumes but because we want them to be people who think about the world beyond themselves and strive to make it better. Should they be involved in lots of activities? Yes, if they are truly interested in them and those activities get them excited about life or meeting their own goals.

I found, with teenagers, that if they find something that they are passionate about and that gives them a sense of purpose, then they will work incredibly hard. With my own kids, staying focused on some long-term goals and that sense of purpose, and of making a difference with people in the world, helped them avoid a lot of the teenage behavior I was worried about. It caused them to stand tall, feel confident, and know they were important by the end of high school.

I for one want to raise young adults who live full, authentic lives. Lives that include things like being excited about what they get to do when they wake up in the morning. Lives where they know they make a difference to someone and their impact is appreciated. Lives where they are more concerned with who they are than what they do.

As a parent I am far from perfect, but I have learned to keep that big picture in mind when I decide what battles are worth fighting and what words of encouragement or redirection need to be spoken into my kids' lives.

Who my children are (in 10 or 20 years) because of my influence, and because of who they have developed into as people, is way more important than a lot of the nitpicky things I could worry about when they are teens. Are they living a life that is interesting and engaging? Are they making a difference in someone's life? Do they know that they have worth because of who they are, not all the things they do? That is my highest calling as a mom, to help them discover who that person is and live their lives to the fullest they can.

Author Bio:
Christine E. Goodner is a writer and Suzuki teacher in Hillsboro, OR. She is the mom of two girls (ages 18 & 20) and is passionate about helping parents work with their children to help them reach their potential both through her teaching and writing. Her unique blend of expertise in music, child development, and leadership gives her a holistic approach to writing & working with teachers, students and their parents. Christine has been published in the American Suzuki Journal, and she writes regularly for her own her blog "The Suzuki Triangle." She is also the author of Beyond the Music Lesson: Habits of Successful Suzuki Families.

Website: **www.ChristineGoodner.com**

Training Kids to Be Helpful Is So Much Work; Is It Really Worth It?
by Leilani Orr

I wake up to the sound of little feet pattering around the house. I open my eyes and notice the light filtering in through the window. Dang it! I slept in, like an irresponsible stay-at-home mamma. The smell of fresh coffee and pancakes griddling on a buttery surface hits my nostrils. I think to myself, *Is it the weekend? Is my husband home?*

No, this isn't the weekend; no, your husband isn't home. It's Thursday morning, just another normal weekday that is calling—calling for your motherly duties.

If Bryan's not here, what the heck is going on? Has an angel come down from heaven to attend to breakfast for this weary mother? Nope, not that, either.

The scents and sounds from the kitchen are coming from my kids. My kids! They've risen, and though I am usually the one that is up early and tending to daily morning breakfast tasks, the kids have seen to it themselves this morning.

As I walk into the kitchen in my sock- clad feeling somewhat sheepish that I slept past my alarm, and expecting that the kitchen will most likely look like a hurricane came through it since I haven't been coaching the kids while cooking, I see that not only have coffee and pancakes been started, but the mess from making pancakes has been thoughtfully cleaned up!

This is surreal.

After years and years of day in and day out of taking care of babies, cleaning up after toddlers, attempting time and time again to teach one or two or nine kids at a time how to do this and that, I am finding that the investment of time and all those moments of wanting to give up and forget about doing anything right, but still pressing through, is paying me back. Big time. In some really grand ways.

Like waking up one morning and realizing that my kids do actually know how to do all those things I've been showing them for the past 14 years and have made breakfast for the whole family.

Before we go on, I want something to be understood. My kids are far from perfect. I am even further from perfect. I am not a "patient person," I am not always a calm mother. I am not a great example of finding the perfect balance between being a responsible and fun mom.

No, indeed. Many moments in my life have been spent with me putting my hands on my face in dismay, in near despair, in crying out to God to please help this very imperfect mother.

Motherhood stretches us all. It pulls out things from within us that we didn't know were there. It presses upon us in some of the worst and simultaneously most beautiful ways.

My season of only having only little ones at hand has passed. I now have a teenager, a couple of tweens, as well as toddlers and a baby.

I'm entering that new phase that so many other moms before me have talked about. The one where my helpers are actually helping. Where the older ones can tend to the younger ones while I work on something else (like writing this story, ha!)

While there are so many take homes and good things to learn about what being a good mom is, one of the points I want to share with you today is this: despite our imperfections as moms, despite that it may seem like an eternity before your kids will be independent, your kids need YOU to be teaching them. To be showing them how to be helpful. How to care for others. How to cook a meal. How to clean their room.

We are training and raising our children to one day be leaders themselves. To one day leave our home and start one of their own.

And you know what some of the best ways to instill that in them is? By teaching them diligence in the small things, even if we as moms aren't always diligent ourselves. I know a lot of people who say, "If I as an adult don't clean up my room, how can I expect my children to do it?"

While there is some truth to leading by example, we must also lead by nurturing healthy desires and coaching our kids on how to attain those things, such as "I may not always keep my room perfect, but I would like to, and the more I practice it, the better I will become at making it a habit. And so can/will you."

By teaching our kids to be responsible with tasks around the house, we're not saying that we're perfect. We're saying we want them to become capable adults. And to become capable adults, we start first as capable children.

A couple of ways that I feel have helped me in pushing through some of those early and tough younger years with children have been remembering that there is a bigger picture than what I'm seeing only in this moment. I mustn't lose sight of the long term, but simultaneously live fully in the moment.

It's one of the more difficult things about mothering. Combining the

Macro (bigger picture) with the Micro (all the daily nitty-gritty little stuff) at all times.

Good news! I don't think any of us do it perfectly. BUT it's so good to have a foundation beneath your "why" of training and mothering and enjoying and loving on those little ones day in and day out.

Because in the insecure and emotional times we can go back to our "why" and let it carry us through our more tumultuous moments.

Find your "why" behind doing what you do as a mom.

And don't think you're perfect, and don't compare to another mom, 'cause they're not perfect either. We can all learn from each other, but we mustn't solely focus on how others are doing it. Get confident in your own mothering skin while gleaning from others.

Teach your children simple tasks and make sure they follow through with them.

Find things around your house that are daily chores and have your younger children come alongside you on a regular basis to help you with them.

I found early on as a mom, that it was waaaay easier to cook and clean and work by myself and let my kid(s) be entertained elsewhere, be it a movie or toys, etc.

But I didn't want that for my kids! I knew that if they were to someday help out around the house and be capable, I had to let them work alongside me.

That's when I found out I could be a super impatient and controlling woman. Ha!

Over time, and doing this regularly, I am now reaping the benefits of, yes, waking up some mornings to hot coffee and fresh pancakes. Or maybe it's running to the kids' rooms and seeing that they've actually done a pretty dang good job of cleaning the rooms and making the beds themselves.

And sometimes it's on a more relational level—I see my older girls and boys caring for the younger ones. Changing them, comforting them, or sometimes just including them in their play.

It's so beautiful. And it doesn't come without trial and error and pain. But it's so worth it.

Our Responsibility to Our Children!
by Lindsay Hack

According to research, a little girl's confidence peaks at the age of 9 years old and decreases every year from there right into adulthood. This statistics gives me chills every time I say it. My oldest daughter is 8 years old.

We live in a world where women are bombarded with unrealistic expectations, and self-loathing begins way too young. I believe that as parents, we have an obligation to give our children the best chance, and in order to do this, we MUST start with ourselves.

How many times have you looked in the mirror and made a comment about the way your butt looks in those jeans or commented on not being able to eat something because of how it will go "straight to my thighs?" Our children are always listening, learning, and depicting how they should act and what is acceptable. Little girls do not grow up to hate their bodies—they are taught. Little boys do not naturally think it is OK to comment on girls—they are taught.

I have two daughters who are growing into beautiful, strong, independent young girls who will grow into teenagers, young adults, and then parents themselves. As parents, we have so many responsibilities: teach them manners, learn to have fun, read, write, be great friends, to name a few. It often feels so overwhelming. I have been a mother for almost 9 years and there are moments when I still ask myself if I am qualified and ready to be a mom. I am almost 40 years old and often wonder when did I grow up enough to be responsible for shaping and molding little people. BUT it is our responsibility as parents, as role models, and as a society to set our little people up for success and push past all the noise that comes piling in a million miles a second. With our children growing up in this technology-focused world, there are more ways to learn and find information, both positive and negative. When I was growing up, regular schoolyard bullies were the worst it got. When I got home, I was in a safe place. I could forget all about it and not have to worry until the next day. Today, cyber bullies can attack any time and ALL the time. When I was growing up, I had to worry about strangers who might offer me candy at the mall. Today, the dangers are online and are everywhere. My daughter plays a game on her iPad called Roblox, which is an interactive game with other players. Her innocent brain cannot imagine how this can be unsafe, yet it can be. As parents, we need to teach them about the dangers of people, and she asks, "Why would someone pretend to be a twelve-year-old girl and want to hurt me?" Great question, little one, and I wish I didn't have to even explain why! But I do, and I need her to understand why it is important to be careful.

As their mom, I am expected to be perfect. I am expected to always know the right answer. I am expected to always be able to make their pain go away. There are times when I fail. I cannot always be perfect and I don't want to be. I want my daughters to know I am not perfect nor do I want to be. I want them to know that I'm OK with failing as long as I keep learning, trying, and not giving up. I do not always know the answers. I cannot always take the pain away even though I feel it so deep every time.

The one thing I can control as their mother is to treat my body and my mind in a positive way. I can never say negative things about my body or anyone else's body. Even better, I can actually BELIEVE it. Imagine never having to change an outfit because you don't feel good enough.

Imagine looking in the mirror and truly loving what you see. We have an obligation to our children to be the best possible version of ourselves from the inside out, and teach them that is the best way.

This is our responsibility to our children. And to ourselves.

Author Bio:
Lindsay Hack, Owner of Evolve4You, is a mother of 2 beautiful girls who are her passion and motivation to focus on transforming women from the inside out through meals, movement, and mindset. By focusing on all 3 pillars in your health and wellness journey, you will have more success with sticking to your lifestyle changes and finally looking in the mirror and truly loving what you see looking back. With over 15 years experience, using her education and passion, Lindsay offers online LIVE Interactive group classes and personal training. Evolve4You also offers a monthly VIP Inner Circle membership for people all over the world. To learn more about Lindsay and Evolve4you.

Website: **www.Evolve4you.com**

Bad Case of the Shoulds
by Shannon Lanzerotta

One of the things I found most shocking about being a new mom is how disgusting we can be. I mean, seriously, a regular human being would not wipe her coworker's nose with her hand if tissues weren't available. You'd just say "Suck it up, buttercup." And what about crawling around on your hands and knees through a dirty office? Or walking around with your boss's spit-up on your shirt? The probability of these things being okay doesn't even enter the picture... Until your new little bundle of joy arrives.

As a fairly new mom, I understand that lack of sleep and time can make us lower our standards. Heck, I just drank from my kid's water glass, where I can clearly see backwashed food floating around. But nothing disgusts me more than the socially acceptable practice of moms shoulding on themselves... in public! I'm telling you. It happens. And you've probably done it yourself a time or two. I know I have.

As a single, child-free woman, I had no idea this public practice even existed. I went about my day virtually unaware of the shoulding all around me. Don't get me wrong, I would should, in private. We all do. It's totally natural. But motherhood takes shoulding to a whole new level.

Public shoulding looks something like this: two moms are talking and one will say, "I think I should homeschool Johnny, but I'm not sure what age I should start. What do you think I should do?" And this is childless me with my eyes open and mouth agape thinking, *Did she just ask someone to should on her?? Yuck!*

When I got pregnant, I got a bad case of the shoulds. I don't want to be too graphic, but the shoulds were running out of me. I could barely even leave the house (I didn't know public shoulding was a thing yet).

I should breastfeed my baby for at least a year. I should have a natural birth in a bathtub. I should immediately put him in his own bed, on his back, in shavasana position (as opposed to downward-facing dog). I should stop yelling at my husband.

Okay, the last one I just threw in to make my husband feel good. I never once thought I should stop yelling at my husband. I only thought he was an unsympathetic jerk. *Edited for husband* Which, post-pregnancy, I realize isn't true. My husband is an amazingly supportive man, whom I love very much.

ANYWAY, I knew you were supposed to have all kinds of weird symptoms when you're pregnant, so I thought I'd get over the shoulds. But I didn't. In fact, once I gave birth, it got worse. Not because I was shoulding myself—I was much too sleep-deprived for that—but because... Now this one is going to be a tough one to comprehend. Get ready for this. Okay, here goes... Other people started shoulding on me! Without my permission! *Gasp* I know!

Who would should on a first-time, snot-wiping, crawling-on-the floor, spit-up sporting mama? The answer: family, friends, strangers. In fact, yesterday my nail lady told me I should have another child. I was like, "Ummmm, I'm kind of busy getting my nails done right now." I mean, I was trying relax, and the least relaxing thing you can do is give birth, right?! Sheesh.

And don't even get me started on all those contradicting mom articles. One is titled, "You should always do A, never B, or you'll traumatize your child" and the other one is "You should always do B, never A, or you'll traumatize yourself."

It's a no-win situation, and when you're new to this everyone-has-an-opinion-about-your-parenting-decisions world, it can be overwhelming.

So here's the deal. My son is 3-years-old. I've finally gotten a little sleep and have enough energy (insert sarcastic laugh from anyone who has ever had a preschooler) to speak out against this craziness. I'm just going to come right out and say it:

As moms, we need to stop shoulding ourselves. And, I can't even believe I have to say this but— we really need to stop shoulding on other moms. The word "should" implies obligation, and obligation restricts freedom. If I say "I should go to a baseball game," it sounds like I'm dragging myself there for someone else, but when I say "I want to go to a baseball game," it sounds so much more fun. One word can change your entire perspective.

Next time you start shoulding yourself, stop and ask yourself what you really want. Here's an example:

Should: I should eat healthier.
Want: I want to have more energy and feel good about my body.

You have to look past the superficial should and figure out what's really bothering you. Find the motivation behind the should. Notice, the answer is not "I want chocolate cake." You have to dig deeper and find out why you started shoulding yourself in the first place. (Although chocolate cake does sound really good right now.)

Let's try another example…

Should: I should be a stay-at-home mom (Let's pretend you love your job)
Want: I want to feel connected to my child.

Identifying what you want gives you power. It also gives you the opportunity to problem-solve so you can create different solutions. In reality, there is no such thing as should. You either choose to stay home with your child or you don't. *Should* is just an abstract concept that makes you feel pretty crappy (pun intended).

Now, I can already hear some of you chattering in my ear about how sometimes those shoulds are things that you just have to do. "Oh, but it's not just about fostering a connection with my child, I should do it because it makes sense financially too. I feel like I don't have a choice."

Well, you may feel like you don't have a choice, but here's a little secret: you always have a choice. No, you cannot always choose your circumstances, but you can choose your perspective regarding those circumstances. Should is a feet-dragging, nail-biting, anxiety-inducing perspective. Identifying the want behind the should is the first step to releasing all that crap (again with the puns), so you can create choices and begin to live life on your terms.

Now, you may end up choosing to be a stay-at-home mom, but it will be your choice, and a chosen future feels so much better than the shouldy future you would have had otherwise.

As for other people shoulding on you and your parenting skills. That's just totally unacceptable. What they think should happen with your family is what they want, and it really has nothing to do with you. The next time someone mentions something they think you should do, just jump back and yell, "Ewwwww, gross! Stop shoulding on me!" They may think you're weird, but are you? They're the one shoulding in public.

Author Bio:
Shannon Lanzerotta has a Bachelor of Art in Communication and a

Master of Science in Community Counseling. She is considered to be a perspective expert by fortune 100 companies who have paid her to train their employees. She is also a licensed counselor whose mission is to support moms through her Perspective Program™. In addition, she has a handsome Italian-American husband and feisty Italian-Irish-Native American son. When they go to bed, she stays up late at night looking through her old rodeo queen albums, therefore, she often lacks sleep. In addition, she loses her cell phone/keys/mind constantly... so take all those degrees and accomplishments with a grain of salt, like everything else in life.

Website: **www.realmomsupport.com**

The Different Phases of Motherhood

"I'm Just a Mom"
by Katharine Barrows

You know, when I was younger, I was sure that I was never going to have any children. I was firm in my decision until I was 19. That was when my life took a different turn. I realized I was pregnant… and I was terrified!

I had run off to North Carolina on a whim that life would be better there. That was where I realized I did not have the flu—I was pregnant. I burst into tears and was on the phone with my mother begging her to help me get back home. Of course she helped me, because that's what my mother always did.

Once back "home," the days went by so fast. I was in no way prepared for being responsible for another life. Day by day I collected things I would need for a baby, not really knowing what I was doing. The first time I heard my baby's heartbeat, it became real for me. There was a life growing inside of me! "It's definitely a girl," the technician said to me. I remember thinking *A GIRL. It's a girl. I'm going to have a daughter. Me.*

The days turned to months, and before I knew it I was 16 days past my due date. I was enormous and very uncomfortable. The day finally came and it was time to go to the hospital. I remember feeling absolutely terrified. My mom didn't really teach me much about having babies. We just never really talked about it growing up. My family was broken years before. Was I going to be a good mother? How did I know if I was doing it right? After 19 hours of very hard and exhausting labor, she was here. She was the most beautiful baby I ever remembered seeing. And she was mine.

Ashley was a very good baby. We could take her everywhere and she was always the center of attention. As she grew older, the terrible twos hit very hard. This once beautiful baby was now mouthy and very strong-willed. I'd call my mother and ask her for advice. I would ask anyone who would listen. I was sure I was doing something wrong, because this well-behaved, quiet child had turned into a screaming, tantrum-throwing, mouthy brat! I knew I would never survive this. I was going to lose my mind. Now, obviously, I lived to tell this story, but at that time I was just sure I was doing everything wrong.

The years went by and things got easier, but I was sure I wasn't going to have any more babies. I liked our life the way it was. It was simple.

I gave birth to my second child on July 28, 1994. Yes, I know, I was never going to have any more children. Surprise!! This time around I was more tired than the last. The pregnancy had taken a lot out of me.

CJ was a quiet baby. The boy hardly ever cried! He went to sleep on time. There was just nothing I could complain about. Ashley was 6 years old when CJ came along, and very jealous she was not the only child anymore. Still, we managed to make everything work. Oh... and I was sure I was stopping here. No more children. This was all I could handle.

Sam was born on January 30, 1997. It was a very hard pregnancy all the way down to the delivery. I had been in labor for two weeks. Finally, after doing an ultrasound, they discovered he was very large. Much too big for me to deliver. He was a C-section baby. I had the perfect little family. An older sister to help me take care of the boys, a really easy-to-take-care-of little boy... and Sammy.

Sammy was different than the other two. I just knew there was something different. I just had no way of knowing that my life was forever going to be changed by this tiny little person.

When it came to my parenting ideas, I was SURE I was not going to be like my mother. My mother yelled a lot. She spanked us with a wooden spoon. She never let me go anywhere without meeting the other parents first. I was determined that I was going to be easier on my kids. After all, I wouldn't want my kids to go through what I did as a child. (By the way, my mother was not a monster. She just insisted that we listen to what we were being told. Imagine that!)

Thanksgiving morning of 1999, I awoke like any other Thanksgiving at the crack of dawn to ensure that the turkey had enough time to cook. I got out to the kitchen and looked at the floor. Sammy had gotten up early today, it seemed, for there were broken eggs all over the oriental rug I had in front of the refrigerator. I gave a big sigh and proceeded to clean it up. Anyone that knows me knows I have a weak stomach, and cleaning up these eggs was the worst! Heaven knows I should be used to it by now. That child was fixated on eggs! I really don't know what the attraction was, but he really loved doing it.

I finished cleaning up that mess and went to go find out where this darling child ended up after his kitchen bombing. I made it to the living room and then I saw it. This beautiful child who I loved with all my heart had smeared three pounds of margarine all over the living-room carpet! I was furious. I could not believe what I was seeing. I went a little bit further to his room and opened the door. This precious child that I loved so much was sitting in his room, covered with margarine and showing me the cutest smile I had ever seen. I remember a lot of crying that morning as I used a spatula to get the margarine up off the carpet. Then came the Dawn dish detergent and hot water. I scrubbed and scrubbed, but every time the carpet dried, that stain kept coming back.

He finally grew out of that stage months later. He had a new hobby now! This beautiful child that I loved with all my heart learned how to unlock the front door to the house. Knowing that he kept getting out, we put a lock way up towards the top of the door. I fixed his little rear end, right?

One night while cooking dinner I went to his room to check on him and found his room empty and the front door open. In front of the front door was a chair he pushed up to unlock the door! I went into full panic mode. Where was my baby? I ran out the door and onto the porch. I looked to my left wondering where he could have gone. I mean, he was just here!

I turned my head to the right and saw the image that will forever be burned in my memory. This child in nothing but a diaper was running down the middle of the road like a robber running from a crime. It gets better, though! There was a police car following very slowly behind him. This is it, I thought. They are going to think I am an unfit parent. I showed the officer what we had done to try to keep him in and he made a few suggestions but never made a report. He gave me a pat on my shoulder and said, "It's okay, Mom. He's home now. You can breathe." This was about 18 years ago. Things were much different then.

Through the years, we had the normal trials and tribulations with all three children. I handled things differently than when I was raised. I love the closeness that I have with all three of them. I didn't have to spank them. They knew if I gave them the "look" they had crossed the line. They also grew up knowing that no parent is perfect and mom and dad did our very best to give them everything we never had. They knew no matter what time of night it was, if they were in trouble they could call me, no questions asked.

Today my daughter has given me two beautiful grandsons and my older son gave me two beautiful granddaughters. And Sammy, well, he turned out to be a wonderful son. He and I are very close. He finished high school and graduated. He got the first job he applied to and it was a perfect fit. They love him! So I guess all in all, I didn't do as bad a job as I thought.

Let's face it. Kids don't come with a manual. It would be terrific if they did! Looking back through the memories in my mind, I think that my daughter came along at the perfect time for me. I was ready. I just didn't realize it until I saw that first little face staring back at me. I wouldn't change anything that happened for all of the money in the world. I was meant to be a mother, and I'm so proud.

Mom Is Not Just the One Who Begets
by Angela María Saldarriaga

"To everything there is a season,
A time for every purpose under heaven..."

Ecclesiastes 3: New King James Version (NKJV)

That is my favorite quote! It has been with me through tough and joyful times. Every time I read it, I feel a powerful presence holding my hand. Every time I am going through challenges, this is the first thing that comes to my mind. It comforts me, and fills my soul with hope and trust. Not all is exactly as I want, but all is always perfect and happens at the right time.

One of my dreams, since I was a little girl, was to have a family, with a lovely, romantic and responsible husband and three smart, joyful, and very caring kids. Well, this wasn't the exact result of my soul's desire. At least, not to end up with kids that weren't mine biologically. Let me explain. I was a teacher for 23 years, and I had it very clear that I wouldn't have kids without a father. I dated some of the purest souls a woman could want, although there always seemed to be a problem: they either didn't love me back the same way I loved them, or didn't want a serious commitment. So, after many tears, frustrations, sad moments, and a fierce determination of being happy without a guy in my life, I began this journey of self-love. I committed to falling unconditionally in love with myself, a love that I always dreamt of from a man. I was almost in my forties and I finally had understood that my happiness was not in a man's hands. So I took it into my own hands and worked consciously to make that happiness happen. Everything was going great. I was enjoying the time with myself, I learned how to enjoy going to the movies and restaurants by myself and spending

Friday and Saturday nights at home reading a good book or watching movies. I was so proud of the friendships I had created around me, and the life I was experiencing.

Suddenly, one day, out of the blue, one of my coworkers, who was going through a lot with his kids' mother, the one I had been listening to and cheering up for months already, told me he was falling in love with me. Here is where my adventure as a mother began. After some meditation and conversations with my angels, we talked and decided we would try to make a relationship out of this friendship. Nobody knew about our relationship, especially not his kids. I asked him to keep the secret until we were sure this would work. His two children attended the school where we both worked, and those two angels were dealing with a tough situation already. I didn't want to make their issues bigger. From that moment on, all my actions with them were guided from the question: How would I like my own kids to experience this?

Some months later, we talked to them and told them about our relationship. The girl, who was ten years old, was in heaven. She had always asked her dad to take me on a date, without knowing he already had. On the other hand, his son, eight at that time, didn't express anything. His heart was hurt. He was dealing with lots of internal anger. His mind couldn't understand what was going on, and in his innocent heart, he wanted his parents back together. There were long talks with him; it was so hard to get him to talk and express his feelings. I felt his rage and confusion was not against me, or against his dad or his mom. It was against the fact that his parents were not getting back together.

I could feel his pain. As already mentioned, I was a teacher for 23 years, and had helped lots of students in the U. S. and back in Colombia, my country of origin, to deal with this pain. A pain they didn't choose, or did anything to make it happen. I knew those eyes were sad, and he really didn't want to see a noisy Colombian woman with his dad. I understood that, but because it was me, I was not the right person to help him to take that pain out of his chest.

We dealt with the situation as well as we could. Everything seemed OK. After a year, their mom was going through a tough financial moment, and we decided to move in together and rent his house to her. That is how they moved to my house and kept dad's house with their mom. We had shared custody, so I saw them twice a week and every other weekend. The boy was now accepting this new life a little better, and so did we.

I never imagined I was going to be a mom in this way. These two kids were hurt, and their mom has made some decisions in life that weren't aligned to what we would have done. She hasn't made the wisest choices, not even when dealing with her kids. They went from shared custody, to being full time with us, as she chose. The same question was going on in my mind and still is, "How would I like my kids to experience this?"

These two children have stolen my heart. I have been there through their sickness, the happy moments, the first kiss, lady's stuff, and disappointments with friends, games, parties, birthdays, holidays and even with their tumultuous relationship with their mom. We have grown into such a loving, caring, and fun family! I cannot ask for more. This is the life I have always envisioned. I feel their love and have all their respect. We are a normal family with rules and consequences in place. I have put into action all the suggestions and advice that I had given to the students' parents all those years. It was easier to parent from behind my desk, as a potential parent.

Putting all that advice to work has given good results, but don't get me wrong. Oh man, it required time, effort, CONSISTENCY, and much love.

This motherhood adventure has also included the undesired friend: FEAR! I am a Soul Realignment Practitioner, Certified Spiritual and Life Coach & Reiki Master. I work with people to help them find the root of the blocks they deal with, acknowledge them, and overcome those blocks to be able to create the life they want and deserve. Fear is one of the biggest blocks. Guess what? I was here, at night, waiting with my husband for the time to pick our daughter up from her first Sweet Sixteen party. While our boy fell asleep on his lap, dealing with FEAR. We were thinking about how much we have grown as a FAMILY. We were also thinking about how much I love them, and how I do everything a mom would do. We realized how proud they are of having me in their family. Nonetheless, we were feeling fearful because of how many more challenges they must overcome, asking ourselves what strategies we have helped them to develop to deal with the pressure of a society where the values seem to be falling apart. Feeling fearful for their emotional development. Even though I have been a mom for them in the good times and in the not-so-good moments, their mom has made some choices that have affected them despite this fact. How will this impact their lives in the future? After some moments of venting our thoughts and fears, we became aware of the power of those fears, and their power to destroy joy, and create more negativity. We also saw the power to transform out of these challenges. We chose the transformational option. We have taught our kids to see the positive in every situation and in every person. They are now seeing with more clarity the opportunity behind every difficulty. We have worked tirelessly on accurate communication of our personal feelings and emotions, and to distinguish the difference between decisions and choices. We trust in what we have seeded. Yes, we accept that we are not perfect parents because we are not perfect human beings. However, they know that we are the perfect parents for them. They have endured some challenging situations, and have come out of them as more beautiful souls. I can confidently say that they are now a mature, responsible, gorgeous and outspoken lady and a crazy, smart, sensitive, and sweet young man.

Five years have passed since they moved in, and with those years, we have created a healthy relationship as a family, where three cultures have mixed. We are a "Colombo-Mexican- American" family, where love, respect, and acceptance have been our flags. They have taught me about love and respect, and made me the mom I always dreamt of being. Even though I didn't have them inside me for nine months, I have supported them for six years with all my heart. I will always be grateful to my husband, for trusting me to be the stepmom of his three (one more in Brazil) treasures; to their mothers, for whom I pray every night, for their choices, which brought the children closer to me; and for the children's ability to see me as the crazy Colombian woman who is not their biological mother, but their mother by heart. I will be supporting them, loving them, cheering them on, crying and laughing with them until the end of this life. We will continue incarnating together. We now know why we are together, and why everything has conspired for our souls to reunite again! That is why "Mom is not just the one who begets."

Author Bio:
My name is Angela Maria Saldarriaga. I was born in Medellin, Colombia, into a beautiful family. I married the man of my dreams and we have created a fun, loving, and spiritual family together. I am a Human Energy Scanner, I provide the information needed to restore the flow of energy by taking ACTION. I guide Empowerment Processes, so, people can reconnect to their manifestation powers to create the life they want, dream and deserve. I guide you to live heaven down here on Earth!

A Better Mother
by Chantel Kirby

I have had the blessing to be a new mother at two very different phases in my life. I had my first son at 19, my second at 22. My daughter was born when I was 36. Over the past five years, I have often shared my feelings on how vastly different motherhood is for me now, as an older, more mature mother. Dare I say better mother? If I do, am I putting down young mothers everywhere, and somehow saying that you can't do it right unless you are older and have more life experience? No. The only person I am judging here is me.

When my eldest son was born, I was 19 and still a kid myself. I had no idea how to be a mother or that I had choices beyond that of matching my nursery decor to the print on my stroller. I didn't know I could give birth without drugs. I didn't know I didn't have to circumcise. I didn't know vaccinating was a choice. It wasn't that I gave my power away. The truth is, I didn't know I had any.

I knew breastfeeding existed, but I had never actually seen anyone do it. The hospital encouraged me to try it. I have always been a well-endowed woman, and I just couldn't find the right position. He was so tiny and I felt so big. As I struggled to feed this little tiny life that was somehow now my responsibility, I felt like a failure. My boyfriend, who is now my husband, tried to help, but it was just way too embarrassing. I gave up. When I think back to all the things I did or didn't do when I was raising him, I feel terrible. But then I always forgive myself. I didn't know any better, right?

When my second son was born three years later, I was still just a kid, but I had a little more mom experience. I went into it thinking I would do better this time, especially with breastfeeding. Then he was born with a mild cleft lip. Was I lacking folic acid? Was it that beer I had before I knew I was pregnant? I felt like it was my fault, and to this day, I still wonder what I could have done differently. I did manage to nurse him for the first four months of his life. I am proud of that, but it should have been longer.

Fourteen years went by and to our surprise, I was pregnant again. By this time in my life I had gone to school and learned all about child development and earned my master's degree in education. I was a teacher, and a beloved one, too. I was more informed about health and the body. I had been eating clean food and practicing yoga for years before I got pregnant. While pregnant, I read books about babies' brains and development. I took my vitamins daily and ate lots of healthy fats. I was determined to have a birth without drugs and breastfeed for the first two years.

Two weeks after I turned 36, she was born. Everything about it felt natural, from the minute my water broke, and until this very day, it has been a vastly different experience. We co-slept. Cloth diapered. I made my own baby food. She nursed until she was 4 years old. Our bond is stronger than I ever imagined it could be between a mother and child. She came at just the right time in my life. I was ready for her, and as proud as I am of what we accomplished together, there is always a mirror of regret that I didn't have this with my boys.

As I sit here, trying to write this earth-moving, emotional essay about the differences between being a "young" mother and an "old" mother, I honestly just feel like a shitty mother. As I sit here and feel this big ball of love and pride in my heart for my daughter and how strong our relationship is, I also think of how much I let my boys down.

I should have co-slept and breastfed longer. Are they emotionally scarred because of the circumcision?

Do they have health problems because of their vaccinations? If I wore them close to me at all times, would we have a closer relationship today? I should have known how important human contact was to a developing human. Why didn't I?

How can I tell my story without turning inside and feeling regret for the things I could have changed? The choices I made could have made their human existence better. Choices I didn't even know I had.

Yes, my daughter is thriving. She healthy and happy, very much like her brothers were at that age. She's bright, with an immense vocabulary. She can memorize song lyrics after the first listen, just like her oldest brother. She's sharp and witty and she literally brightens people's day with her personality. And she is also very stubborn, just like her older brother.

So how do I keep her from being depressed? From giving up too easily? From losing her passion for life?

The age-old question. Is it nature or nurture?

If the answer is nature, then no matter what I do differently this time around, it won't matter. She'll still end up struggling as she enters into adulthood, because that's what my babies do. If the answer is nature, then I can let myself off the hook a little bit with my boys, knowing that maybe even if I didn't make the best choices for them, it's not entirely my fault.

If the answer is nurture, then my daughter should be golden. In theory, she will thrive. Hopefully, I will never have to worry about depression or sickness. When she is finally the age my boys are now, she will be off to college, pursuing her passions and chasing her dreams.

Was I a terrible mother? No. But I do believe my choices today are much better than the ones I made 20 years ago.

I hope my boys never think that I don't love them as much as I love my daughter. That's not true.

I love them every bit as much as I love her, today and every day since the day they were born. I just didn't know the power I had as a mother until now. Please don't judge me. I am already judging myself.

Author Bio:
Chantel Kirby is a proud mother of three children, two young adult boys and a five-year-old girl. After teaching elementary school for many years, she is now pursuing a writing career in young adult fiction. She has also made the decision to take her daughter's education into her own hands, using a bit of homeschooling, unschooling, and everything in between. An Arizona native, she currently lives in Chandler, AZ.

Motherhood: The Soul and Breath of the World
by Girija Devi

Mother, the most divine word in this universe—as old as the origin of Life.

Thinking of motherhood, memories of my mother first come to my mind. She started her married life as the better half of the senior member in a joint family. With her kindness, love and hard work, soon she became the supporter of the whole family. To express my mother's personality I will need to say a bit about my father too.

The welfare and progress of any community is mutually interlinked with the education of the people of that place. The goodwill and foresightedness of my father made him realize this truth and he decided to start and run his own school in his village. His aim was to give free education to the children—for the better future of his village. He provided food and clothes to the poor and needy children so that their parents would send them to study. In this way, he led the helpless young generation in the direction of progress and helped the poor parents realize their dreams of educating their children. He started the school in 1935. In reality it was not an easy task at all, to establish and to manage such an educational institution in India, still under the British rule. Since the day my mother became his life partner, she strongly supported my father with her unique personality—an amazing combination of steely mental strength and warm compassion.

Whenever my father was busy in his own field as a teacher, social worker, and politician, my mother handled the large joint family comprising of around 15 members, not to mention the several helpers and support staff of the school who practically lived with us, in an appreciable way. When we, the children, were worried about something, she realized it immediately and would solve it. In my mind's eye, I can still see my mother waiting with hot food for us to get back from school. Further down the years, when we were in college, still waiting restlessly, because we had to walk long distances from the bus stop not knowing if there was a breakdown or cancellation of the bus.

Life turned quite unexpectedly. We suddenly lost our father— the greatest protector and guide of our life. Even though we were unstable financially, my mother handled the situation carefully and with a lot of strength. Without any moral pre-education she taught us all the moral lessons of life. I am proud of being her daughter. The day I moved to Dubai to join my husband, she wept silently, thinking when we would next meet. Now she is no more but is still living in my heart. Yes... Amma, no one can replace you.

No doubt, motherhood is the greatest status in the life of any woman. I understood that when I first became a mother—a baby girl with her thick black hair and large blue eyes. She was my angel and I hugged her to my chest. She felt my love, my touch, my sound and even my smell. We enjoyed the day and night in each other's company. From that day on, I was her best friend and she was mine. We shared our happiness and sorrow. She understood each expression on my face and vice versa. When I laughed, she would laugh louder and when I was angry, she would start to weep. I enjoyed it all.

Months and years soon passed, never waiting for anyone. It brought about a lot of changes. My baby became a young lady, a wife and a mother. The day she became a mother, she too realized the actual happiness of motherhood, the satisfaction, felt the protection over her life itself. I also enjoyed the new status as "Amoomma" or grandma. Today I am grandmother of two. With their love and a friendship, I am experiencing my youth again. With them I forget the stress and strain of my life. Now we live in separate apartments but in the same complex. When the kids come from school they want to sit with me and we play together. But they always think of the time when their mom (my daughter) will get back from the office and they can sense the time without any alarm or clock. It is already set in their heart.

I remember one day my daughter was late getting back from her office, the little one told me "Amoomma... can you take me to my home, my mother might have to come. Let me give her a kiss then I will come back and play with you." Did I feel a little jealous? Oh, no... I realized once again that this was the true love—the greatest gift towards being a mother.

Any creature born immediately feels the love, touch and care of its mother. She promises immense love, care and security to the growth and well-being of her child. They say that God could not be everywhere at the same time so he created the mother to take care of each of His children, thus making her status equal to that of the supreme level. No child needs to have a language to communicate with its mother. There is no other link in the universe as strong as the mother-child relationship.

It is very important to make studies and discussions about subjects like motherhood because today's generation's thoughts and beliefs seem much deviated from the moral values that bound humanity through the ages. Much of today's society seems to be selfish, seeking only to enrich their own personal life. Though physical distances can now be reached easily, it is the mental distances we need to bridge. For this, in each of us, we need a lot more of the qualities we associate with our mothers: selflessness, forgiveness, patience, maturity, and above all the unconditional love to make this world a better place.

Oh... Mother,
Thou... my Goddess,
Thou... my Wealth,
Thou.... the Soul of Myself.

Author Bio:

Mrs. GIRIJA DEVI (B.Sc.) is from Kerala, India but have been living in UAE since 1978. For about 31 years, she worked as a medical technologist in the pathology section in different sectors of the UAE government's medical department. Both her children are now working in the UAE. She loves reading and writing and also loves to travel. She has written two travelogues in the Malayalam language.

Email: **girijadevi0112@gmail.com**

Mom, You Can Overcome Your Fear

Love Never Fails
by Danielle Bernock

The first time I held my daughter in my arms was the first time I had ever held a baby. I was both in awe and terrified. I felt so inadequate. I didn't know what I was doing. This tiny life was utterly dependent on me and all I knew to do was love her, the best I knew how. Inside my heart swelled emotions I had never experienced before. They were larger than me and fed the hope I clung to, that I might not fail her.

She was born on Christmas day. That brought a whole other set of challenges, one in particular that I could relate to: she had to share her birthday. I had grown up having to share mine. I had been born the day after my mom, so our birthdays were always celebrated together. No, actually, that is not entirely true. It just felt that way. And because it felt that way it was the truth to me. So I held a personal compassion for my daughter's dilemma.

Over the years of her growing up there were many voices chiming in on this subject. There were the compassionate ones that would say things like "You get to share your birthday with Jesus, that is so special," or something like that. And there were times when it felt sincere and special, but there were the other times too. Times when people would say:

"Wow that sucks."
"I'd hate to have my birthday on Christmas."
"You probably get gypped out of presents."

Funny thing is the people who validated the challenge of sharing your birthday with the biggest holiday of the year were the same ones who would give a single present to cover both. I never really understood that.

Over the years we tried many things to make our little girl know her birthday mattered separate from the holiday, that she mattered. We tried celebrating in the summer, in the fall, and even the week before Christmas. Still, it was always evident that she had to share. Another thing we tried was a card first thing in the morning with a small gift validating this was her birthday and we were not ignoring that. Then we would open stockings, then presents, then off to our family gathering where in the evening we would depart from focusing on Christmas to focus on our precious one.

That became the tradition. She still is quite aware that simply because of the day she was born, she will always have to share her day. She knows that there will be those who will not want to take away from their Christmas to celebrate her. One Christmas evening after the happy birthday was sang, and the presents were opened, someone said to her that her birthday was now over and it was Christmas again. Yes, having her birthday on Christmas has brought her challenges, but I believe it also has built in her things others cannot understand. She knows her value. She has had it challenged. She has had it attacked. And yes, she has cried. But she has emerged stronger. The one she shares her birthday with gives her the strength. It was forged even stronger through her own mommy story.

The day my daughter held her son for the first time was hours after he was born because he came too soon. The emotions in her were raw and large. She felt she had already failed him. She whispered to him "I'm sorry." And when she had to leave him at the hospital, going home with a framed photo of him instead, the pain was off the charts. He was in the NICU for nine days. Her feelings of failure were traumatic. She has worked hard to overcome that.

Four years later my daughter held her tiny daughter for the first time

THREE DAYS after she was born. Three days earlier she almost lost her ability to hold her at all. Death came knocking. She developed severe preeclampsia, causing her liver and kidneys to shut down. She was only thirty-one weeks along, but to save her life and hopefully that of her baby, an emergency C-section had to be done. God saved them both.

On that "first hold" day, I was there video-recording the moment, calling it pure bliss. And it was. But in her heart was the same sorrow she experienced with her son—she felt she had already failed her daughter. Again, her first words were "I'm sorry."

My daughter was allowed to hold her daughter for only an hour. The little two-pound baby became quite distressed at being taken from her mommy to go back in the incubator. It took so much effort from the medical staff to calm her down that it was decided she needed to be moved to the larger NICU in a hospital further away. So they took her by ambulance with mommy and daddy following behind. The emotions screamed fear and failure. She was in the NICU thirty-six days. It was traumatic. But it was not failure. Sometimes emotions lie.

Now it is five years later again. I watch my daughter demonstrate amazing love. The kind of love I hoped to show her when I first held her. I see her share her life with her precious children, instilling value and individuality in them with an expertise I didn't know existed.

When I first held my daughter in my arms, I was afraid I would fail her. When she held her children in her arms, she felt she had already failed. I loved my daughter, and look what love has done. God taught me how to love along the way. I'm still learning. My daughter loves her children and it is evident in them.

Have we failed? No we have not. We have made plenty of mistakes along the way, but we have loved, and love never fails.

Author Bio:

Danielle Bernock is a published author and member of Tribe Writers. Her first book, E*merging With Wings: A True Story of Lies, Pain, And The LOVE that Heals* (available worldwide) takes you on her journey of personal transformation. Her blog addresses issues of the heart, encouraging readers to embrace their value and freedom. Born and raised in Michigan, the granddaughter of European immigrants, Danielle's been happily married since 1980, has two married children, and four living grandchildren she adores who call her Mima.

Blog: **www.daniellebernock.com**
Twitter: **@dbernock**

A Question of Purpose
by Deborah Carson Weekly

This is a story about how I entered my worst time as a mother and emerged with my true purpose in my children's lives. Both my grown son and a daughter became terribly sick from different invisible illnesses at around the same time. Invisible illnesses, you say? Well, you know the kind of illnesses I am referring to, the kind that are considered the fault of the sufferer; that may not be accepted as bona fide illnesses; that provoke shaming instead of pity and, by constant association, evoke a lifetime of disgrace instead of admiration for survival. Their illnesses left them debilitated and emaciated. After seeing them, I walked around in a state of shock for a bit, shook it off, and then got about the business of shouldering their projected rage while listening to them rewrite our history into one where they had no responsibility and I had it all. It was as if they released my hand and were fading farther and farther into a deep fog. By the time I became fully aware of the impact of their illnesses, my grandchildren were in danger and I was actively ideating suicide.

All I had were questions. Why was this happening? Why didn't I see this coming? What had I done wrong? What was I to do? I worked hard to provide my children with a fun, safe, and loving environment in which to grow up; had disciplined them appropriately but not harshly; had given them opportunities to express themselves; and had supported their childhood endeavors. In short, I showered them with all the love and attention I hadn't received as a child, believing their lives would be even better than mine and that we would have a better relationship than I had with my parents. I loved my parents, but I was raised in a different time, with different values, influences, and consequences.

When my kids were little and acted out, I simply exerted tighter controls over them until they responded with acceptable behavior. I thought this was my purpose as a parent. They grew up polite and well-behaved. And it is with this history and those expectations that I embarked upon a disappointing and painful relationship with them as adults. As we all grew older, my well-intentioned responses to their demands and cries for help only managed to weaken them and our relationship. Upon reflection, it seems that I often did for them exactly what they should have been doing for themselves in order to grow and learn. I was so afraid that they would fail and of what that would say about me. The years flew by. I hardly considered how spending so much time on them left my own life unattended.

Now, I blamed myself for their illnesses and measured my parenting with a retro yardstick.

Many of my family and friends took pleasure in doing so, as well. When you think about it, society does a great job of holding parents eternally responsible for their children's actions. It is still widely accepted that only good parents produce good, healthy children, and vice versa. Whether behavior leads to illness or illness causes unacceptable behavior, it is the parents (and most often the mother) who are held responsible. With two children sick, I saw myself as doubly guilty of bad parenting!

I finally came to the conclusion that my inability to control everything in my children's lives was the problem—doctors, hospitals and care decisions—everything! Yet all my attempts to gain said control failed miserably. Nowadays, you cannot even gain access to information about your children from their caregivers without their permission. My feelings of uselessness led to depression and my considering ways to end my life.

Thankfully, I am blessed with a great husband and best friend, both doctors who knew to take my talk of suicide seriously. My husband provided extra comfort and support, while my friend (a psychologist) set about helping me trace the origin of my desperation. In her expert opinion, my children's situation triggered a mom-must-jump-in-to-save-her children-from-drowning response in me. The realization that I was powerless to save them and all my grandchildren was too painful for me to bear. Copious days and nights of weeping and talking followed. Somewhere beyond my tears was a place where I could actually hear what she was saying. It was then that my real purpose, my work with myself, began.

I started by asking myself some significant questions. What if I was always powerless to resolve my children's issues? Can one ever really resolve anyone else's issues? What are my issues? What if all those excursions into the lives of my children and grandchildren were only excuses for not moving forward with my own life? I started to research and read about my children's illnesses. The subject of co-dependency was introduced and, like magic, subsequent information about support groups and volunteer opportunities within various organizations materialized. I experienced the profound effect of looking into the eyes of a family member of a person with my child's illness and seeing myself reflected. Along my journey I was prompted to seek answers to a different set of questions. What if everything was unfolding just as it should? What if all of this is somehow for our highest good? What would happen if I let go?

The positive energy I put into getting to know and heal myself netted amazing results. I woke up one morning with a newfound understanding of the words: "When you change, so does everything around you." I concluded that my true purpose in my adult children's lives was to let go and love them unconditionally. My greatest gift to them was to get out of the way and let the universe operate in and through their lives. In this way, love is a verb, and no other action is required. As of this writing, my children are alive and dealing with their illnesses and the consequences of their decisions as best as they can. Just like everyone else! I am happy to report that my precious grandchildren are all safe and well.

I accept that things will definitely change in our lives and I hope it is for the better, but whatever may come, I won't look at it as my responsibility or fault. I am only in control of my reactions. Sure, my family doesn't look or function in the way it used to, but that doesn't matter; there is no less love and I am no less a good mother and grandmother. I stopped shaming and blaming myself and entertaining that from others, which left loads of space for creating more health and happiness in my own life. Prayer and meditation are relieving my stress and helping me connect with everyone and everything around me. I am at peace.

Following are the top twelve pearls from the shell that was once me.

1. Your body, mind, words, and actions all carry clues to your mental and physical health.
2. Pay attention! Don't be afraid to ask for help, especially when sadness and disappointment lead to depression and suicidal thoughts.
3. Your martyrdom is not the price you must pay to be called a good mother. You are entitled to happiness and a good life at every age, even when your adult children have not created this for themselves.
4. We are all connected, individual expressions of the divine. Your children came through you but are not you. They are on their own path and so are you!
5. The shame and guilt you are feeling as a result of your children's actions and illness are a choice you are making based on self-judgment. You can choose differently.
6. No matter what your early relationship with your children was like, you are not their only influence. It is unkind to yourself to

underestimate the influence of the other parent, heritage, culture, peers, institutions, technology, society, etc.

7. You have to decide whether you will be fueled by comparisons, competitions, and the negative opinions of others. Your decision on this will be life-changing.
8. Even though it feels weird and really wrong at first, get into the habit of letting go.
9. Everything changes and nothing is permanent by human standards.
10. In response to the chaos swirling on around you, find the love and peace within. Forge a path directly to your source through whatever method works for you. Some considerations are prayer, meditation, self-hypnosis, or yoga.
11. See yourself and your children as perfect and whole, regardless of what is showing up in your experience. This is a powerful relationship shifter.
12. There is a reason for everything. You won't always be able to see or understand as you are experiencing it, just trust that everything is in divine order.

My affirmation:
My children came into this world through me as wonderfully unique individuals. Our lives are in divine order and everything is happening for our highest good!

Author Bio:
Deborah Carson Weekly is a semi-retired HR business consultant, writer, and editor who is a mother of two, stepmother of four, and grandmother of thirteen. She and her husband, Carlos, love living in Phoenix's East Valley and traveling.

Mother Shadow
by Ashley Arnold

The shadow is made up of all the parts of ourselves that we hide, deny, suppress, and don't see in ourselves—both the positive and the negative.

—Debbie Ford

I remember the day we found out I was pregnant. The doctor laughed as she told us they barely even started the test before it showed it was PREGNANT! We decided to tell our parents and not wait. My pregnancy went smoothly minus a few hormone-infused scares/freak-outs. I was pregnant and my husband is a very patient man! Depression and anxiety were both things I wrestled with from my early twenties. The possibility of postpartum sat perched up on its stool looming. Those close to me told me not to put energy into it and I let it go. I enjoyed the rest of my pregnancy, and the day my daughter was born was unlike any other day, experience, or moment in time I have ever experienced!! Your heart grows beyond your knowing, and electric energy filled the air as we welcomed a new being to Earth.

Today I still feel the shadow loom, even after days and months have passed. Postpartum is more than depression; it has expanded to an array of mood shifts: depression, anxiety, and OCD to name a few. For me the shadow didn't present as lack of support. My husband and family were beyond supportive. Especially my husband. During the painful nursings and emotional roller coasters, he kept me grounded.

The first time I felt the postpartum blues was during a quick trip to Target with my husband to get a manual breast pump. I bawled my entire inner ocean out in the car and walking through Target. I felt like an empty, cold, dead-inside cave. The rawness of my emotions and being just me in my body after sharing space for 10 months was terrifying. My daughter was safe at the house with my parents and I was surrounded by love and support. Still, the depth of the darkness that swallowed me from there on has been the ocean I swim in. As a new mom, you wonder if you are doing things right with your new little one. The shadow adds in the self-doubt, the aren't good enough—not good enough of a mom, aren't doing enough around the house, never giving yourself any time to breathe, heal, enjoy being a mother, and ultimately enjoy your child.

From the day I fell into the shadowy ocean, I have learned to swim and almost drowned in my extreme attempt to cling to the past: past me, pre-mom life, the Ashley I had known and grown for 27 years. A representation of a Shadow Ashley. I didn't know how to allow myself to move into the next chapter. Uncharted Shakti mother and feminine energy.

After my daughter turned two, and with the full support of my hubby, I dove into the 500-hour yoga teacher training with additional 300 hours in yoga modalities, yoga nidra, and holistic nutrition. This training gave me the tools to truly care for my body, mind, and soul through yoga and holistic nutrition, to move forward from the past, and to stand in my power as a mother, among other facets of myself. It also gave me the ability to hold space for others, to explore the shadow side, and honor the duality of the light and dark sides in their practice in every aspect.

The shadow is always there. Same as the light. Some days we have coffee and chat, other days I give the shadow acknowledgment and love. There are also days the shadow and I just be. Healing is painful.

Allowing yourself to feel—not become—the pain, that is the lesson. The integration and clarity as another layer falls away.

Every mother has her facets and her duality. Good days and not-so-good days. We all learn from those experiences and send extra love. If shit gets intense... BREATHE! You are supported, you are loved, you are enough.

Every day is a new day to experience the now with my daughter. She is my ultimate divinely sent teacher of patience and limitless love to name a few. She keeps my husband and I on our toes! Being a mom is the highest honor.

You are not alone. Shanti.

Author Bio:
Ashley is a mama to a 5 year old ball of love and energy Ella, wife, yoga teacher, holistic nutrition coach, and graphic designer & creative consultant. Ashley and her family like to hike, read, paint, cook, get frozen yogart (mostly for the toppings!) and practice yoga. Being a mom is the highest honor. Ashley honors all mamas, especially those that have or still walk on the shadow side. You are not alone. Shanti.

How Emotional Abuse Affects Mother's Love and Children's Emotional Health
by Rolie Lybl Manne

My emotional abuse lasted for 18 years. I have 2 children: a 15-year-old daughter and an 8-year-old son. My diamonds, my precious babies. Let me explain first what emotional abuse is:

"It involves a regular pattern of verbal offense, threatening, bullying, and constant criticism, as well as more subtle tactics like intimidation, shaming, and manipulation. Emotional abuse is used to control and subjugate the other person, and quite often it occurs because the abuser has childhood wounds and insecurities they haven't dealt with—perhaps as a result of being abused themselves.

They didn't learn healthy coping mechanisms or how to have positive, healthy relationships. Instead, they feel angry, hurt, fearful, and powerless." [Live Bold and Bloom.com]

I did not know that I was emotionally abused. I was constantly interpreting my words, my actions, doubting myself and trying to do the same for him. I was always left with this feeling of total confusion and not understanding what was really happening and if I had a role in it.

Traumatized by violent domestic violence from even beyond my birth, I knew that in my case I would not be a battered woman like my poor mother was.

Funny enough, I did my best right from the beginning of my 18-year-relationship to warn my ex that any violence towards me would end up with the police intervening and me leaving.

He knew I meant what I said. He did not hit me once. I imposed this because I wanted to make sure that there was no abuse in any way, shape, or form in our home. Imagine the shock when I realized that I had been emotionally abused. Me! After all that I did to prevent it! Me! No!!

How come and how did I let abuse enter my home?

I had imposed that there would be no shouting, no rows, or no raised voices at home and in front of our kids. Any arguments between him and I were done when the children were away or us out of the house. There was no argument in front of the children.

So how come it still happened? Why didn't I see anything coming? In fact, my ex was skilled, very skilled.

I saw the immensity of the iceberg once I left him. I just could not understand how it could have happened. I made sure not to repeat history. I really thought that I had succeeded in breaking the pattern of abuse.

But emotional abuse is not physical abuse. Emotional abuse is sly. [And I had never heard of emotional abuse before!] This is what you need to know: emotional abuse enters your psyche without you knowing, and it's with my eyes full of tears that I must admit and accept that my children witness and absorb the abuse too.

An over-anxious teenage girl and a clinging little boy:

Now that I have left the relationship, I see a beautiful girl walking in our house, over-anxious and very passive, putting herself last, being a people pleaser and ever so harsh with herself. Having expectations so unrealistic that she set herself to fail every time. She has social anxiety and only 2 girls to call friends.

In his bedroom I see a young boy clinging to me and telling me I am the best mom whenever he sees me. But I would find him crying his eyes out on his bedroom floor telling me he cried because he felt suddenly sad. He calls himself a loser and gets confrontational in school with his teacher.

What did I do? What did I do, me who wanted to protect them from abuse so much? I put them right in it! But thinking of it, all the signs were there warning me from day one, but I did not understand what they meant.

So how does the emotional abused mother love her children, then?

Well, she loves her children with all her heart, but she is broken and emotionally unavailable. She loves them the best she can at the time. Why? Because she is riddled with

- Negative Feelings: guilt, shame, helplessness and self-hatred, and
- Mixed Feelings: she feels empowered [she left him] and selfish [the kids live separately from their father]
- Relieved [free at last] and depressed [what is she going to do now]
- Strong [showing a brave face to her kids] and weak [she is so confused, she is alone with her pain] happy [the children are safe] and angry [why did she let this happen]

So yeah, she is not always available emotionally to empower her own children.

The routine of work, school, and shopping trips must carry on no matter what, though. She shows affection at times and other times she shouts.

She is trying to be available for them all the time, putting her painful emotions aside, but the triggers play tricks on her. She realizes she cannot stuff them down anymore. She admits defeat: she can't cope with her own feelings. [She has PTSD and anxiety]

So she decides to face the pain and deal with it. She makes decisions for her own sake and her children's. She wants to be happy and her children deserve to be happy too.

She learns, she educates herself on her abuse, her symptoms; she asks for help and reaches out.

Little by little she understands her abuse, she makes time for herself and time for her children. Healing has become a priority now.

She sets new rules and explains clearly to her children the reasons for them and how they will promote everybody's well-being.

Day by day she improves herself and feels better about who she is. She sees herself laughing and showing more affection, more spontaneously, more freely, more eagerly. [Journaling was a great tool in releasing her buried emotions]

And one day she realizes that her children were the reason she made it, she survived and recovered. She wants to love life again. She says it loud and clear with so much pride: My children are my rock."

How children's emotional health is affected by witnessing their mother being abused:

Unfortunately, children are greatly affected when witnessing abuse.

"A child witnessing abuse is just like abusing the child itself."

They hear, watch, observe, sense any tension and feel uneasy emotions without really understanding why. They feel sad, depressed, and cry uncontrollably. They don't know themselves why they feel so hopeless, why it hurts, why they are confused. That is what emotional abuse does, it gets into your child's head and simply crushes them.

Here is a list of symptoms that my children have been experiencing [healing is a long process]:

- Low self-esteem
- Helplessness
- Damaged self-worth
- Stress and anxiety
- Bedwetting
- Fears
- Clinginess
- Depression
- Fear of the dark / nightmares
- Becoming a people pleaser
- Social anxiety
- Self-harm
- Avoiding confrontation/arguments

Therapy work has helped both my children, but it's the "everyday" work that I do that brings the transformation:

Here is what you can do to help your child:
- Rebuild stronger whatever has been damaged
- Positive language [no name-calling, no put downs, NONE WHATSOEVER!]
- Showing them how to set personal boundaries and explain why they are so important
- Encouraging them to express their needs clearly, telling them they have the right to do so
- Boost their feeling of deserving happiness [not suffering; when my daughter said to her the-rapist that she did not deserve to be

happy, it crushed me to the core]

- Boost their self-esteem at any opportunity
- Explaining to them that they are responsible for their own behavior but not responsible for others' or how others respond to them
- They are allowed to think of themselves first; it's self-care, not selfishness
- Organize activities that teach them a skill, support their talents [guitar club, swimming, karate, etc.]
- Organize "friend parties" where they invite their friends for an afternoon or sleepover, encourage them to be social [we do movie night, it's so much fun and great memories for all of us!]
- Teach them to learn from their mistakes and not beat themselves up [my son calling himself a loser for leaving the tap on, etc.]
- Lots of "I love you" I'm proud of you! Are you proud of yourself? How do you think you did? What came to your mind at the time?
- Help your child understand their own behavior before they condemn it or belittle themselves, show them how to speak positively even when they do wrong.
- Finally, use this key question: What is the solution to any problems or situations, because it offers your children an exit to see and find a positive outcome instead of remaining in the negative one.

To conclude, yes, it was the best decision I ever made to leave their father for my children's best interests and mine too.

Staying for the sake of the children is no more a valid excuse.

No mother has given birth to her children for them to grow up in a destructive home.

So it is our duty to remove them from harm. Abuse is abuse. And emotional abuse is worse than physical abuse and leads to permanent mental illness.

Removing your children from any abusive relationship is allowing them to live in a healthy and safe environment where they can flourish and learn to have healthy relationship themselves in the future.

Author Bio:
Rolie is a wellness and resilience coach and the founder of LYBL Wellness Retreat and the Facebook group A.W.S.E.A; Amazing Women Survivors of Emotional Abuse. She was a Special Education Teacher who had been in the education field for 20 years working with students with emotional difficulties. Using her teaching experience and her own experience after overcoming 18 years of NPD abuse, her emotional struggles turned into passion to help other women survivors of emotional abuse. She is an advocate of emotional wellness and creates e-courses and playbooks helping women nurture their emotional health. She offers workshops using journaling techniques to help them fall in love with their life again.

The Ripple Effect
by Kristen Held

As a little girl I was the victim of sexual abuse. I waited a very long time to speak about it and work through it. As a matter of fact, I waited until I had a child of my own. Why, you might ask? Because, once I had my daughter, the floodgates of fear opened and poured out. I could not bear the thought of leaving my child alone with anyone. Not even family sometimes. I struggled letting her go to the nursery at church, the daycare at the gym, and even to start school. The intimate part of my marriage began to deteriorate due to my rampant thoughts of my childhood. I thought I was going crazy, seeing the whole world as predators, and having no peace. I sought help.

It was then in those dark months after first becoming a mom that I learned I needed support, and someone to reassure me that what happened to me wasn't a normal childhood. I needed to hear that my child wouldn't be destined for the same experiences. I found comfort and joy in life again after seeking help, in the form of a female counselor at our church.

I sought the comfort of the Lord, and did so with the help of my husband. Our marriage grew. My mothering became love-centered rather than fear-centered. When asked to write about a moment or significant experience in being a mom or wife, this is what comes to mind. I am a military wife, a mom of three, and no longer bound by fear. That isn't to say I don't have bouts of fear for my kids. Sometimes more than other moms, and sometimes just the "normal" healthy amount of fear, but nonetheless, not at all what I used to experience.

My husband and I chose a life that required us to make new friends, for both ourselves and our kids, frequently. This is not easy when the fear starts to creep in. Although what happened was over 20 years ago, it spills into my life, causing a sort of ripple effect. I second-guess every new person. I struggle to see the immediate good in people and sometimes restrict my children's time with others more out of fear in the extreme than basic caution. I often have to re-evaluate my feelings when I see men around my children because I have a burning desire to scream "get away!" even when I know the person is okay. I have learned that through my own experiences I have to watch how I see things. I have to remember that not every person in my surrounding area is out to hurt me or my children. This may all sound either incredibly relatable, or insane. Either way, it's what I as a mom have gone through. It's a part of my life that has impacted my marriage, my mothering, and my ability to make new friends.

I am always working towards peace and calming. I am always trying to remind myself not to project my fear onto my kids, and teaching them how to be safe and to protect themselves when I am not around, without overdoing it.

It's a crazy balance, one I pray many women don't have to face, but if they do, they will know they are not alone. I sit with my kids daily, praising the Lord that he protects them, heals my soul, and watches over all of us. I work daily to be emotionally and physically strong, to show my daughter there is strength in truth and knowledge to never be scared to tell someone if she's scared of someone she comes into contact with. Teaching all three of my kids that no matter what, they can come to their dad or I.

In the end, I want the world to know there is life after victimhood. There is a big beautiful world full of amazing people, some not so amazing, but still more often than not, there are great people to have your back. You do not have to be defined by something that has happened to you, or that you have done.

You do not have to live in fear and let it ripple into all you do. Love fiercely, love unconditionally, and be brave. There is only so much we can control as parents. Only so much we can say to, and teach, our children. We have to do our best, and pray our children never see harm. I have promised my husband and my children to focus on filling our lives with joyful and loving experiences, and teach them well. Not to focus on fear, or panic, and just to love.

The Good Mom
by Elisha McCardell

It all came surging toward me at once, a firework with a bad fuse. Bills, kids, school, all things I had a plan for when I was 20, but none of which panned out the way I had imagined. I was 30, and I felt helpless. Like a baby needing her mother, I could not move. So I sat there in the car and did what I always do when things became overwhelming: I cried. Not one of those "this is a hard day cry." I cried one of those "your eyes will be large and puffy when you wake up the next morning" cry. Had anyone been looking through my slightly tinted window, they would have felt pity for me. A grown woman sitting in the parking lot of McDonald's crying.

I pulled the shirt from the passenger's side seat and blew all my emotions into it, and I pulled off. I didn't have any solution for the dilemma I faced, but I did feel like the 50-pound weight that was on my chest became 20. I pulled up to the kids' school and placed on my mirrored sunglasses.

The last thing I needed was for my little ducklings to take on a pain that wasn't their own. They had enough to deal with balancing the emotions that come with divorce.

"How was your day guys?" Immediately the bombardment of requests, complaints, and other kid-focused topics began to fill the car. Usually with such a stressful day I would snap. Maybe say a word or two I regret and keep it moving, but this time I didn't. I looked at them with a blank expression and responded, "I am tired, guys, and I understand you have all these things going on, but before you begin to give me a list of demands, consider this. I had a long day today. The teachers did not show up for work. I had to cover two classes. I didn't eat lunch, and my breakfast was a cup of coffee without sugar. If your day could top this, I give you permission to spill it on me." Immediately the car became quiet. A little too quiet. I had to look in the back seat to make sure I had them all.

I turned the corner of our quiet street and pulled into our driveway. I sat for a moment—really an attempt to catch my breath, but the kids probably felt it was something different. They didn't move. They sat paralyzed in the energy that exuded from me. A Star Wars force field that prevented them from moving. I opened the door, and instead of grabbing my bag with my computer, files, and folder for the work I can get done at home, I left it in the trunk. My body had decided for my mind that whatever was in my inbox could wait until the next day. The normal prepped food was not in the refrigerator waiting to be cooked, and I felt okay. I did not care that the lack of preparation may equate to a later bedtime for the kids. I did not rush to check homework, nor answer the blinking light that beckoned for me on the answering machine.

I went into my room, took a long bath, and decided an hour later I should at least attempt to feed them. When I walked back into the living room, the kids were all at the dining room table completing homework. They weren't arguing, pushing, or fighting over whose turn it was on the computer that did not stall. I opened the pantry waiting for an idea to pop out, and I remembered the kosher dogs I'd placed in the freezer from Gabrielle's party two weeks ago. I found a can of chili, placed it in the large pink microwavable bowl, and pressed 4. I put the buns on the table and all the trimmings, and I told my oldest that chili dogs were for dinner and he needed to fix their plates.

I wasn't sad. The house didn't blow up. They did it. WITHOUT ME! The guilt that usually creeps up into the corners of my mind when I feel I am being less than a "good mom" did not occur. Even if it had, I would have pushed it away with everything else I chose not to do that evening. I finally thought of myself and did not have any regrets. I felt good the next morning. I woke each kid up with a kiss. Breakfast was already on the table. The pancakes had the house smelling sweet. The kids got dressed and looked at me with caution. I told each of them why they were so important to me.

We sang all the way to school that morning, and I let them choose the song. I made a promise to myself that day. I will never wait until I am out of control before I begin to take care of myself.

Author Bio:
Elisha McCardell is a loving mother of four beautiful children who resides in the U. S. When she is not writing short stories, she spends her time as a principal at a charter school in San Antonio, Texas. Her 13 years in education has fueled her passion for writing.

My Fears Raising My Children in This Society
by Elizabeth Breuder

I fear for the health of women in this country. I fear for the female race as a whole, for their children, and their children after that, because the fate of our population and of fertility is greatly at risk. While many people are worried about the fate of our planet (which, I, also, am greatly concerned about), I intensely fear also for the pillars of our human race.

Since the beginning of time, women have been greatly revered, even long before there were written records. They have been mystified, glorified, and venerated in many forms for central characteristics: beauty, sexuality, fertility, and motherhood.

The women's liberation movement in the 1960s brought new life to female empowerment, and central to this movement was the quest for "reproductive freedom." During this time a large majority of women were indoctrinated to the belief that birth control would liberate their lives and reproductive rights, but as time has gone on I fear now is the time to re-examine this perspective.

I can recall from when I was as young as four or five years old, my mother commenting on the state of "society," and where it was going in relation to the family unit. My mother was born an Italian American Catholic in a family of six children in the late 1940s; her own Conservative mother raised her traditionally from home. My mother would often say that the integrity of the family unit was disintegrating, with divorce and abortions on the rise, more and more mothers comprising the work force and leaving their roles as stay-at-home moms, and the public materialization of homosexuality and gender issues infiltrating even children's worlds. In response to my mother's lamentations, I would roll my eyes and vehemently pronounce her "old-fashioned," "unprogressive," or "anti-feminist," merely for the sake of thinking differently than she did.

At the age of 17, I got pregnant with my oldest daughter. A high school friend of mine who happened to be pregnant at the same time as me had chosen a different route: abortion.

She wasn't the only teenage mother I knew of who had chosen this route of foregoing single motherhood. Although I was greatly saddened at their choices, I also didn't judge them; it was a situation I empathized with as I myself had sat in the clinic's office contemplating the same "choice," faced with the same fears: How will I raise my child? How will I better myself and seek my dreams if I am saddled with a child I can't yet provide for? Ultimately, the only decision I could live with was the one that gave my child the same opportunity at life that I had been given.

Fast-forward a few years, and my daughter is now 8. She is at that age where she has started to learn about sex, and I myself am starting to come to terms with my duty to sift through the wealth of other topics and information pertaining to sex which she will need to learn about and comprehend, most importantly of which is her own fertility. This is an undertaking I do not take lightly. The new journey of properly educating and guiding my child has forced me to not only re-examine some principles that were passed to me in my youth, but to find a way to merge those values with new ones I have learned, as well as contrast them against society's.

Becoming a mother has shifted my perspective of sex and society, especially when it comes to my daughter, even though I am still considered a "young mom."

I am much more protective of her, now that she is getting older. I am amazed at the number of sexual references, inappropriate scenarios, scantily clad girls, and explicit music lyrics that are so easily accessible in my child's media. My daughter easily picks up on these insinuations from certain TV shows especially, and I can see an almost immediate change in her persona and attitude. At eight years old, she instantly becomes way too moody, sarcastic, and even flirtatious for a young girl.

As a young kid myself, I never gave a second thought to the things I absorbed. I do feel they influenced my own choices in life that perhaps I am not the most proud of; however, I do have learning experiences that I wish to pass on to my own child, though in a more enlightened manner.

When it comes to raising my prepubescent daughter, I am greatly concerned over the general attitude towards girls and sex that is too often portrayed and targeted to younger girls, especially through television and music.

Furthermore, the prolific attention the homosexual and transgender community receives has infiltrated even the most seemingly innocent media platforms for kids. I, in addition to other moms, have been taken aback to see scenarios played out on popular kids' networks like Nick, where two boys prepare to go on a date together and make out in a movie theater. I was amazed to overhear references to boys secretly dressing like girls in a Disney show, and I was blown away when I saw a commercial for Caitlin Jenner's reality TV show, "I Am Cate" advertised at seven thirty in the morning on Nick over the summer.

While I don't believe I can really shield my daughter from some of the inevitable growing up, I do seek to protect her innocence and spare her unnecessary confusion in her formative years, as well as to perhaps shed some light on other topics regarding sexual decisions and managing fertility. Introducing the idea of homosexuality or transgenderism to kids at such a young age, I believe, leads to only more confusion.

Something as simple as a mom and a dad get married, and 'are you a boy or a girl' becomes an immensely complicated subject that doesn't quite require it to be so. I am sure the opposing argument would be to preach acceptance and tolerance, however I believe quite the opposite is happening. These agendas are being promoted to kids; they are promoted through celebrities, through music, television, radio, social media, you name it.

The messages my daughter receives from society about sex and sexual identities are further compounded with confusion even about the female body at the doctor's office.

I am concerned for the future of all young girls, because at a very young age they are being pushed to take vaccines (including the HPV vaccine) that contain a cocktail of chemicals, in addition to being coerced into going on contraceptives, from prescription birth controls to shots, to even getting contraceptive implants, for a variety of female health concerns (other than preventing pregnancy) that can more than likely be more gently treated with more holistic and natural methods first.

I am greatly concerned over the pharmaceutical industry's hold over women and the misinformation so many women receive. Most women never really learn about their bodies (particularly, their hormones and menstrual cycle), and how they truly work. Sex education in our schools has been a far cry from truly educating youth about how women's bodies function. Sex education has been more like a lesson in how you have sex, and it has even been introduced to kids at an incredibly young age (some schools as young as kindergarten and first grade). Furthermore, parents are usually not involved in this process and are left in the dark as far as what is going on in the Sex Ed classes.

When young girls or even grown women go to their gynecologists with questions about their bodies, fertility, or hormones, almost the first course of action is to be prescribed some form of birth control. This has become the ultimate solution to almost any hormone-related issue that arises. It comes in patches, shots, creams, pills, and implants. Most girls and women are not properly educated on the possible side effects that can, and many times, do occur when using these contraceptives. Many women suffer from deadly blood clots, strokes, and fertility problems (including loss of fertility) in addition to the numerous list of other, "milder" symptoms like depression, weight gain, or stomach problems, though the medical community continues to sweep all this under the rug. As far as natural family planning or fertility awareness goes, there is such little knowledge of it, that it is sad. The average woman, let alone hormonal teenager, doesn't know her basal body temperature, or how to read her mucous signals or gauge the position of her cervix. With knowledge, there is power, and unfortunately, women have not gained the knowledge of their own bodies, and so that "power" had been given to the hands of something larger, like Big Pharma.

From yet an even broader perspective, there is also an epidemic of women in the US who either have extreme difficulty in conceiving, or cannot conceive at all. In fact, according to the CDC, there are about 7. 5 million women ages 15-44 in the US who fit these descriptions of impaired ability to get pregnant or inability to sustain pregnancy. That is staggering! 7. 5 million women! It's time we stop and ask ourselves, why are there so many women and young girls now that are experiencing this level of fertility issues?

Society seems to have glossed over the fact that birth control has not really been studied over the long term. Every year it seems there is another contraceptive on the market, each with a laundry list of ingredients and side effects, yet the pharmaceutical companies are still making money hand over foot despite the fact that these contraceptives are incredibly new and haven't been studied long term, (and this especially applies to contraceptive implants). If women as a collective, societal unit were to truly examine the data of the number of infertility cases, the number of reproductive cancer cases, and contrast it to the number of years birth control has been around, as well as the amount of money the pharmaceutical companies have made, (including contraceptive drugs, fertility drugs, as well as reproductive cancer treatment drugs etc.), wouldn't some dots start to connect?

Now if there were such an epidemic of infertility, wouldn't it make sense that there would be fewer women on birth control, and fewer women getting abortions? Not so. According to the CDC, about 62% of women of childbearing age (15-44) use contraception. Of those women, 77% are married women versus non-married women. Furthermore, the Pill is also the most widely used contraceptive among teens, college students, women in their 20s, and cohabitating women. Let's contrast these stats with those of abortion: In 2011, 1. 06 million abortions were performed in the US. 51% of all abortion patients were using a contraceptive method during the month they got pregnant. From 1973 through 2011, nearly 53 million legal abortions have been performed in the US.

Does 53 million aborted babies sound like American women are "controlling their births?" How is it that half of all abortions were from failed contraceptives?

I fear for our women. I fear for our babies. I fear for our population. We have gone down a rabbit hole, and I fear that we will not be able to come back if women don't start a different kind of liberation movement.

Disclaimer: The views expressed in the story are solely of the Author and should not be construed as medical advice. If the reader or any other person has a medical concern, he or she should consult with an appropriately-licensed physician or other health care worker.

Author Bio:
Elizabeth Breuder is a mom to two girls, Hailey, 9, and Laela, 2, and is a stepmom to Jane, 16. Elizabeth prefers a holistic approach to life, and is always seeking to learn new ways to live more healthfully and fully. She is a lifelong dancer and an advocate of the Paleo lifestyle, red wine on Sundays, fertility awareness, and recess for all school children. Elizabeth is a contributor at Thrive Global and is the Founder and Editor-In-Chief of Primal Kidz Mag, a new digital natural parenting magazine.

Website: **www.Primalkidz.com**

Insecurity of Every Mother
by Meghna Thakkar Joshi

Every woman dreams of becoming a mother, or rather the best mother to her child, and expects the child to love her unconditionally.

Where there is love, there is insecurity and fear of losing the love of the loved ones, be it any relation—parents, children, siblings, couples, or friends. We always want our loved one to be with us and are very protective and possessive about them.

A mother is a girl's best friend, guide, and philosopher. When in doubt, I always looked up to my mother and I had a solution to my problem. However, I didn't have her by my side when I conceived my first baby, as she had already taken a heavenly abode. At this crucial time in life, when a girl only trusts her mother for tips and tricks to handle her baby, I had my elder sister to guide me.

She had brought up my niece singlehandedly in the USA; she didn't hire domestic help there and she was quite possessive about her baby being with her always. This set up my mind to do everything for my baby and not trust anyone else, (even my in-laws).

Possessiveness creeped into my mind the minute my daughter was in my arms. I had decided that she would always be with me and I would be her sole caretaker. I thought that if she stayed longer with my in-laws, she would love them more than me.

I was surrounded by tiredness, frustration, baby diapers, feeding bottles, and not to forget the colicky nights, but still I used to massage my daughter, give her a shower, and took care of her singlehandedly, except for the first 40 days after delivery, where I had to take my mother-in-law's help at nights.

I would carry my daughter everywhere I went, would plan my exercise routine while she was asleep, eat with her in hand or while she was sleeping, and I would not let in-laws pick her up too much, saying that she would get used to being in the lap always and that she needed to be independent. I made sure she was always around me and with me. In fact, my husband and I, in spite of having the luxury of staying in a joint family, did not go for movies until she was one. Only after my husband insisted a lot that my daughter needed to learn to stay without us for a while so that we could spend some time together did I start leaving her with my in-laws. However, my heart and mind would be with her—whether they fed her, whether they put her to sleep—hopefully she wasn't crying.

It took a few times for her and me to get used to staying away from each other, but it did work and she got used to staying with them for a few hours. I was not convinced to leave her with them much, till I started working part-time with my cousin.

I had to leave my daughter with my mother-in-law whenever I went to work, as neither did I believe in letting nannies take care of my one-year-old, nor did I believe in the concept of day-care. I thought my daughter was most secure at home with her grandparents. I would still feed her well before leaving, would make sure that she slept on scheduled time and had a lot of instructions for my mother-in-law.

My mother-in-law was really sweet to take all the instructions from me, maybe because she knew that every new mother behaves the way I was doing. My daughter would happily stay and play with them while I was away. Nevertheless, the minute I returned home, she would come running to me and she would have the best smile ever on her face. This smile used to take away all my tiredness and made me realize that although she loves everyone in the family, no one can take my place whatsoever. I was her world and she was mine. She is almost 4 now, and still she has no doubts that she loves me the most.

Later when I was pregnant with my second child, I had to give up on some of my earlier notions as my elder one was just 2. 5 years old. She needed equal attention as my younger one (son), the only difference being that my younger one at that age would not mind staying with anyone after he was well fed.

There were times I felt horrible, and told my mother-in-law that my younger one would not know who his mother was, as he was with her all the time. I felt that I was ignoring him because I was caring more for my daughter's emotions as she was at such a tender age. I would feed my son and then give him to my mother-in-law; she would put him to sleep in the afternoon and also hold him when we were out while I took care of my daughter.

Although I still had my set of insecurities in mind, at times I just felt relieved that I could take a break from everything and relax while he was in safe hands. I could go for a nice shower while my elder one was in school and younger one playing with grandparents. I could complete my exercise routine every day while my mother-in-law put my baby to sleep, and most important I would have proper meals, which is required to manage two young kids. In fact, I am so used to them being around us that while we went to Singapore for a holiday, I was really missing my in-laws. Now, every day when my father-in-law comes back home from work, I hand over both kids to him to play with. They enjoy and he enjoys while I relax. Thanks to them I have also restarted my career as a health coach and am conducting various workshops while they take care of my kids.

So, to all the moms and would-be-moms, your child is always going to love you the most, whomever they stay with the whole day. Having in-laws to take care of your kids is the biggest boon for every mother.

We might not like a few things that they tell our kids or teach our kids, but they also are our kids' well-wishers.

Leave aside all your insecurities and fears and enjoy the benefits of letting your children stay with family.

Website: **www.meghnajoshi.com**

Without a Father
by Tiina Kapela

"There's not a lot of space in a small heart. But there's always room for mum. Happy Father's Day from Oskari."

My son had made a big and beautiful Father´s Day card for me in school. I was speechless and the tears burst from my eyes; I wondered what that little and lovely seven-year-old boy might be thinking. Big words spelled with little letters and written carefully on yellow paper. The card was filled with strongly colored hearts and stars. Once again I woke up to thinking what he might be missing. Or is he missing anything at all?

Along the years as the child grows to be more understanding towards things, these sentences and questions have flooded my mind hundreds of times.

Yes, he does not have a father. At all. Well, he´s proven to be someone´s blood and flesh, but can someone who abandoned his child without ever even seeing him be called a father? No questions about how he is, not a word about wanting ever to meet him. Only silence all these years.

In my memories, I return to the moment when we split up. During the last moments before the child was born I moved from our home to nothing. I lost my job, my home, and I had to move to another town. I was left with nothing. That is how I thought. With teary eyes the world collapsed and I was scared. I was on my way to an unknown world where I would be responsible for the life of a little baby. I had no money, no companion to support me in parenthood. At least I found a roof above our heads. In that moment the only option was to move back in with my parents to have at least some support and safety around us. There was bread on the table and a warm home around it. The fear of making it and of failure played a big role in my mind, although the facade was OK.

On a hot summer day it was the time to go to the hospital. After two days of struggling in pain with my mother by my side, the labor started. The night fell. But how the fear gave way at the same moment when the midsummer sun shone its light on that feared moment! The light of love appeared that night as a little innocent messenger of love with dark hair and big eyes. Everything gave way around me but the little boy, unconditional love, and the midsummer sun in the sky. It was the midsummer when the sun shines all night in Finland. I knew I had gotten a child of light. And that moment I decided that we were going to be fine.

After that day I never gave fear in my mind power, although there have been hardships on the way such as the death of my father. The great sorrow touched our family when my son was one year old. On his deathbed, my father's words to me were "What are you doing here? Go with your child. I will be OK."

And so I went back to my child, who at that moment needed me more. My emotions were contradictious because I wanted to be there when my father moved from here to eternity. Those words were the last words my father and I shared. At that moment I allowed my father, who had loved and supported us, to leave us.

With the support of my mother my life went on day by day with my little miracle. There were ear infections, sleepless nights, but all in all happy life surrounded by the scent of a new baby. It was time to get back to the working life again, and I searched for a new job actively. In Finland we are in that lucky position that it is possible to stay on a paid maternity leave for nine months. I was at home over a year until it was necessary to push forward with my career. I returned to my profession as a real estate agent, only in a different company. And soon I found myself working as an entrepreneur in my own office. I thought I would do everything I could to give my child a good life where he would lack nothing, although he was missing so much already with the lack of a father and the grandfather who moved to the heavenly home too early.

I was selling apartments, building our home, and also working as an entrepreneur with my brother by constructing a hundred row house apartments. But that was not all. I was still a single parent. However, I was happy and the train kept moving forward fast and joyfully. Until the fatigue caught me. And I lost everything again. I was faced with days filled with emptiness again without a source of income. The companies were sold one by one. But I had the beautiful home and the son. Once again I was picking up the pieces of my life.

However, I felt no fear anymore due to the decision I had made at the moment I first held my son. Now I had time. I had time to be present for my son every moment. I lost nothing. Life has given me such a great gift that it can't be measured with anything: my own child, which the creator does not give to everyone. The great gift of the heart is expressed in that beloved little person who trusts life and teaches me to think more than anything else in the world. I have received more from life than I have given.

Every single day, when I see my now already seven-year-old wonder's sleepy eyes and the smile on his face upon waking up, I know that that is happiness. A person can ask for nothing more. I'm grateful for all the misfortunes and the moments I had to grow, but the child is the greatest and grandest travel companion of all. And he is lacking nothing. He is perfect. And we live a happy life. So you, don't you feel fear—trust life! Everything will fall into place as it should, no matter what the situation.

Author Bio:

Tiina Kapela is a writer and entrepreneur who was born and raised in Finland. She attended Seinäjoki University of Applied Sciences School of Business and Culture, where she attained a Bachelor of Business Administration, and also the University of Jyväskylä, where she studied writing and literature. Children's literature is Tiina's forte, and she has written a total of 5 so far, with more planned in the coming months and years. In the future, Tiina would like to see her books do well and be an entertaining force in the world of children's literature.

Infertility, Death, Adoption & Hope!

Mothers We Know. Mothers We Become
by Stephanie Kripa Cooper-Lewter

My biological mother, I don't consciously remember. Left in a cradle on the doorsteps of an Indian orphanage during the early years of my life, I often reflect upon the potential circumstances surrounding my entrance into the world. Did my first Indian mom love me? What was she like? During my own pregnancies, my connection to her was especially strong. Knowing nothing else about my Indian mom's life, we share one life-transforming experience: motherhood.

My Indian foster mom, I fondly remember. She welcomed me into her home, giving me a break from orphanage life while my adoption paperwork was finalized. With her husband, she successfully raised four beautiful children together. Before grandchildren graced their lives, they showered affection and love upon me in the 102 days I stayed with them in foster care in India. Over time we lost contact, but we reunited in 2005 and I shared nearly a decade more of memories with her. She passed away right before her 90th birthday; I attended her funeral and helped carry her casket. Reflecting on my Indian foster mom's legacy, I am proud to share her love for others.

My adoptive mom, I know well. She embarked on parenthood as a single parent in the 1970s, when transracial, transnational adoption by single women wasn't well known or popular. Her parents adored me and warmly embraced the bright-eyed Indian girl that she brought into their lives. The woman I am today reflects many of the values my adoptive mom instilled in me: a love for reading, education, stories, traveling, social work, and a faith that kept her strong which helped her face cancer twice. Given my childhood years together and the years ahead with my adoptive mom, I am shaped by her never-ending love.

Nurturing life within and bringing two beautiful humans into this world filled my heart with love, excitement, anxiety, and the weight of responsibility as they were placed in my arms. When my daughter arrived, I was a single mom struggling to make ends meet on $436 a month through Aid for Families with Dependent Children, $127 in food stamps, and $50 child support pass-through. At 20 years of age, I committed to teach my daughter to listen, value, and use her voice. After marrying and miscarrying, fourteen years later my son entered the world. My labor was traumatic due to his positioning; the doctor's unsuccessful attempts to rotate him and failure of descent resulted in an emergency C-section and a five-night hospital stay due to post-operative complications. In the weeks that followed, I was awakened by nightmares and experienced months of post-partum depression. At 34 years of age, I was determined to raise a son in a world that might not recognize or misinform him of his worth. I cherish my daughter and son; they are the only biological connections I have in this world. I can see parts of myself reflected in them. I love watching them grow into all that they are destined to be.

I have walked the path of motherhood for more than half of my life. I understand and know firsthand how relentless, hard, exhausting, heartbreaking, beautiful, and rewarding being a mom can be, whether our children are young or in adulthood. Motherhood is messy and imperfect; no matter how our children come to us—through birth, kinship, foster care and adoption, we are shaped by the mother figures in our lives whose presence and quiet wisdom nurtures and heals. I hope to pass on to the two children I birthed into this world from the mothers who influenced me their courage, resilience, strength, and ability to defeat the odds. One day my children will add to the stories of my three mothers with stories of their own from the memories we create together, long after I am gone. Speak to me of mothers. Ones we hold close, those far away, whose presence and absence shapes us. Mothers we know. Mothers we become.

Author Bio:

Social worker, personal and executive coach, speaker, author and philanthropist, Stephanie Kripa Cooper-Lewter, Ph.D., M.S.W., came to America through international adoption from an orphanage in India, giving her tender heart a deep desire at a young age to understand her "why." Believing a person's present circumstances never determines their ultimate destiny in life, her life's work is to uplift, connect and inspire, especially women and girls. She is Co-Founder of Lost Sarees, and Founder/National Chair of Roshni, Lost Sarees National Women's Giving Circle. Coaching and Positive Psychology Institute graduate and former President/CEO of Big Brothers Big Sisters of Greater Columbia.

Facebook: **@StephanieKripaCooperLewterPhd**

Passing the Baton: The Continuation of Motherhood
by Reshma McClintock

I cannot think of a relationship with more potential for intimacy than that of a mother and her child. While the potential is not attained by all, there are many who enjoy the fullness of the relationship tapestry between mothers and their children—a unique, tightly woven bond.

A mother is a beacon. A mother is home. She holds the key to her child's history. Each detail of one's life is written on their mother's heart. She knows everything: likes and dislikes for specific vegetables, a preference for milk or juice, timidity versus fearlessness. A mother knows when her child is getting sick before the first snorted sniffle makes its audible debut. She can see the first signs of sleepiness creep into her child's eyes, and she can feel when their heart is aching. She just knows. My mom certainly did.

Many would suggest a mother's intuition and love stems from a biological connection, but as an adopted child, the lack of biology between my mother and I suggests otherwise. My relationship with my mother confirms it is possible for a woman who did not carry a child within her womb to take on the role and love of a mother; for her intuitive nature to come alive despite the absence of ancestral association.

My mom's intuition baffled and irritated me for much of my childhood. It also saved me many times over. I never understood it; she knew the truth behind every lie, she could see the deceit behind each omission. Try as I frequently did to keep her in the dark, my mom just knew. Children don't often view their mother's intuition as a gift, but when you become a mother yourself, you can see the beauty in it—a true testament to how well a mother knows her child.

When my own daughter was born, I finally understood how my mother felt about me. I understood her fierce protective nature and profound intuition. I experienced a deeper, more intimate love than I could comprehend prior to my entrance into motherhood. My first experiences as a mom gave me a greater respect and appreciation for my own mom. From that moment, and all the moments that followed, I was finally able to fully grasp her side of our connection.

Experiencing motherhood with my mom was a highlight of my life. In every exchange we basked in the fullness and privilege of being moms; in the joy of our daughters, the frustrations, chaos, and hilarity that were now integrated into the fabric of our individual identities. I loved sharing this with her; a mother/daughter full circle, exhaustive story of motherhood.

My mom passed away four years after I became a mom. My beacon, the keeper of my history, gone. In the days following her death, my head swirled with questions I'd forgotten to ask, with answers I couldn't remember, with fear and sadness over everything she was going to miss and everything I'd miss about her. I was devastated and lost. How could I be a mom without a mom? It wasn't a question I'd entertained until I had no choice but to live it out.

When the light from my beacon dissipated, the loss and grief were immense. And the aforementioned tightly woven tapestry began to fray. The love was not undone. The memories not reversed. But the once solid connection I shared with my mom was now missing a vital piece—the piece to which I was linked. Her. I was now missing her.

As I trudged through the grief, I did begin to see some light. Perhaps the light even came from my missing beacon. A light from the mother I lost; dimmed and distant, but not extinguished entirely. The beauty in the missing piece is that as the fog of grief lifts, it can be found again in the continuation of motherhood. I will forever be missing the living, breathing connection to my mother, but I am equally as connected to my own daughter as her mother.

While there will always be an intimacy between my mother and I, the closeness did transform upon her death. My mother will shine on. I will remember her fondly; every success, every failure. Each day I will ask myself what she would do as I navigate motherhood; I will call on her wisdom even in her absence.

There's been a passing of the maternal baton from my mother to me. I carry it with pride and conviction. I carry it with great determination; to not only be as good as my mother, but to do better; go further, push harder, and love even more deeply, if that's possible. I will honor her by passing on everything she taught me about motherhood to my own daughter; and so goes the continuation of motherhood.

Author Bio:
Reshma McClintock is an international adoptee from Calcutta, India. She is an avid writer and speaker, sharing her story and encouraging others as she lives out motherhood and endures the trials of life. Reshma recently returned to her birth country as the subject of the film, *Calcutta is My Mother*. The documentary is expected to premier in 2018. She currently resides in Denver, Colorado with her husband and daughter.

Website: **www.writtenbyresh.com**

Dealing with Miscarriage or Secondary Infertility
by Nikki Hartley

It's one of those subjects that nobody really wants to talk openly about. We pretend that we all easily get pregnant, have seamlessly easy pregnancies, and then go on to have an euphoric, albeit painful live birth. That's not always the case. In fact, I had a miscarriage—twice, actually—in 2014. The first was a fairly early miscarriage, but the second dragged out for over a month, and that resulted in a D&C. It also happened to be my third (which makes me officially a recurrent miscarrier), and it sucked. Actually, it still sucks from time to time when I think about it because of the grief that goes along with it.

This was all a huge shock to me, as with my first pregnancy, it happened so easily, and I just assumed that was how all pregnancies happened. I didn't have to temp or track my ovulation. We fell pregnant our first time of having unprotected sex. So when I was ready to conceive my second child, and it was met with a few miscarriages and lots of heartache, only then did I discover that secondary infertility was a thing.

For those who haven't lived it, I think you're pretty much all aware that it happens. You know someone, or you know someone who knows someone, who lost a baby. And it's terrifying, and sad, and maybe makes you feel a little icky or uncomfortable and you can't even talk about it. Maybe you don't know what to say, or do, to make it all better when someone brings it up, so you change the subject, or you assure the grieving friend/family that it was for the best, or that it's normal, or that it wasn't really a baby yet, or that there will be another baby. And as someone who has had to deal with that, I can assure you that the words are appreciated, but they don't help. You can't help. You can't fix what has been lost.

So, here's where awareness is needed—pause and back up, let's let that sink in a bit more. You can't fix this. It doesn't need to be fixed. I don't need to be fixed. What I did need to do was find a healthy way to deal with what was going on with my body, my heart, my soul, so that I could go on to have the baby I so desperately wanted. I had all the tests ran, did a HSG, and everything came back normal. It was unexplained infertility I was up against. I also had already had a viable pregnancy that resulted in a live birth, which stumped the doctors even more. I was just told "we're sorry, this sometimes just happens." That is when I turned to more holistic methods of healing, specifically meditation and acupuncture.

For me, I was lucky, and a year after I started actively trying to conceive, I finally fell pregnant, which resulted in the birth of my daughter. But since then I have started working with other women who are going through similar issues, and I can tell you that we are not alone. This is something that more people care to admit happens to them. I think we should all be able to support each other as mothers, as women who want to be mothers, and as friends who just understand the heartache of loss.

Prior to my experience, I didn't know that miscarriage was such a common thing, I didn't know that it could take a long time to actually fall pregnant when you were ready to have a child, and I didn't know how to talk about these hardships because nobody ever talked about them. That was the most surprising thing about motherhood. That and how the first bowel movement you have after giving birth is actually worse than the birth itself. HAHA.

In conclusion, my advice is to just be aware. People lose babies. People grieve in lots of ways, comfortable and uncomfortable. It's an important part of life. And, if you and I are both up for it, we can do it together. It doesn't need to be a secret. It takes a village, and we are all in this life together.

Author Bio:
Nikki is a certified integrative holistic therapist. She has developed a program to help those who are looking to heal the mind, body and spirit naturally, by using various modalities such as hypnotherapy, Reiki, crystal healing, aromatherapy and intuitive guides. She believes that the body achieves what the mind believes, and when the mind and spirit are in balance, than the physical stuff falls into place. She is a member of the American Board of Hypnotherapy, a Reiki practitioner trained in the Usui Ryoho Shiki system.

Website: **www.mindbodymana.com**

Finding a Miracle
by Payal Raghuvanshi Mukund

I am sipping my tea in my favorite mug, which says, "I am a mom, what is your superpower?"

I am a mother now, but it wasn't easy getting here. They say good things come to those who wait but better things come to those who are patient. And guess what? My utmost patience blessed me with this miracle of a super baby who turns 4 in December, 2017.

There were times of anxiety when I thought I would never become a mother. On other days, I was extremely positive that I would become one. What kept me going was the endless love of family who never made me feel that something in my life was amiss. For that matter, they never made me feel that not having is a child makes you incomplete.

I did go through a lot of ordeals mentally and physically before I had a baby. There was a phase when we were ready for parenthood but some health issues were hampering the plan. The doctor visits, societal pressures, and stress were adding to my woes. But one thing was constant: my husband's belief that we would be just fine and that we should stay positive as much as we can.

Then came a phase when I tried to change my outlook about the whole parenthood thing by believing that this unnecessary stress was only taking me away from what I truly wanted. I started involving myself in activities I always loved, which not only distracted me from the negative thoughts but also made me a more positive person. My husband and I even decided that if nothing worked out, we would adopt a baby. That was always an option for us.

They say miracles happen if we give as much energy to our dreams as we do to our fears. We finally conceived after 6 years, and it felt no less than a won battle. I was enjoying every scan, hearing the heartbeat of the little one, the nausea, cravings, kicks and swirls in the belly. I was in the happiest place! My boy arrived and I couldn't be happier. He was the most beautiful thing I had ever seen in my life.

I remember the days when I was new at this. Beginning this roller coaster ride they call motherhood.

I took a break from my career, as I wanted to completely focus on the little one, give him my complete attention and not miss out on any of his milestone moments. I was fortunate enough to do that; not all women can afford to take a sabbatical like that. I was not ready to juggle work and baby at the same time. So here I was, a stay-at-home mom with a single focus in life, and I was loving it!

I had an overwhelming first few months. I was often clueless as to what to do in a certain situation. The baby would poop, puke and pee at the same time and I would almost pass out. But I learnt from every situation, and with every passing month, I was turning into quite the supermom!

Every moment reminded me of the unconditional love that our parents have for us. I realized how much they must have gone through and we take them for granted, don't we? They tolerate our tantrums even now.

Each day surprised us with precious moments, and I found myself changing into a more patient person with the determination to be a better parent.

Days flew by as he grew too fast before my very eyes.

The house was messy, so was the hair,

Chuckles and cries were a daily affair

Tripping over toys, singing lullabies

Naming colors and counting butterflies

Getting lost in those button-like eyes that stare, dazzle and mesmerize

Stealing a kiss or two when you sleep

The love for you is so pure and deep.

As much as I want you to grow up

I still want you to be a cuddly little buttercup

Today, I would like to share the lessons I learnt from my experiences. They may help another, though I am sure your journey may be uniquely challenging.

My experience taught me to be hopeful. Hopeful of things that you never thought you would get. Before you give up, think of the reason why you held on for so long.

Keep reminding yourself that you are doing an excellent job of bringing up your little one. She looks up to you and you are the guiding light in their life.

Advice will come from everyone. Which one to take and which to ignore is completely your discretion. Don't let anyone else's advice or comment bog you down.

Try not to compare yourself with others. Everyone is different and each one will have different ways of doing things.

Try to focus on yourself too. We tend to forget ourselves when the baby comes and many a times we ignore our health.

Most importantly, don't let the feeling of guilt overpower you. I used to feel guilty when I went out to the salon, leaving baby with my husband or catching a movie while the little one was in daycare. But over time I realized these are some stress busters you need frequently.

With my little boy, I feel all is right in my world. I see the world all shiny, happy and joyful through his eyes. He is the closest I will ever come to magic. Of all the things I have done in my life, motherhood is the most rewarding experience. And yes, I have found my miracle.

Author Bio:
Payal Raghuvanshi is a Digital Marketing Manager in one of India's top IT companies. She is a mother of a hyperactive 3 year old boy. In her free time, she likes to write blogs, pursue her musical interests, exercise and participate in marathons but above all spend her time with her family.

A Miraculous Journey
by Jody Katter

At 11:03, on July 24 two years ago, my sweet little miracle baby was born. She was tiny and perfect and all the things I had been wishing for since we started our journey.

Becoming a mother, it seemed, was not in the cards for us. We started trying for a baby a year after we got married. For the first two years everyone said we were young and it would happen. Doctor after doctor kept telling me there should be no reason to proceed with fertility treatments because there was a 3% chance of problems. As it turned out, I was in that 3%.

For five years we went to numerous doctors. We had a plethora of tests run. We took pills. We did shots. I can probably tell you everything you want to know about the reproductive system and more. After 7 rounds of IUI and 3 rounds of IVF and 1 surgery, we decided to be done. At this point we had spent over fifty thousand dollars in medical expenses and, emotionally, it was best to put it to rest.

I'll never forget the week that we found out that I was pregnant. I was up, down, sideways and could not get a handle on my feelings about life. It was almost like I was back on all those fertility hormones. I even threw a plate at my husband (which believe it or not is not the norm for me.) I went to have a metabolic screening done for my insurance, and the nurse that helped me was my fertility nurse. I told her everything that was going on and she told me to take a test. But I just couldn't. I'd had so many negatives, I just couldn't handle another one at that moment. AND if the doctors couldn't make it happen, how would I have done that?

Well, Friday I woke up and took my test. I don't know why I did. Why was I going to subject myself to ANOTHER negative pregnancy test? But I did it.

Have you ever looked at something and you just couldn't believe what you were seeing? It was like you were in some sort of dream or a parallel universe. This was me. I sat on the floor of my bathroom, sobbing, staring at a POSITIVE pregnancy test. In seven years I had NEVER seen hope. I had never been able to even know if I could GET pregnant.

Now that we're two years and two babies in, I know that God was looking out for me and my husband. He knew when the right time was. I also believe he wanted us to go through the emotional roller coaster so we would lean on Him. We would come to Him. He loves us and He does not want us to suffer. Our faith in Him has grown, and I'm so grateful for the time my husband and I had to be able to learn and love and grow as a couple before we brought our babies into the world, because babies are hard!

Am I right?!
The last 9 years have taught me so much. So many lessons that I am so excited to share with my friends and family. And the one I want to share with you is this: Find the joy! Find the joy in everything in your life. It really does make those hard times a little more bearable. Maybe out of the pain and suffering a miracle will be born.

Author Bio:
Jody lives with her husband and two beautiful babies in Virginia. She loves reading, going to concerts, spending time with her family, and lots of coffee. You can find Jody across all social media platforms, where she is helping moms everywhere find their sparkle!

Website: **www.thriveathomemama.com**

Burial Vault
by Kaylee Garling

I place my palm against the cool rock. It warms under my skin. I think of my baby, how her body is as cold as the stone I'm touching. How it should be warm like mine instead.

The granite burial vault holds her tiny body. It's been two years since we laid her to rest. Two years for me get used to her name on the grave. But it still feels too fresh to be real.

Too many wishes crowd my mind. Wishes of life. Of smiles. Of hugs, and kisses. All the things children are made of. If only I could experience those things with my precious little one. But I'll never know if she'd stick out her tongue when I said something funny. Or if she'd hold my hand when she was scared. Would she stare up at me with big blue eyes? Or would she have springy curls that bounced when she walked?

She will never need me like a child needs her mother. She's not here. But I am. Alone. Wanting. Wishing for a life unknown.

A tear slips down my cheek. The wind chills the trail of moisture. I shiver and wipe it away. Pull my coat tighter.

How do I go on? How do I keep moving forward when my life has come to a halt? How can I help others when I can barely help myself?

I send up a silent prayer, asking for strength. Strength to keep going. Strength to live another day. Strength to smile when all I want to do is cry.

I pull my hand away and stare at it. If she's not in my hands, then I pray she's in God's hands. That she's with my father, sister, grandparents, uncles, cousins. All my relatives and friends that have transcended this life. Do they surround her? Give her all the love she deserves? Do they tell her of my thoughts unending?

A tingle of jealousy fills my breast. They know her better than me. How unfair. Unjust. The fact lingers in my mind, making me wish I could join them. Join her.

My son tugs at my coat and looks at me with eyes as wide as the sea, his curls waving in the cool breeze. He looks so much like his father. I am not alone.

Crossing my empty arm against the chill, I step away from the grave. My son stares at the name plaque, holding my hand. Remembering her. The moment her fragile body came into this world. Small. Broken. Unable to take a breath of life. But her spirit, strong and endless, set free. Free to return home. A home filled with more love than I could imagine. No pain. No sorrow. A place where dreams are more than just a wish. They are reality.

I cling to that hope. Grab on to it like a lifeline. Even though my arms are empty, my heart is full of love.

God's love. And someday, I will look back at this moment and realize it was just that, a moment. Pieces of a shattered life made whole through Him who created it all. A life to find out what true happiness is made of. Because without pain, would I realize true happiness?

I breathe. Live on. Remember the great Creator, and His love for me. The pages of my story are not over. They never will be. I will keep on writing. Living. Hoping. Enduring. Will you join me?

Goodbye
by Kimberly Gladden-Eversley

August 22nd, 2014

Alongside the pier at Naval Air Station North Island stood the Carl Vinson (CVN 70) aircraft carrier in which my husband was one of 6,000 headed out to sea. As the horns of the ship sounded off and the bells chimed through every ear of loved ones drenched in tears, it began to sail away. I watched as the ship the size of 3 soccer fields became smaller and smaller until I could no longer see an inch of its existence. I looked at my father for a sense of comfort and just like that, I'd become a single mom of 2 in a state I barely knew.

My father and I drove back home, and questions quickly raced throughout my mind. What do I say when the "where is daddy" questions arise? How do I explain to a teething toddler and a 2-year-old barely out of Pull-ups that daddy is deployed? How will this affect them?

I walked through the door and was quickly greeted by my mother. My children were full of joy from the excitement in the air. Mama and Papa were in town to see my husband off, which was a great temporary distraction. As soon as my parents left, it was time to roll up my sleeves and become super mom. I like to call us stay-at-home military moms the silent ranks.

My daily planner was full; I had a to-do list the size of what I assume would resemble Santa's Christmas list. Find a doctor, a pediatrician, a new church home, places for family-filled fun and more. I had to learn budgeting and how to pay bills after never paying a bill in my life. I googled everything on parenting that I could find. How would

I discipline my children going against my nurturing instincts? How would I protect my children's innocence in a society that is designed to destroy it? Although Google was a great help, it surely wasn't the "cure-all." Over time I was able to get settled in and develop a weekly routine.

Unfortunately, sleep didn't make the list. I found myself staying up all night, wondering if my husband was safe, and even worse, wondering if a day would ever come that my son would just stop breathing. My son was born with laryngomalacia, a rare birth defect that affects the opening of the trachea which allows oxygen to flow within our bodies.

Unfortunately, due to floppy tissue in his trachea, his ability to freely intake oxygen was restricted. I would watch my son every night as he slept. His breathing sounded like a loud snore as his chest retracted deeply into his ribcage. I am so thankful for God and the gift of discernment.

One night I felt tightness in the pit of my stomach as I was cleaning the kitchen and preparing for the next day. I rushed downstairs to find my son was unable to breathe; he tried to cry but couldn't create a sound. I rushed to the hospital and stayed overnight along with my daughter and thankfully after treatment and a team of amazing doctors he was fine. I had no clue this would mark the first episode of many more nights like this. I felt as though the ER was our second home. You know it's bad when nurses, doctors, and hospital security begin to remember you and your family by name. After all, they see hundreds of patients a day!

Peace and a sound mind, the fruits of God's spirit, seemed nonexistent at the time. I grew weary, frustrated, and at times angry. I questioned things I have never questioned before. God...do you even exist? Do you remember us? Do you even care, or does anyone? I remember as though it were yesterday. The night I almost lost my son to a combined battle with laryngomalacia, asthma and RSV. The night I rediscovered God and myself. My son had just turned 1, what a blessing! Although his birthday party meant daddy wouldn't be there, nor family and faces that were slightly familiar, celebrating his birthday meant much more. It meant he made it to see an entire year!

I started to worry less about him. I developed a sense of security knowing he would be OK—except for this particular day. My son had a fever and was breathing faster than normal. My daughter walked over to me and said, "Mommy, there are angels in the room with MJ." Immediately I knew this was something much more serious than Tylenol and TLC could cure.

Once we rushed over to the hospital, I knew it was serious. A team of doctors mustered up the courage to tell me with fear woven through their voices that MJ would be transferred to pediatric ICU at a different hospital. The nurse added that they must move quickly before he lost the energy to fight for air.

At that moment, I remember having an out-of-body experience and felt as though I couldn't function. I cried after hearing my mother's voice over the phone. Her voice was familiar, soothing, encouraging, and reminded me that I was not alone although it may look that way. I was able to cleanse myself from all fear and worry to develop a sense of boldness I hadn't felt in such a long time.

Once we were transferred in pediatric ICU, a pastor entered the room and offered prayer. My first thoughts were, *is this a sign I might lose my son?* My heart raced but all I could think was, *God, if you are real, please show up for my son tonight.*

A nurse later entered the room and offered the American Red Cross service to fly my husband to the hospital from Bahrain. I wanted to be excited to see him, but being a wife had to take a seat at the back burner. I was mommy now and didn't have time to switch roles. After many breathing treatments and countless cords connected to his small body, he became semi stable. I looked at my baby girl with a forced smile on my face, reminding her everything would be OK. I walked over to the white board in the room that was used as a friendly reminder of your assigned doctor and nurse. I remember erasing everything on the board and writing the number 23. Twenty-three represented the day I believed by faith we would be discharged from the hospital even though the estimated time was several weeks.

Every day felt like an eternity. I hadn't washed and barely ate a cracker. I focused on keeping my baby girl happy, making sure my son was getting better, and counting down the days, believing on the 23rd we would leave the hospital. I didn't care about what it looked like, I truly wanted to test out the power of faith. Finally, we were discharged from the hospital. It wasn't the 23rd... but a day earlier! I felt a sense of power. We fought a battle with the help of God and faith as small as a mustard seed.

I often hear others say, "Don't lose yourself in the midst of being a mom!" I wouldn't say I lost myself, but what I did lose was the false idea of who I was. Truly in motherhood I found myself. I discovered who I truly am from the good to the very ugly. I discovered parts of myself I wish I didn't see. But in essence I am thankful because now I can truly appreciate every lesson learned to become better than I was before my children entered my life.

We live in a society that constantly challenges the significance of a mother. We are often challenged by individuals that would never dare walk a mile in our shoes. I am thankful for my chosen position as I leave my shoes by my bedside and dare to wear them over and over again.

Author Bio:

Kimberly Gladden-Eversley, an aspiring author, was born and raised in the city of Brooklyn, NY. At the ripe age of 28 years she discovered her voice through her writing. She has written short stories to poetry and gospel music. She also uses her voice to raise awareness and bring inspiration to all. As of May 11th 2017 Kimberly has become a Certified Life Purpose Coach. She uses her gift of faith and encouragement to ignite the light in those who have lost their fire. She acts as a guide leading the young generation to their God-given purpose. As a navy wife and mother of 3, she understand the true definition of love and sacrifice.

When Hope Is All You Have: My Journey Through Loss to Acceptance
by Melissa Berg

I've conquered a huge fear that I've held captive for so long. This is only the beginning of my story, which has been living deep inside of me for so long. My fragile heart is still hurting; I am still grieving. But I know it's time, time to share my story for them, and so here it is, just a snapshot of a time so profound, still vulnerable, and very much still real.

This quote has remained top in my world for a very long time: "Anyone can give up; it's the easiest thing in the world to do. But to hold it together when everyone else would understand if you fell apart, that's true strength." I have been through many losses in my life that have tested my patience, love, understanding, and faith. I am blessed with three beautiful children here on earth and three angel babies I never got to hold in my arms. Years of infertility and pregnancy loss became an unwanted pattern that shaped my reality spanning over a decade. It was such a lonely time. No one really talks about pregnancy loss, nor are we really allowed to. Miscarriage is death. It brings with it all the agonizing grief that comes with losing a loved one. There are no funerals. No memorials. You don't get sympathy cards or flowers or bereavement time. Instead routines go on, you take sick days.

The emotional and psychological "toll" that miscarriage has on a woman is often profound. Each loss brought its own feelings and emotions. It was not just about "that loss," but the losses and the hopes, wishes, and dreams for my future family were shattered each time. Coping with so many difficulties and changes in such a relatively short time of being pregnant, losing the baby, and medical treatment and intervention.

Well, what about my plan, our plans, our hopes and dreams, our love? All your hopes and dreams for him/her and for you as a family were now gone forever, crushed. Nothing in the world can help heal the pain loss causes. It's overwhelming, stifling, it crushes your very soul. No one can heal that hurt for you. So alone in your grief. Grief is overwhelming, suffocating, life-sucking.

Grief completely shocks you down to your core. You never know when it will come, how long it will stay, what it will do to you or how it will leave you...unraveled. There was no one to talk to or process with. I needed someone to understand, listen, comfort and heal, provide compassion. Instead I was isolated. And to not be able to take that previous baby home with you, hold him/her in your arms, smell their baby scent, snuggle them on your chest...you can't go anywhere without it in your face. Pregnant women and newborns at the zoo, television commercials for diapers, social media people posting about being pregnant, babies all the time, 24/7 in your face. People asking you if you have children, how many, do you want more, how come?! And then to hear those awful words... "Just move on," "try again," "it was meant to be," "it's God's plan." It became too easy to ask "Why," "Why me?" Why is my struggle so different from others? What did I do wrong? Why am I being punished? What did I do to deserve all this pain and suffering? Why do others have it so easy? But I have known that has never gotten me far, to question. I have had to reach inside my very soul as I have hit some of the darkest periods of my life so far. I know I have lost my way, gotten off the path, and completely given up at times. I lost my faith, my way, my reason...

I have to go on, go through my day, I have to survive. Am I still working on restoring my faith? Yes. I know I need to share my story with others so they know they are not alone. We need to come together. We cannot stay silent and suffer anymore alone. There has always been something that has always been there—even if I couldn't feel it or know it, it was there. This everlasting shining light within me that has allowed me to persevere, to keep moving forward despite the challenges I have faced. The process of becoming a strong person is not easy. Often we can emerge from the darkness of grief as a stronger person for having gone through it. I take strength in knowing that while my arms may not have held them, His do.

Author Bio:
Melissa is a School Psychologist, Wellness Advocate and Success Coach who educates and empowers others on natural and healthy ways of living. Melissa has a passion for empowering stressed, over-scheduled women to seek balance while creating a lifelong healthy lifestyle. Melissa works with inspired women who are ready to integrate and manage their health through natural, holistic activities to nourish their mind, body and spirit.

Website: **www.melissabergwellness.com**

Mom, You are Brave & Strong!

A Priceless Gift
by Miki Bennett

As I sat beside her hospital bed, I stroked her hair as she tried to sleep. The pain medication she was receiving via one of the three IVs she had was helping, but not enough. Ever since she was a little girl, every time she was in the hospital, she would always ask me to sit and run my fingers through her hair to help relax her. Little did she know that this simple gesture was helping me too. To be able to touch my sweet girl, trying to reassure her that everything would be okay, made me feel like I was doing something, anything, to help her feel better and take away some of the pain.

This was her fourth surgery in three weeks to remove metal rods that had been holding her spine together as she grew over the years. Except now, at the age of twenty-five, that metal was causing complications in her body. The rods were rusting and breaking down, creating a severe staph infection that was very hard to treat. Each surgery was supposed to be the one to fix the situation but instead it seemed to be worse than the one before. And for the first time since she was born, with everything she had been through, my little girl opened her eyes and told me she couldn't do this any more. She was ready to give up.

This was her twenty-eighth surgery for her congenital scoliosis that she had been born with. It was part of a set of birth defects called VACTERL Syndrome. And it seemed like we had spent a good portion of her life at the Children's Hospital. Now, though, she was an adult, but that didn't matter. She was still my baby, hurting so bad that she didn't care what happened to her. She just couldn't handle the pain anymore. And my heart was breaking.

I had always called Holly my "Energizer Bunny" because, despite the odds of her disabilities, she kept going and going. She walked when they said they didn't think she would. She danced. She went to a regular school. She was a straight A student despite surgeries, doctor's appointments, IV therapy at home, feeding tubes at times. She was a fighter. But that day, the defeat I saw in her eyes was almost too much for me to bear.

As I continued to sit by her side, she finally fell back to sleep. But memories started to flood my mind. Of handing her to the nurse when she was six weeks old for her first surgery, so scared as a new mom that I was lost. Of having to put her in a plastic body cast daily from the time she was eight weeks old, hoping that it would mold and shape her little body as she grew. Of the countless hospital visits to her seven different doctors to make sure she was growing, thriving, and keeping her the healthiest we could as parents and doctors. Of the hospital waiting rooms, sitting as patiently as I could, waiting for the surgeons to come out to tell me that, yet again, a surgery or procedure had been successful. Of the other parents who were at the hospital with their little ones, feeling emotions very similar to mine. We were kindred spirits in a place we didn't want to be, wishing what all parents do for their children: to be healthy, whole and happy.

Over the next several days, Holly continued to fight the infection that was ravaging her body. But it was only that one time when she wanted to give up. After that, we all encouraged her, prayed for her, and supported her in any way possible to let her know she could do it. She would come out on the other end a survivor, and we—I—would survive this battle too.

Today, I talk to my daughter via FaceTime. We try to make sure to chat each day.

She has had more surgeries since this one but has faced each one just like all the others she has endured. She still faces daily challenges and continues to amaze me with her strength and courage.

As for me, I still see her as my baby. It doesn't matter her age—she is my daughter and I fight to protect her, love her, help her, each and every day. Now Holly has a wonderful man by her side, her husband, who supports her and is such a blessing not only to Holly, but to our whole family. He accepts my daughter just like she is, and that is an unbelievable gift. And because of my daughter's courage under such incredible circumstances, she has enabled me to handle a divorce, cancer, and now a very rare chronic illness I deal with on a daily basis.

The love of a mother and child is priceless. It is beautiful. It is a gift from God. And God gave me a beautiful present the day my daughter was born.

Author Bio:
With a passion for wholesome adventure, Miki Bennett is the author of two contemporary women's fiction series: Florida Keys Novels and Camping In High Heels. A deep love of the beach and lifelong experience in the RV and camping world led her to write romance novels that bring humor and paradise to readers' fingertips. Miki lives in Charleston, SC with her husband Jeff. They are empty nesters with three grown children.

Website: **www.mikibennett.com**

Searching for Safe Haven
by Noushin Mazlaghani

Here I was in Tehran, Iran in 1985 as I celebrated my daughter's first birthday on March 22. Tehran was under attack from Iraqi bombing. Missiles were being fired at the capital; the war had been going on for about 3 years now. I remember one day it got so bad that I had to put my daughter under the dining-room table and cover her with my own body to protect her. It sounds like something from a movie, something not real, after almost 31 years, even as I remember it and share it with you.

Fast-forward to 1989. I had my son on November 09, 1989. He got infected in the hospital with a urinary tract infection and we couldn't do anything. My daughter had been infected with salmonella at the same hospital during the war when she was born.

There were so many major events that led us to choose to leave the country to find a safer, more promising future to raise my children. I felt so small and not able to do anything.

We arrived at JFK airport NYC, USA in July 28, 1990. The rest of story is about my challenges as an immigrant mom raising my two precious kids, of fear of uncertainty of the future, adapting to a brand-new culture, and detachments to what was in the past. I had to study with my daughter to be able to help her with the homework and watch my 9-month-old son as well. Even though I knew English, it had nothing to do with learning American English language.

The First Halloween party was a major shock, as I didn't know the culture. I was standing in the middle of my daughter's school's gym holding my son, and she wanted to go to run with her new friends with their costumes and play. All I wanted to do was make sure that I could see her and follow her around the gym. The environment was not familiar, my son was scared of the masked faces, and my confusion and frustration didn't abatetill we arrived back to our new home that night. The lifestyle, noise, and traffic of NY wasn't to our liking, so we moved to a small town in VA for a safer, more relaxed experience.

I remember one day in the cold, wintery weather my daughter, now in second grade, came home in the middle of the day by herself. I was shocked that she could find the house after she got off the bus. They had closed the school because of the heavy snow. I hadn't been listening to the news and so had missed the announcement, but thank goodness she was home safe and knew the way. Later on I opened my own daycare, as I didn't trust or know anyone to take care of my kids.

I remember the first day of school, I followed the school bus to make sure it took my son to the right place (he was going to a magnet program and a different school from other kids). The driver stopped the bus, came out, and asked me, "Are you going to do this for the rest of the school year?!" I mention this because I want to express the amount of pressure and separation anxiety that I felt over making sure I was raising healthy, happy children.

The new job of my then husband took us from VA to MD and then AZ since 1997. We faced the challenges of finding a right school for their education, securing their future, and providing them with a great, healthy lifestyle. We also all had to deal with bad situations, from being bullied in school, to not being picked up in a sport team, to receiving an unfriendly letter that directly asked my daughter to do NOT sit with others at the same table because of her hair color. The story goes on and on.

My strong belief in my faith encouraged me to face these challenges of being an immigrant mother and made all of us better human beings, teaching us to have compassion for others, be kind and do our best.

My daughter works for Maricopa County as an attorney now and my son runs a multimillion dollars franchise. They are both very successful, healthy, happy people in love and active in their communities. I am happy to have found a safe haven for them to grow and serve the community, state,and country as we made USA our home.

Author Bio:
Noushin Mazlaghani is passionate about body, mind, spirit well being. She dedicated her life to bringing world peace through her services such as cranial therapy, Polarity raining, Kundalini yoga and meditation. She lives in Scottsdale, Arizona for last 21 years and loves nature, hiking, photography, writing, story telling, dancing and laughing.

Website: **www.delanguagehealingarts.com**

Being a Mom
by Betsy Anciani

I became a mother eighteen years ago. I have two daughters who every day fill my life in the same way that letters fill the pages of a notebook, in the same way that the sun illuminates the sky with its light during dawn, in the same way that the water cools an arid terrain. When I got pregnant with my first daughter, I remember I was full of questions, dreams, and fears. At that point in my life, I had all my family close to me, offering their unconditional support. My daughter, as well as being my first creation, was the first grandchild, the first niece, the first baby for all of us in a long time. Her arrival was a big event. Six years later, the same would happen with the arrival of my second daughter.

When I was a child, I used to draw my adult life. I wanted to be a teacher, a doctor, or maybe a lawyer. However, sometime in my early maturity, I became aware of the sacrifices my mother made: a divorced woman with two children who were taken care of by their aunts, uncles, cousins or neighbors while she was away working to ensure a good quality of life for them. When I was ten years old and my brother was only five, I began helping my mother with his care. I helped him to eat, bathe, dress, do homework, and of course, we played together. At that moment, without realizing it, I started my training as a mother. Today, thirty-three years later, I still worry about him as his mother. That, undoubtedly, was my best training.

However, nothing prepared me for being a mother who would move from country to country every two or three years. The day that I left my home country for the first time, I faced one of my biggest fears: living with my daughters of ten and four years old in a completely different country. New home, new school, new classmates, new friends, and a significant amount of new challenges. How was I supposed to teach my daughters to adapt to such a big change? I had been born, had grown up, studied, and worked in the same city of 975 km2 (376 sq. miles), with an average of 250, 000 habitants, for all my life.

The city of Villahermosa in Mexico was our first home outside of my country of origin. The average temperature of the city was too high; we had to learn to survive strong heat waves. Air conditioning was not an option due to the high cost of electricity. Mexican food is a delight, a real heritage of humanity. However, we had to get used to the spicy dishes that locals don't even consider spicy. We were surprised to see Mexican children from a very early age consuming fruit sprinkled with hot pepper. The schedule of the meals in Mexico is different from my country, so in that aspect we also had to keep pace with our host culture. In terms of the language, although Spanish is the official language in Mexico like ours, there are different words for certain objects, vegetables, fruits, meals and general expressions. We learned to call things by the name they used, so that we could understand each other. In our country, we used to have a variety of tropical fruit juices, but in Villahermosa there were only three customary drinks to have with your meals, very different from ours.

The most shocking part for my daughters was making friends. This city didn't have any international school, so they entered a private school, where as usual kids have been together since kindergarten. Every day my oldest daughter came home crying because no one wanted to be with her or even include her in their teams. I went to many school meetings looking for advice from local mothers, who suggested that I should take her to all the parties to which she was invited. Three months later, my daughter had a party every Friday and I had to check with her agenda so that I could organize my own free time.

While my husband went to work, I went to school activities, I enrolled in a fitness center, participated in the society of wives sponsored by the company my husband worked for, and during the evenings I took my daughters to extracurricular activities to escape the heat waves in our home. I had a hectic social life; there was no day in which I was not invited to a breakfast for any motive: welcoming, farewell, baby shower, philanthropic events, and many more. Certainly my public relations experience multiplied; meeting people of different nationalities and with so many different stories was filling my days in a very interesting way, because I was learning tips about the city, the country, entertainment for my daughters, doctors, and crucial details to adapt to our new city. I even enrolled in a school of writers, which I attended every Saturday for a year, greatly enriching my cultural heritage.

The experience of living in Mexico was also unforgettable because of the villages, cities, and landscapes that we visited. Without a doubt, this country has a lot to offer to humanity. They were two and a half years filled with lots of learning of all kinds. When the company told my husband about the transfer to Bogotá, it was as if I had to say goodbye to my native country and my family all over again. My husband was born in Bogotá and had lived outside his country for about fifteen years. Colombia received us with open arms, and since it's a bordering country with my country, Venezuela, I discovered a lot of similarities in our customs.

In Bogotá, my daughters enrolled in an international school with a high quality academic level. Once again, it was hard to make friends, but this time it was less traumatic or shocking. My youngest daughter made friends the quickest. Younger children have fewer prejudices when it comes to welcoming a new kid to their group. For teenagers, it's a little more complicated, but it was easy to find other teens with international lifestyles. These schools have a figure called "buddy," which is another kid of the same age as yours that show them around the school, teach them the way the school routine works, and introduce them to other classmates. This time we had the same meal hours, the same language, and fewer variations in vocabulary in general. Colombians are extremely cordial, not that Mexicans aren't, but Colombians really try to please you with their attentiveness. This time the society of wives was larger; the list of activities was longer and more varied, including a Reading Club in which I still participate today.

In Colombia, I had the luck of finding a cooking academy for beginners, where I studied for a year of delicious discoveries and lots of entertainment. My daughters were quite occupied with school work and extracurricular activities offered by the school. We also had the opportunity to travel a lot in this country, since the amount of holidays is considerable. We visited beautiful places in Colombia, and got to learn about its cultural heritage and customs. As a family we spent lots of time in amusement parks, cinemas, restaurants, plays, and musicals at the level of renowned international shows.

The cuisine of Bogotá is surprising. I always say that there's not enough time nor money to enjoy the wide variety of restaurants that this city offers, with some delicious dishes from any country you can imagine.

The only drawback of living in Bogotá is the traffic. Like any great capital city, it has a high level of mobility, which taught us to leave the house really early to be on time for any engagement. However, the benefits that you can enjoy in Bogotá make you forget the sacrifice of spending so much time driving. The government is constantly working to fix this issue; for instance, we have the "Ciclovia." Every Sunday and holiday, important streets of the city are closed for family entertainment with bicycles, rollerblades, and hikes during which you can enjoy green areas and a varied gastronomic offer.

Colombia has a vast historic heritage in architecture, customs, and cuisine. Its most famous advertising tagline confirms what you feel when you live there or simply visit any of its cities: "The only risk is that you'll want to stay."

Our next destination took us to Houston, Texas. After three fabulous years, we left Colombia with due homesickness, but full of expectations heading to our new host country. This time my oldest daughter only had a year and a half to finish high school. The younger one would go to elementary school. Despite receiving information about excellent school districts in Texas, we decided to choose an international private school, thinking about the exchange with other families with similar lifestyle and, as we saw in the previous school, receptiveness for new students.

For each move, we received advice from outsourcing companies contracted by the company my husband works for to facilitate the school hunting, house hunting, and legal paperwork. They give us suggestions in each field, and we evaluate them and make decisions that are more adapted to our interests.

In USA, there are not as many holidays as in Colombia. The difference is very big, so the getaways were minimal. However, we found some time to visit the emblematic places of Texas and to visit New York. The social activities for the family in general were drastically reduced. The social gatherings were limited to those with friends from work, most of them Spanish speakers, and not so frequently, since we didn't live near each other. The social exchange with locals was very reduced; their lifestyle is very different from that of the Latino culture. So we invented our own festive evenings in the privacy of our home.

While living in Houston, we truly missed the delivery service that Colombia offers, where you can ask for anything, from a screw, to medication, to a full supermarket purchase to be delivered to you. Homemade food is not the general rule in the US; frozen meals are more common, while we love fresh food that had just been prepared. We were also surprised to see that the locals were happy with a sandwich for lunch.

My daughters got adapted to the school and to their new friends, but their social meetings weren't so frequent. I continued participating in the society of wives, which, just as in other occasions, kept me occupied and gave me the chance to meet a large number of women with a greater ethnic diversity.

In the previous two cities, I had participated in an international festival organized by this society. This time, the participation was massive. An average of 200 women gathered to share their gastronomy and culture. Most of the continents had representation in a memorable gathering. Without a doubt, this was one of my favorite moments. However, I should mention my physical exhaustion.

The lack of domestic help was something that affected me in a considerable way. In my previous locations, I could afford the service of a maid every weekday. Maids are expensive in the US compared to what we had been paying. So I had enough workload which I strategically shared with my family, but it wasn't enough for me to feel healthy. This was the favorite topic of conversation among women, always seeking the best service and the best price.

The US is an incredible country, very well organized, with very clean streets and with an excellent observation of all type of rules. It may have some imperfections like any other country. Physically, there is not such place as an ideal place. You make your own ideal place with your spirit and attitude towards life. Something that made me particularly happy during my stay in Houston was meeting this sweet woman from India. She is a Health Coach who taught me to know more about the food I bring to my family's dining table. She taught me about organic products, how to organize my pantry and new kitchen strategies, but the most important thing is that she heard me, she was really worried about me, and despite the distance now, she keeps sharing her knowledge and love with me up until today.

We only spent one and a half years living in the US. The critical situation of the oil industry changed our plans, and four months ago we returned to Bogotá for a short period of time. We are waiting for news that will change, once again, the course of our lives. But here we are, as if we were sitting at the movies eating popcorn before the film begins. We are ready and we have plenty of tools to deal with what the universe has prepared for us with the best attitude. We are ready for adventure and more learning.

It's been little more than seven years since then, moving twice within my home country and four times internationally. Four different countries, six different schools, several cultures and multiple idiosyncrasies, innumerable first times for such a brief period of time. Somehow, my family and I have been put in a type of life boot camp. I have always thought that my daughters have the great advantage of being more than prepared for change. *Challenge* became our favorite word. Our experiences are full of large difficulties, fears and tears, but our attitude, our work as a team and my desire to be the best support for my daughters, have given us the necessary tools to overcome every obstacle in order to keep going and set aside the stones that made us stumble along the way.

During my experience as a mom, I have observed the lack of communication in many families through different cultures. Many parents do not know what their children do or what they like to do; they don't even bother asking what they ate at school or if they were able to adapt to their new classmates. I have seen children arrive to school holding hands with their nanny, their driver, or even with the bodyguard. I can't help but remember my school days; I was the one who picked up mine and my brother's report cards. I can't forget what it felt like. My parents gave us the love and the attention that the situation allowed them to give us, but there are emotions that definitely marked us.

I decided that the best thing I could do for my daughters in this new nomadic lifestyle was to stand by them in every possible detail of their lives, giving them even more support and presence than what my family's situation allowed me to enjoy. If I was going to have difficulties working in my profession due to our constant moving, then I would stay at home to be the best mom my daughters could have.

The day that they returned from school, competing for being the first to tell me with careful detail about their first day with their new classmates and the information they'd learned from their new country, that day was one of the most powerful and important days in my life. Since then, I have been working hard so that all our days are that way.

I've certainly had moments of weakness, especially those when I have seen my daughters crying because of the unknown, their loneliness during the school recess when they are the "new girls," their sadness at the departure from the place which became their home for two or three years. In those moments of weakness, an unknown force devours me and returns to me the desire to stand by them and tell them that it's OK to cry, it's OK to miss, and to start drawing for them a new destiny with faith and hope. I always tell them that they are fortunate to initiate a new school every so often, a new city, new interesting places to know, new cultures to learn from, and most importantly, to complete a rainbow of wonderful friends and unique experiences.

I hope I'm doing well. I hope that my daughters are becoming dignified human beings, global citizens and respectful of the diversity that surrounds them. I hope to keep carrying this profession with pride, since it's the most beautiful of all professions: Being a Mom.

Author Bio:

Betsy is a Mom, writer and an avid reader. She is certified by the Universidad Juárez Autónoma de Tabasco in literary formation and also certified in professional coaching by CoachSI. Betsy is a Licensed Master Practitioner of Neurolinguistic Programming (NLP) and a specialist in international relocations,change management and the necessary emotional adjustments that derive from frequent moving.

LinkedIn: **www.linkedin.com/in/betsy-anciani**

Being Mom: Blessing from Above
by Pooja Malik

The moment I realized that I was going to be a mom soon filled my heart with immense happiness, but also lot of fears started developing in my mind. I feared whether my child would be able to complete its journey from inside me to beside me safely. Fear of my child being healthy. I questioned myself. Was I capable enough to raise a child, and was I ready to be a mom? Basically it was a fear of the unknown, like all moms have.

When that magical moment arrived and I heard that first cry, felt that first touch, saw that first glimpse, my heart melted, and with a gust of wind all fears disappeared. Two small innocent eyes looked towards me and silently we both took a vow of being together with each other forever. At this moment I felt both the weakest and the strongest as a person. When for the first time I took her in my arms I felt like a weak and vulnerable person who would do anything for that little soul. That little girl also made me a mother, which made me feel powerful and strong. I was now a person with a lifelong commitment and responsibilities towards my child.

During the past 5 years of motherhood I faced lots of challenges in raising my child. Playing the dual role of being a parent and breadwinner to my family increased my anxiety even more. There were lots of questions popping up in my mind, major among them if I would be able to raise my child in a healthy, safe, and happy environment. Being a mom was now my priority and my major concern, instead of being a dentist by profession. So initially I wanted to have everything done perfectly for my child, but soon I realized I was being overambitious. Soon I realized in life perfectionism doesn't exist and I needed to set my priorities and balance my personal and professional life.

And I started setting up small, easy-to-achieve and realistic goals. I try to spend as much time I can with my child; together we have made a few routines so that we can spend time together, like I read her one book every night, on weekends we both do some cooking together, we go for swimming, do groceries, and many more things like going to parks, riding the bicycle, and movie nights occasionally.

I realized that my personal sufferings evolved me as a better and stronger person both personally and professionally. This made me more empathetic towards situations and people, especially children and the underprivileged. It inculcated a desire and need in me to help others, maybe because I can identify myself with them. Furthermore, it motivates me to do a lot of volunteering in my child's school, which benefits me in many ways. First of all, I get to spend more time with my child. Secondly, it boosts the self-confidence of my child. And lastly it gives me immense pleasure if I can be of some help to others.

Occasionally we also try to attend workshops organized by the city for kids and parents, like Christmas and Halloween craft workshops and many more. Recently we both attended a Halloween workshop and we spent a wonderful time together making monsters and comparing whose was more creepier.

Kids at this age have a thirst for learning and discovering new things and are always ready with millions of interesting questions. My daughter has had some amazing questions for me to answer, like, "How did dinosaur go extinct?" "What would happen if they were still alive?" "How do whales breathe in water?" "Can I become astronaut?" And the list is endless. I try to answer her questions as much I can. I also plan our outdoor picnic visits to places that can answer her questions and even develop many more in her little mind, like museums, the zoo, and library.

I make sure to ask her daily about how was her day spent at school. I really like to hear her long stories about her school, friends, teachers, music, and gym classes. I feel that listening is very important for me as a mother, as it keeps me aware of how things are going at school, and for my child I feel that my concern for her makes her happier and even more eager to learn and perform at school.

It's been couple of years and we have moved to Canada from India, as I got the opportunity to pursue a specialization in my field from one of the world's most renowned institutes. This not only helped me further consolidate the base that I have built, it also exposed me to a broader spectrum of knowledge while giving me a deeper understanding of dentistry. But again it was not an easy decision to make as a mother leaving your country and getting settled in a new country. Again I was feeling the same as I was at the time of the birth of my child. I had a fear of the unknown again. While discussing about it with my little girl, as I have a habit of doing always and trying to explain her according to her capacity, she said to me, "YOU CAN DO IT, MOM! YOU CAN DO IT," and all my fears vanished upon hearing these magic words and the decision was made.

I had always been so fortunate to be surrounded by wonderful people who helped me in my problems and made my journey so smooth. Now I realize that coming here exposed us to lot of new things like new cultures, different people, their beliefs, festivals, food, sports, and many more. That helped me to teach my girl respect for all and respect for humanity. Now she knows and celebrates many different festivals, from Diwali to Christmas with her friends. I feel it makes her wiser and an even better human being.

Being a parent, there is no bigger reward than seeing your child succeed. It gives me immense pleasure to see my little ballerina performing on the stage in front of large audiences. When I'm sick, she tries to help me with my daily chores.

I recently got a comment from her teacher saying that "she is such a smart, sensitive, generous, and polite young lady. She often gives up what she has to share with her friends. You have done a wonderful job raising her." What else could make a parent happier than hearing these words? These words encouraged me and made me feel that I'm moving on the right path as I'm raising my child. Moreover, it gives me more strength to continue my journey with my daughter in the path of our lives.

Family Is...
by Stephanie LaBonte

Our family is ball games, camping, hiking, concerts in the back yard, movie nights, homework, Legos on the floor, home-cooked dinners, dinners out when we don't feel like cooking dinner, skinned knees, brotherly fights, and so much more. Our family is amazing, and incredibly boring, and normal at the same time.

In our dining room we have a painting over the table with these words:

Family Rules... Use Kinds Words. Do Your Best. Always Be Honest. Forgive and Forget. Help Others. Work Hard. Try New Things. Be Yourself. Love One Another.

This speaks so directly to what we strive for in our family. We value kindness, helping others, and respecting the differences that God has created in all of us.

Our household is an LGBT blended family living in Alabama. Some are surprised to hear this, given how "normal" we sound. As far as our children see it, our family is also a family of 3 moms, 2 dads, and 4 kids. How does that math work out? My wife and I were both married to men previously, and we each had two boys from those marriages. My wife's ex-husband remarried. Thus, we have 3 moms, 2 dads, and 4 kids. Our household is currently 2 moms and 3 boys; my wife's oldest son is living in another state with his dad and stepmom.

But our family life wasn't always so "normal." Until gay marriage was legalized, we were forced by custody agreement to live separately, not as a family. We lived in two separate houses, had twice as many bills, and my boys did not know that my wife was their stepmom, nor did her children really view me as part of their family. We lived this way for a year and a half.

In many circles, it feels as if we would be the family you'd invite over for playdates with the kids and backyard barbeques—if only we were a heterosexual married couple. Being nontraditional in that way seems to carry a stigma with it and present its own set of prejudices and complications. Sometimes it's hurtful; other times it makes us feel sad for others and their inability to accept people who are different. Then, of course, we have to add in our unusual blend. I had fair-skinned, blond-haired twins, and my wife had boys 3 years apart—the oldest being African American. Our family pictures are nontraditional in every sense. Though we can't truly speak for others, we often feel like people see us simply as a same-sex couple living together with their kids—and not the blended family that we are.

We experience all the same things as (I would venture to say) every other blended family. Family meetings have been a must, because one way or another, we had to learn to live together. We never stop learning how to do that. Our boys had been raised differently, and we have to make it a point to continue to recognize the differences in our parenting styles and work through compromises. We've been very fortunate that our boys mesh very well, even with their distinct personality differences. Of course, it's not all about the kids. My wife and I had to learn to come together, especially after having been married well over a year before actually living together (or even being "allowed" to act like we're married or a family in front of my boys). That brought its own set of stresses we had to work through, on top of deciding things like where the coffee cups will go in the cabinet and how the refrigerator will be organized. I know those may seem like trivial matters... but you haven't met my wife. My point is that we had to blend and compromise like any other family.

But then, as we step out into the world and meet new people, we are constantly reminded of what others see and the perceptions they have about families "like ours." We have to "come out" over and over again. And so do our children. While we have to continually learn how to live together as a family—combining our ways of doing things, our rules, our routines—we also have to be aware of other situations we encounter that many other families just don't see. Like many parents, we're trying to raise our boys to be kind, responsible, and inclusive adults, but when they go to school, they're often faced with the hateful rhetoric of children who are simply regurgitating what they hear at home, on the news, at church... It's difficult to have that component added into our everyday blended family challenges. In the aftermath of that, we're faced with trying to explain to our children why people feel so much hatred and discontent over our family. It's not easy explaining unfounded hate to children while also not wanting to discourage them from forming their own opinions as they become young men and adults.

Our middle-school-aged son was recently bullied at his school. We do not take the word "bully" lightly; there were multiple kids saying horrible things about our family and our son on a daily basis. The principal had never dealt with a situation like this before. She did not know how to handle it, but as a whole, the administrators seem to be educating themselves and talking to students about tolerance and respecting differences in others. We were pleasantly surprised by how well the situation was (and is still being) handled, but it doesn't change the reality that our family faces daily. We teach all of our boys that they can't choose how other people behave, but they can choose how they respond to the actions of others; that they have a tremendous amount of power in whatever situation they are faced with. They are children, though, and as they make their way through these years of their lives, they will undoubtedly face difficult times in southern Alabama.

In a way, being an LGBT family makes the "blended" part of our family reality seem not so difficult. We can make our own choices and change together as a family to become a better family unit, but the way other people view us and accept us in the community—that can't be so easily changed. So we continue to focus on being the best people we can be and let our example speak for us. That, and time, will change hearts.

Even amidst all the craziness, though, what we can always be sure of is that our family will continue to be ball games, camping, hiking, concerts in the backyard, movie nights, homework, Legos on the floor, home-cooked dinners, dinners out when we don't feel like cooking dinner, skinned knees, brotherly fights, and so much more—because we are a family like any other. And these are the things families do. We are amazing, and incredibly boring, and normal at the same time. And we wouldn't have it any other way.

Author Bio:
Stephanie LaBonte is a wife, mom of four boys, runner, planner addict, blogging novice, and lover of motivational quotes. She is passionate about helping others determine the goals that set their souls on fire and pursue those goals with intention. She believes in the power of positive psychology, and that focusing on strengths is more powerful than improving areas of weakness.

Website: **www.stephanielabonte.com**

Forgive
by Ursula Carbajal

We were at a local judge's office waiting for some documents when we heard a teenage girl crying, begging her mom not to send her dad to jail. The mom had anger in her voice (we assumed he was late on paying the alimony).

"This will teach him!" But I did not pay much attention to the mom. All I saw and heard was a little girl begging for her father's freedom... and being ignored.

I turned to my husband and made one of the most important promises of my life. "If we ever divorce, I swear I´ll be never be that woman."

7 years and 2 beautiful girls later, we agreed to divorce, but this was just the beginning of many changes. A week after the decision was made, the doctor told us he had cancer and needed urgent surgery.

Suddenly life felt apart. I found out he had many investments that didn't go as he expected, now he was telling me our financial situation was bad, and I saw myself being in charge of the bills, house, kids, him(!) and still working and doing my best reorganize our life.

We sold the house, moved to a small apartment and stayed living together not as husband and wife but as two people doing their best to survive thorough this. I know we both did our best to keep the relationship as friendly as possible—for the sake of the kids, I kept telling myself—but something wasn´t right.

Seven years have passed and he has been fighting not just with the cancer but an aggressive diabetes, as well. Seven years of going in and out of the hospital.

Around the third year I realized some things were not OK, none of us were OK. I didn't know at that time, but later I learned that I was still resentful for the whole situation. I haven't had the time to grieve the end of my marriage; all this time I felt I had to stay strong and busy and I haven't allowed myself to release the pain and the anger, and this began to affect the kids, so I asked for help.

Help came as a Buddhist psychologist who helped me to accept the fact that there are going to be situations I can't control, and most importantly he taught me to forgive, to accept that my ex-husband is not perfect, that I have to let go of the idea I had of him and what I used to expect from him, because none of that is going to happen.

Slowly life began to change. My relationship with the girls improved. I discovered myself being more present in their lives; now we can all sit at the table for dinner, tell each other our stories of how the day was, and the girls share their own stories from school. It is good; it is better.

But it was not an easy process. Eduardo was officially disabled and I had to keep working; we both agreed it was time to follow our separate ways, but who should live with the girls? It was a painful decision, but we agreed they should live with him and I would visit them daily and stay there until they fell sleep.

We both knew that living with me meant lots of hours with the sitter or grandma while mom was at work. Living with him meant having dad at home for them, to help them with homework, cooking for them, being with them, loving them.

I used to blame him for ruining the marriage and everything, but it was my anger, my frustration, what was wrong. Learning to forgive has given me the tools to improve not just my life but my kids' life; it has giving me the strength to help Eduardo through his new battle against cancer and stay by his side, showing and teaching the kids we are family. We might not be together anymore—we might not be married anymore—but we are always going to support each other.

It's a Boy!
by Simran Bhatia

I turned my head to the side to hide my tears. I drifted back to a few years before when I was sitting on the hospital bed holding my mum's hand. She had woken a few days before from a coma she was in after her cancer treatment had gone terribly wrong. I heard her say, "I had this vision that I had to be here for your 2 daughters. I had to come back."

Since then I had convinced myself that the first time my mum held my daughter would be this magical healing moment that would wash away all of the angst of the last few years. But we were having a boy.

Instantly I felt guilty about being sad. We were having a healthy child. I should be grateful. An hour later I told my hubby, "I feel ashamed. I'm already projecting so much onto this child. When does the baby get to be himself?" I held my belly, looked down, and said, "Mommy's sorry. I'm making you a promise today... I am not going to burden you with being who I want you to be. You just be you, okay?"

My mind drifted back again to another promise I had made a few months before: to break a habit that was turning me into a shell of who I was before. With my Mum's sickness, the day-to-day of becoming a caregiver had started to feel like too much, and so as soon as a feeling crept up I went into major avoidance. I would delude myself that I'm just going to stuff my face with food for the 22 minutes this show lasts on Hulu and then I'll let myself figure out what I'm feeling.

And then one day I finally had enough—of myself. I made a promise to myself that I needed to feel my emotions, experience life, and move through. Three weeks later I found out I was pregnant, and my mind played the stupidest trick on me. It said, *now this, THIS is the experience that will break all your bad habits. You should do an unmedicated birth and feel everything.*

Forty-one weeks later, all the physical exercises and mental preparation in the world couldn't have actually prepared me for what happened. I asked to FEEL, and the Universe delivered—BIG TIME. For three days I felt like I was in labor for 6 hours a night, and then it would... fade away. The fourth day things really started, but 44 hours later I kept fainting, so my birth team convinced me I needed an epidural at this point to get through. But even that wasn't enough. Another four hours later my little boy came out in an emergency C-section.

Every imagination I had about my perfect natural birthing story was lying like shattered glass all around me... and in that I found the healing I had so desperately been seeking.

For the first time I filled up with this feeling that I wasn't the story—of how this birth had taken place, of my Mum's cancer, of the things that had "gone wrong" before. I could feel the story, let go, and move on. And celebrate having received the most beautiful gifts in the world: a son with a bright, strong spirit; and knowing that I was no longer afraid of feeling all life had to offer me, as I learned how to be his mother.

Author Bio:
Simran Bhatia is the founder of Flowation. com, a marketplace for spiritual-minded business owners to sell their online courses, products, and services. She lives in the Chicago suburbs with a husband who wishes he were Batman, and a son who...probably is. She spends her free time dancing around the kitchen, doing yoga, writing, and dreaming up new ideas on how to help soulpreneurs have a bigger impact on the world.

In Sickness and In Health: My Child's Daily Gift of Grace
by Sylvia Ronnau

Ten weeks. My body shook, the fourth contraction in the past hour. Tears crawled down my cheeks as the pain blasted my lower stomach area. I grabbed the phone, labored breathing.

"Hello. May I please speak with Dr. Wells?" I screamed as the inner parts of me quaked. "I think I am going into labor," I cried.

"Relax, Sylvia. How many contractions have you had this hour?" Dr. Wells asked calmly, always calmly.

"Five, and another may be on its way," I belabored my points to the doctor. Bedrest for ten weeks almost drove me insane; anxiety and depression twisted together to describe my state of mind.

"You are fine. Remember, six contractions, and then call us." Eye rolls accompanied his answer; I could feel it, sense it.

Pillows were strewn about everywhere on the bed and on the floor, many touched like kittens in a new litter. My lower back burned, flicks of baby kicks fluttering. My stomach balled up into knots; the pain penetrated my back up to my shoulders. It was time.

The car flew to the hospital, slipping in puddles. My husband sprinted ahead while I ambled along. I became friends with chronic pain years ago, so the labor pains intensified with each step with screams, shrieks, yells. Jesus kept me going even when I wanted to depart the earth.

I peered into my doctor's eyes. "OK, Sylvia, push HARD!" I pushed and screamed and howled and cried. "You did it!" Dr. Wells said with great pride. Little one screamed loud, healthy lungs.

A nurse sauntered over with her in her arms and asked, "What are you going to name her?" After many arguments and disagreements over her name, we picked "Zara," meaning "dawn ascending, light."

"Zara Elizabeth," I answered with joy and peace, holding a baby, scrunched eyes, in my arms.

The next weeks sucked all life from me. The chronic pain in the form of horrific migraines, TMJ, fibromyalgia, and sleep apnea grabbed on to me with a vengeance. The migraines rendered me incapacitated; walking was a chore. The knees caved, my body falling to the ground. I contracted MRSA, a deadly staph infection in the hospital. Limping along, I sprayed all surfaces with bleach to prevent Zara from contracting it.

Tears sprinted down my face as I sobbed and sobbed. Motherhood with pain stretched me beyond comprehension. My sunglasses covered my face from the world. "Sylvia, room 7," the nurse uttered. I spoke with the doctor about the pain; I barely functioned and I wanted to be a good mother. Failure. Failure. Failure. Those words pounded my brain. He prescribed medication, one I had used before for my pain. My breastfeeding days were over. This medication would cause growth problems had I used it while breastfeeding.

I broke into five thousand pieces as I sat in the car with the prescription. Functioning mattered much more than breastfeeding, I convinced myself. My heart bled and bled. I loved Zara so much and wanted the best for her, which I could not give her. I sighed and sobbed and sighed and screamed at God. *Do you hate me? What did I do wrong?*

After taking one dose, the pain melted off my body. I smiled at Zara; she smiled at me. Zara always smiled even when life hurt for me. She smiled when I sobbed. God gifted me with a little girl that gave me grace when I held on to shame, guilt, and defeat. God who died on that cross for my sins and saved me with grace gave me a child full of grace so I would understand Him.

My husband desired for me to go back to work, though my body revolted. When he came home, I would rush to give him a kiss, only to be rebuffed. I labored for our marriage, proving my love to him. I grabbed him and swallowed him with my arms and he pushed away, tears falling like rain drops to the ground. Zara ran to me, jerking my finger and then clinging her arms to my leg. I picked her up, kisses everywhere. She was grace.

One time, when nearly two years old, she spotted me in my room sobbing over my life, my pain. She kissed every finger on my hand, sitting with me. God appointed her as an angel for me as I struggled, showing His unconditional love through her.

The guilt gulped me up; tears were my friend on a daily basis. I thought myself a horrific mom. I could not do enough activities with her because of my pain, while the parents of her friends spoiled them with activity after activity. Whenever I looked in her beautiful blue eyes, I never saw condemnation, only grace.

She is not a perfect child—far from it, actually. Even at five years old, she still has tantrums and knows my guilt will always yield any toy for her. Any lack in activity I replace with a doll, coloring books, new markers, a tea set, among many other things.

Despite her normal childlike nature, her love always overpowered me. When we moved from California to Colorado, fear engulfed me upon encountering a dreadful hail storm. Hail sheets tumbled on our car. Golf-ball-sized hail pelted the windows and doors. I screamed and screamed and screamed. She folded her miniscule hands together and closed her eyes, head hanging down. Her little lips moved as she prayed; she grabbed my hand, slipping her tiny one into mine. Her childlike faith put my doubting faith to shame.

To this day, she looks for me, peeks in every room, peers into my eyes. She will ask, "Mommy, why are you crying? Don't cry. I love you." She wraps her tiny arms around my neck, and I bury my eyes into her little shoulder.

Zara is a precious giver, a true gift from God. When I could not wrap my mind around the meaning of God's grace, she showed me one step at a time. She grabs my hand and kisses it, and I cry because the beauty in her spirit breaks me. I thank God every day for gifting me a beautiful spirit. She gives my life meaning, and demonstrates God's grace every day.

Author Bio:
Sylvia Ronnau is a wife, mother to a peppy five-year-old girl, appellate attorney, and writer. She also suffers from chronic pain and felt God calling her to write about His grace in our everyday lives, even when we go through hardships.

The PB&Js of Mommyhood
by Trish Winston

When I think of my experience as a mother, I think of a PB&J sandwich. I know that sounds a bit odd, but it's true. This vision of two light and fluffy pieces of wonder bread with a gooey but satisfying middle just comes to mind. I know.... weird, right? Just keep reading.

My story started off much like most stories about motherhood. I was chasing the fairy tale; husband first, then the home, built from the ground with all the fixings tailored to my liking, paid for with love (at least in my mind). When the time was right, we would add in a couple of perfect kids—one girl and one boy. Next I'd stir in yearly vacations on the beach, a pinch of weekend dinner parties on the deck, with a dash of lavish anniversaries, birthdays, and holiday shindigs, you know, all the ingredients for the American Dream.

My vision of being a mom was directly intertwined with the role of my husband being a dad. It was greatly detached from reality but very clear. My children would obey all of our directives because "we said so" and we would reward them. I would show them love always, and hubby would discipline them when needed to get them back on track and teach them right from wrong. In addition, my husband and I would provide them with the necessities for physical survival along with an abundant supply of tools needed for their inner man (or inner woman) to succeed, to be strong, persistent, ambitious, good-natured, spiritual, and have an abundance of wisdom to escape the many traps that are ever present in this world. In my eyes they would be soldiers and our mission would be to prepare them for the possibility of war.

This was my visualization of the role of a wife and mother in my depiction of the American Dream.

So let's see, I landed the husband, check. Come to find out, it took money (not love) to build a home, so we had to settle for an apartment to start, but we had a roof over our heads, so check. And I was pregnant with our first child, triple check! Life as I had envisioned it was on track and I was off to a great start!

Some time had passed and I had given birth to a healthy baby girl and was pregnant with our second bundle of joy... wait for it... another baby GIRL! I know, I know, not the duo I was hoping for, but what more can you ask for than two healthy babies, right? We were well on our way to being the parents I had imagined with two children in tow.

Life seemed... complete. But I was in for a rude awakening. Little did I know life was just getting started.

Six short years after marriage, my husband passed away, leaving me with two little girls to raise. We went from being co-parents to me being a single mom, from a duo to a solo just like that. I wanted to ball up and die. What do I do now? There was never a plan B. But I guess that's the whole point of a dream; very seldom is there much reality in it.

Anyway, I had sunk very low in depression and was seriously considering ending it all with the sorrow of losing my husband and my dream all at the same time, until I heard my oldest daughter cry. She was just in the other room, and although her cry was soft and lacked conviction, it was just the wake-up call I needed. It brought me back to reality. I still had two little princesses who called me mom depending on me. In that moment I felt ashamed that I even considered checking out.

So I had to pull it together. I prayed A LOT... and cried a lot too, but

I went on about the business of being mom; my perspective and strategy on parenting had not changed. I just had to do it alone now. I had to cultivate my soldiers, but life was about to teach me again.

I started teaching them as soon as they were able to learn, talking to them about life as soon as they could understand. Teaching them right from wrong through lecture, punishment, discipline, and the occasional example. However, there were several things I hadn't taken into consideration. Who knew they would be so unbelievably ADORABLE! Who knew that as they grew. I would be affected and somewhat swayed by their mini minds, will, and emotions; I was not prepared for these variables. I was caught by surprise. So I had to revise my approach to motherhood. I was a bit embarrassed that my strategy, while somewhat sensible in theory, lacked practicality. There was no wiggle room for human error at all, and let's face it, we all need wiggle room from time to time.

But wait, I certainly wasn't going to use my upbringing as a blueprint—I barely made it out. So what do I do? I could read some books, but there was no "parenting bible," so how would I know if I was applying the right strategy to each situation? And after receiving soooooo much input from surrounding loved ones, I was dizzy and more confused than before I started. So I turned to my faith once again—after all, my God had never let me down before. I mean, we were still working the kinks out of our relationship regarding my husband's death, but I was sure the kinks were on my end.

I began praying even more on wisdom to parent and God started to open my eyes to the inevitable truth that my little people would grow up to be big people one day and I had a hand in how whole or broken, how prepared or unprepared, and how knowledgeable or naive they would be when they arrived to adulthood. So when parenting, I've learned to ask myself these questions: is what I'm about to do going to hurt them or help them ultimately? Will it build them or break them? Is this a lesson they need to learn or did the consequences of their actions teach them well? What do they need from me the most right now? Do I punish, do I guide, do I nurture, or do I let slide? Whatever I decide, I am aware that the common denominator in any method rendered should always be love. I've realized from experience that any lesson taught, regardless of the tactic, is only effective if your child/children understand that your methods are love-driven. Love produces patience, while knowledge produces understanding, and understanding is POWER!

So of course I had to throw away my "because I said so" strategy. Children have "The Great Wonder," at least that's what I call it! They reach an age where they want to know everything about everything and it's up to us to teach them. This is natural and as it should be. So when we explain to them, for example, why we pray before we eat, why we don't run in the house on the tile floor, why we put seat belts on in the car, why we must eat, how are babies made, or why we lock our doors, etc. We are giving them the knowledge they need to understand how things work here on this planet which they have temporarily inherited. Giving them the "WHY" allows them to better and more quickly acclimate themselves to this place we call earth, And they are more likely to buy into the concept on a personal level and invest in doing the right things, if not immediately, eventually.

In my experience, I have also come to realize that telling your child "NO" is good. Say it with me! "No is gooooood." Now of course not all the time; they need to hear "yes" as well, this is also important. But my guess is that most parents don't have a problem saying yes. Telling your child "No" (and sticking to it) helps to develop these 5 key essential lifelong tools:

1. **Accountability:** If their yes was conditioned on a task they were to complete and did not, telling them "no" develops accountability.
2. **Rewarding:** Saying "no" after your child misbehaves teaches them

that bad behavior will not be rewarded.

3. **Coping:** Telling them "no" aids in allowing them to develop coping mechanisms; this will strengthen and quicken their ability to recover.

4. **Ambition:** "No" can be a serious motivator; if they want it bad enough. They will learn to keep working to correct whatever behavior or requirement is necessary to get that yes. Most successful people heard a plethora of "NOs" before getting that yes.

5. **Resourceful:** Hearing "no" teaches them to be resourceful. One "no" shouldn't always mean it's OVER. If they can't get it done one way, they will be able to find other viable options to achieve their goal.

These tools can only be developed if you consistently practice "sticktoitness" (yes, I just made that word up and I like it).

VERY IMPORTANT: Going back on your word can be more damaging to your child's growth than if you had originally said yes. So take the time to think your answer through. Don't make an emotional decision. Weigh out all sides. After you've done your due diligence, if your answer is "no," you must do your part and STAND YOUR GROUND!

Or follow my lead and say no *sometimes* for good measure; it builds character!

As I said before, saying YES is just as important as saying no. Children need to be rewarded. Well, while I'm on the subject, we ALL, if we are honest, need to be rewarded for the good that we do in one way or another. It's how we are built! But since we are focusing on mommyhood, I'll stick to the subject.

I've found that rewarding my children for things like consistently keeping their rooms clean, taking out the trash without having to be constantly reminded, bringing home good grades on the report card or showing that they are responsible and can be trusted in my absence goes a loooong way. When they know that I see the good they do and it means something, they continue to do well. Again, it allows them to buy into the process.

Notice that the examples given for rewarding DO NOT include singular acts. We can all do A good thing every now and then. Especially if we know we are going to be rewarded for it. I try to reward them for consistent efforts; it speaks more to what I'm trying to develop in them and keeps the process honest and effective. It also teaches them patience, tolerance, and what it means to attain goals; which are proven to also be extremely essential tools to have in succeeding as an adult.

So now, my daughters are all grown up. One is a student at Sam Houston University studying criminal justice and the other will be well on her way to college life in a couple of years. She's excited, focused and driven. I think for all intents and purposes. I've done well with an enormous amount of help from my Lord and Savior Jesus Christ... AND recently... wait for it... my NEW husband!

Yes, I tied the knot again!! Ten years later I am a proud wife to a great guy! He is definitely one of the good ones, and I'm so blessed to have him in my life and my daughters' lives. He brings new perspectives and a different approach to the table. More input is better than one input. I've found, It makes for a more objective and successful outcome, So I guess my dream of being co-parents was just deferred and not denied, huh?

Life is good again... it started out light and fluffy, then it got really gooey and tough in the middle although sweet because through it all I've learned some very important parenting lessons... but NOW it's light and fluffy again, Remind you of anything?

Author Bio:

Trish Winston was born on January 20, 1977 in Houston, Texas. She lived and attended school in Missouri City, Texas most of her younger years until she graduated high school. She joined the working class at the early age of 17, as her ambitions for independence couldn't wait any longer. At the age of 20, she accepted Jesus Christ as her Lord and Savior for the 3rd and final time and began serving at Fifth Ward Missionary Baptist Church. Soon after, at the age of 22, she became Mrs. Lamont Winston and they went on to have two beautiful baby girls, La Neysia and La Zoriah during their 6-year marriage. Trish became a widow on September 25, 2005 and went on to be a single parent. But on November 15, 2015 she wedded Quintin Murray and acquired 2 more beautiful children, Trayce and Tailyn Murray.

Mom Challenges, Struggles & Triumphs

"One day in July..."
by Tammy Coin

As a mom, we work hard to do our best and to be our best for our children. If we come from a particular background, our goal is often to do the opposite from our parents, because we want to improve for our children. Sometimes this is a good thing, and sometimes it's not. Sometimes we are faced with making decisions that can change the entire trajectory of the lives of our children. Even in those times, we attempt to do the best we can with what we have.

At 16, my dad was killed in a car accident and my life flipped upside down. I had been through so much pain by this point in my life, you would think I would be numb, but this pain was the worst so far. It was just two weeks before I started my junior year of high school. After that, my life became a little foggy. Within a few months, I had met a boy and we had our first date. A few months later in January, I turned 17. A few weeks later, I became sexually active and about a month later, I became pregnant. About two months after that, I got married. A few months after that, my journey as a mom began. I gave birth to my first child, just before Christmas that year. She was the most amazing little girl with a head full of dark hair and these big, gorgeous eyes. All I wanted was to be a good mommy. I worked really hard, took her to school with me and officially graduated mid-term the next month. She even attended the graduation ceremony with me a few months after that. I went on to start a federal career, hoping to give a good life to my little girl.

A few years later, when I was 23, I gave birth to my second child. This little one had a bald head and resembled a little football player. He was delightful and clearly a force to be reckoned with. Our life was often difficult, as it sometimes is, but one thing was clear: I loved these children more than I had words to say. When my little boy was ready to start school, the decision was made for their dad to stay home with them while I worked. He was a great stay-at-home dad. He cleaned the house, cooked the meals, and I often called while he was catching up on The Price is Right game show. He got the kids ready for school. He took them to school and was able to make every event called "Super Kids Day." We had a sweet little family, but as things happen when you start your life as teen parents, stress got the best of us.

Ten years after our teen marriage began, we chose to end in divorce. At this point, our kids were 9 and 4. We both loved our kids very much and we loved each other, we just needed to grow separately. With our divorce came the understanding that we would continue to co-parent our children and be the best parents we could for them. This worked out pretty well. In spite of our difficulties, we still managed to co-parent our children the best that we could. We attended every school function together. At least one of us attended every sporting event that our kids had, and their dad was even the assistant coach for our son's baseball team.

Their dad and I had often discussed if we would rekindle our romance and reunite our family. We felt that our children would have the best possible lives if we could just be a family again. As divorced couples go, we had a lot of healing to do, and didn't want to cause any upset for our children until we had a decision. So they were often unaware of these discussions. At this point, our kids were 14 and 9.

One day in July, just a month after our little boy had turned 9, things felt off. I didn't know why. I couldn't quite put my finger on it, but things just didn't feel right. I received a call from my ex-mother-in-law (who is still one of my favorite people in the world) and she asked me to come over. I didn't want to know why she called me, but I knew.

I asked my mother to come sit with my children, and I left to go visit with their other grandmother.

Their grandmother lived on the other side of town, but it was just about 15 minutes away. About 3 minutes before arriving at her home, I heard the voice of my children's father say, "Take good care of my kids." This voice came out of nowhere. It sounded like it came from the backseat of my car, but nobody was there. It sounded as if he had leaned forward and spoken these words into my ear. A knot tied in my stomach and a lump wrapped around my throat. I felt the air leave my lungs and the tears begin to fill my eyes. I tried to shake off what I had just experienced. There were no words.

A few moments later, I turned the corner to her home and saw the Highway Patrol sitting in front of her house. I stopped the car and got out. As the policeman approached, I began to cry and felt my knees buckle, and I fell to the ground. I knew why they were there. You see, 16 years after receiving the news that my daddy had been killed in a car accident, I was now going to have to give this same pain to my own children. After I got myself together, they began to ask me about identifying marks to identify his body.

It is one thing to tell your children no. It is one thing to disappoint them. It is quite another to have to give them news that completely changes the trajectory of their little lives. I felt frozen in time. How in the world could I deliver such pain to my babies? I'm their mommy. I'm supposed to protect them. I am supposed to shelter them from harm. I am not supposed to give them news that will shatter them.

I had to call my mother and ask her to bring my children to me. At that point, I had to sit my little 14-year-old girl and my little 9-year-old boy down and explain that their daddy was never coming home. I will tell you that I have survived physical abuse, sexual abuse, emotional abuse, and multiple traumas and nothing, and I do mean nothing, will ever compare to the pain I felt when I gave that news to my children that one day in July.

It's been over 19 years since that day, and the pain and sadness still fills my eyes and my heart as I write this. I am happy to report that even through the worst of times, we survive. Our babies are now 33 and 28. Our little girl works for the federal government and is raising our two-year-old little grandson and our little son is now overseas serving our country.

As a mama who has lived a lot of life and carried so much pain, I wanted you to know that no matter what you face, just remember to do the best you can with what you have. Do your best to learn better and do better. Sometimes, even in our darkest times, we still make decisions that let our children know how much we love them and it gives them the wings to fly.

Author Bio:
Tammy Coin is a Mind-Body Wellness Practitioner, Teacher and Speaker. She holds sacred space & helps you locate the unhealed emotions leftover from Childhood Abuse & Trauma that block the door to your authentic self. She then partners with you, using the pieces of her own life, to empower, motivate and inspire you to fully uncover your Soul Purpose.

Website: **www.thedoorsofwellness.com**

Every Fall Makes Me Stronger
by Veronika Quiñones

My story as a mom begins at my early 21 years. A beautiful pink baby with big brown eyes and very red lips arrived to this world through me. It's hard to explain with words the love I felt in that moment. Tears of joy ran through my face. I was being part of the wonderful miracle of life; I was now in charge of a completely dependent being.

Time went by and everything seemed fine, until one day in which I realized that I had to make a decision which I knew would affect my daughter for the rest of her life. I took the decision of separating from her dad. I was very young, insecure, with a lot of temperament, but with little character and will.

It was that day I knew that I couldn't keep waiting and tolerating a relationship full of immaturity, with lack of commitment and responsibility. I wondered, was this what I wanted for my daughter and myself? And my answer was no! In that moment, I filled myself with courage and took the decision of divorcing him, and I continued my life with my daughter.

I can't deny that in some occasions, when I looked at a couple with kids, I desired as a mom and a woman to live a life in a "normal" family made up by a father, mother, and children. But in that moment, I would remember that if my daughter had my love and I felt happy and calm, it was better than being in a relationship with both parents together, but hiding and covering unpleasant moments and holding on to the happy moments.

Time went by and I met a young man with whom I began to go out as something casual, until I realized everything was serious and official to the point that we started living together.

Years passed by in which I dragged guilt, fear, insecurities, inconformity, but always with the hope of giving my child that home I desired her to experiment. In occasions, I felt that it would never happen. I tried several times to get out of that relationship in search for what I truly wanted to live, but in all this process came a beautiful girl, white as snow and with yellow hair as the rays of the sun. From the time she arrived I was captive with her blue eyes and her smile full of love and light.

Since I was very little I wanted to find the answer to some questions, like why are we here? Where do we come from? Where are we going? And it was after Angelina's birth that I felt a sensibility and a strong need to evaluate my life. In this process life showed me a wonderful being that I already knew from a few years ago but only in this moment of internal reflection I made the decision to delve deeper in his teachings, which guided me to fill all those blank spaces and give answers to my deepest questions. It was here when I awoke from a dream of 28 years; it was here when I realized the importance of life, the purpose, and that is when I said to myself "I want a different life, I want to teach my daughters that when one makes mistakes, that person has to get up and continue, and that's how it was—I went on with my life with my two daughters, I got up and connected with the Divinity that exists within me.

It has been a hard job and still is, to forgive myself to not feel guilt of having two daughters of different fathers, and to constantly remind me that, if I want to help the two beings I must guide in this life, then I must be what I want them to be. The problem is not failing; the problem is not realizing, or even worse, realizing and going on because of fear and shame.

I wish to inspire and encourage all those women who feel ashamed of their mistakes, who feel guilty for their decisions, and invite them to forgive themselves. Forgiveness is powerful and will allow them to go ahead and convince themselves that they have the right to be happy and to live their dreams.

I wish that when my daughters are adult women and they have to take hard decisions, they have the learning and inspiration from their mom, that they can have the courage and the will, first to make right decisions by always measuring the consequences, and secondly, if they are wrong, they can extract the teachings and the good from that experience, and discard the rest to save it in the book of the past and use it as a reference only when needed, but never to blame or punish themselves.

Being a mother is a complex task; we never know if we're doing the right thing and if the result will be what we're expecting or what we planned. Each child comes with its own conditions that will make them go through situations that they must experience in order for them to learn to live. We can only be guides, motivation, and inspiration for them and provide them with the resources that facilitate the process of learning from their life lessons.

It's because of all these that our lives should be the example, so that they can really experience what we want to convey firsthand.

Children have what I call energy leaks, and this means that there are things such as school, television, music, friends, etc. which are not always in tune with our values and our lifestyle. This is why even if we want to have everything under control, unfortunately it is not possible; somewhere there will be an escape, and we must be prepared to accept it and take the necessary measurements for it to not harm their lives by strengthening the foundations of a life full of qualities such as love, honesty, righteousness, education, compassion, and service.

It is a journey that never ends. Day by day, as parents we must become better human beings and thus we'll be able to show the right path to our children. If you don't know, ask questions, read, investigate, and most importantly, connect with the Divinity that lives in you and you will be able to express extraordinary virtues that will make you a great mother and woman and will allow you to find the happiness and peace that you are looking for,which is within you!

The Journey of Special-Needs Motherhood
by Giuliana Melo

What is a mom? A mom is defined as being the female parent of a child. Moms are women who inhabit or perform the role of bearing some relation to their children, who may or may not be their biological offspring.

I had been married for ten years when I learned I was pregnant. It was a very joyous day! I performed three home pregnancy tests before the doctor verified I was indeed pregnant. You see, my husband and I had tried for years to have a child. We walked through a very difficult time of infertility. But that is another story. This one is a time for celebration of the miracle of becoming a mother. With pregnancy I felt a deep blessing until the end of the first trimester, when the alpha-fetoprotein test result came back saying that my beautiful baby would most likely be born with Trisomy 21, a birth defect where the baby doesn't survive long after birth. I was devastated. I searched my soul and I cried out to God.

Why? Why? The doctor recommended us to consider a therapeutic abortion. One day, as my husband and I tried to eat lunch, we both decided the response would be no.

We didn't want this story to end in that way. We were going to see the pregnancy to term and see the birth of the precious life we had been given. My pregnancy wasn't easy, with nausea and vomiting almost daily. Still, I loved being pregnant so much. I was ecstatic that God had finally chosen me to experience motherhood. But I also realized the enormity of the job, and come what may I was sure I would be ready.

I had a lot of love to give, I knew that for sure, and I had the full support of a hard-working husband. I loved my growing belly. I talked to it. I sang to it. I rubbed it. I loved feeling the baby move and play and hiccup. Hiccups especially were the funniest thing ever!

The night my water broke I heard this big pop, and as the bathroom was only a few feet away from the bed, I jumped up and ran into the washroom with water streaming down my legs. What an experience that was. After getting cleaned up, we drove to the hospital, where it was discovered that I was failing to progress. I ended up having a C-section.

My son was born blue, with the cord wrapped around his neck 3 times. Every time I had a contraction, he was denied precious oxygen. We didn't know at that time what the long-term effects would be. But he was gorgeous. He was healthy. He wasn't trisomy 21. I rejoiced. I had a beautiful baby boy.

My son reached all his normal milestones, but when he was 3, the babysitter noticed he was having some issues with attention. I have never liked labels, but after medical evaluations he was diagnosed with ADHD, mild cognitive delay, expressive and receptive speech delay, bilateral strabismus, and later on epilepsy and asthma. We became a part of the special-needs world. As he entered school, he received specialized help and support. I loved him where he was at. I gently guided him and advocated for him. When the doctor said he needed Ritalin, I naively gave it to him. When he became disengaged with life, I knew that was my cue to take him off the meds. The doctor agreed.

Sometimes, during our walk through the early years, I longed for normalcy. Or what I thought in my head normal was. When we were in the midst of typical kids, bad behaviors would escalate. I noticed he had sensory issues and sometimes didn't want to interact with other children. The doctor said he had autistic tendencies but never fit into the black-and-white diagnosis in this area. With those words I began to do what most mothers do when things go wrong: I blamed myself; I concluded that I must have done something to cause his special needs. As he got older and more side effects of the Ritalin were published, he read them and began to blame me for his weight gain while he was on the meds. This was an unhappy time for me, as I kept blaming myself. But in retrospect I know I did the best I could and I was always his champion.

During my own walk through an illness, I met an amazing mentor who taught me that as I healed, he would heal too. She taught me that children come to you and through you and don't belong to you. That it isn't your job to control them, but to guide them, to teach them, and to keep them safe. This is when my mothering took a 360-degree turn. I began to learn to trust my child's spirit. I learned that he had his own journey to experience and that I can't control it. I realized that God had assigned me to him to allow him to learn, grow, and expand his own soul. He had his own experiences. I had to trust him. I had to trust God.

Then I learned from Dr. Shefali on Super Soul Sunday that the myth of parenting is this: Parenting a child isn't about the child. Parenting is about you. She goes on to say, "If you don't raise yourself first and parent yourself, you will then aspire to make your child a mini version of yourself. So you are not really raising the child, you are raising yourself. So let's call it as it is. Rein in that ego. Parent yourself and then you will attune to your child. And then you will make space for the spirit of your child to unfold." WOW. I had a serious aha moment. It is true. Just like what my mentor had taught me. Heal myself and I will help him heal too. That really, my son's behaviors were mirroring me. When I was angry, he was angry. When I was sad, he was sad.

As I am healing, I am becoming a better mom. I love being a mom. It is my greatest job on this planet. I don't regret one moment of parenting. I love him with my whole heart. You see, I do recognize that he is the only person on this planet that has heard my heart from the inside. He is a part of me and I am a part of him. Together we are a part of God, and on a soul level we connected to get through this crazy life. Love. That's the answer to all of it.

After all, unconditional love, with faith, trust, forgiveness, and compassion are the five lessons we came to master, and by exercising all of these we can get through anything.

Author Bio:
Giuliana Melo is passionate about nontraditional healing and working with angels. Her own experience of walking through and healing from cancer caused an awakening in her spirit when she was asking WHY ME? When she realized WHY NOT ME? she experienced what GRACE is. She recently retired from a 31-year career in health care and has become a certified Mind, Body, and Spirit Practitioner. She has a strong faith and encourages many through her coaching. She also provides intuitive angel card readings and Reiki. She is an author contributor to the bestselling book *365 DAYS OF ANGEL PRAYERS* and also to *The Book of Love.* Giuliana is a Kindness Ambassador and created the "Kindness Crew CALGARY Society," which is committed to providing a hand up to the homeless and performing random acts of kindness. She has been married for 29 years and has an 18-year-old son who is the light of her life.

Website: **www.giulianamelo.com**

Finding a Village
by Stephani Roberts

When I was in my twenties, the phrase "It takes a village" popped up all around me. Hillary Clinton released her book in 1995 and created a conversation around what it meant to have that village.

As someone raised by a single mother of three, I understood the thought behind "the village." My mother knew she needed to work and loved the idea of going out into the world to make her mark, I think she felt liberated from her housebound status. But it was the 1970s and there weren't a lot of options for someone like her. I'm sure she prayed on what she should she do with three kids under age 9.

Brilliantly and against her parents' wishes, she figured out a way to make things work.

I was four years old when we moved out of our duplex and into a big building on a beautiful New England campus. We had a one-room living space with dormitory-style bathrooms. I learned that this place she moved us to was called a Christian commune. I didn't understand what "commune" meant but quickly felt welcome and surrounded by beauty and a loving community. As nutty as this move may seem by today's standards, it gave my mother a safety net and place full of security.

Our one large room was a big shift from a full home, but there were families nearby, all people like us who'd given up their traditional homes, and lots of moms around to watch us when our mom was working. We had large groups of kids to play with and gorgeous land to explore in a quaint little town. For us kids, it was quite an adventure. It was like being at summer camp year round. There were quirky people, lots of characters, tons of Christian events and social opportunities. I don't remember ever feeling bored.

We gave up a lot, though. Privacy, the convenience and comfort of personal possessions, and we moved along with the ministry as it branched out. One average, every year and a half we moved and started over. As exciting as it was at the time, our nomadic style of living never gave us a firm foundation of friends, neighbors, or people in our lives, and it took a toll on all of us. To this day my brothers and I struggle to find connections because while we uprooted, our commune friends stayed and built the foundation we were missing.

My mother's craving for a sense of adventure and a way to increase her income trumped our need for stability. She didn't want to slow down to see our family struggles, as she was otherwise occupied doing God's work offering Bible studies, helping drug addicts, homeless people, and lost souls. It doesn't make sense to some, but I've learned that this is not an uncommon experience for preachers' kids as well.

I decided that when I became a mother myself I'd do my best to tune in to my kids and see what their unexpressed needs were and attempt to meet them, or even better, encourage an environment where they could share their feelings openly.

But I became a mother in circumstances where, try as I might, even in the kindest of ways my own expressed feelings were ignored or incited arguments.

I left that toxic long-term relationship and found myself alone with my two little girls, a toddler and 6-year-old. Now in a better position to model the behavior I wanted them raised in, I was determined to find necessary social support and a sense of community wherever we would live.

Many of the places I looked at were in the next town over, cul-de-sacs with townhomes mostly full of single moms. I knew we'd be able to support each other and I felt drawn to these living spaces. I crossed my fingers and hoped the landlord would approve me in spite of my modest income.

I was hopeful, but I wasn't the only one who had say in the matter. The schools in the nearby town that I thought were a great choice for us were not as good as our existing school system, and my attorney felt it was risky to try to live there. From her perspective it looked like I could lose custody of my children if he stayed in our home in the better school district. So she spurred me on a mission to find a town with better schools where I could rent.

I was open to the idea—I would have done anything for my girls. Realistically I figured I'd lose my immediate connection to local friends if the distance was 30 minutes or more, but based on my first search in a neighboring town, I felt sure I'd find fellow single mamas ready to help each other out with moral support, babysitting exchanges, and appointments.

I targeted 4 towns in the top 10 school districts and found one that had affordable rentals, a choice of six elementary schools, and an abundance of nature.

Because God has a sense of humor, this town was also the same one I lived in as a baby right before my parents divorced. Life truly comes full circle!

I didn't have time to research the stats of the town, and honestly, that didn't even occur to me. The townhouse I found was affordable, had a garage, a basement, and was on a private street with mature trees.

Plus, I discovered we had access to a pool. As far as I was concerned, the gods were shining on me, and I was filled with gratitude for our new home.

It wasn't until about three or four months into our new arrangement that I realized I was quite possibly one of a handful of single parents living in our town. And though I was excited by the culturally diverse school my daughter was assigned to, it was comprised of married families from cultures where divorce was not acceptable and much less prevalent.

So much for my fantasy sisterhood of the single mamas.

In this town, being a single mom made me different and not relatable. A Scarlet Letter sort of existence began to unfold for me. Living this out day after day my, happiness for my newfound freedom transitioned into outsider depression.

What to do?

I saw that my mental state directly impacted my kids. I upped my self-care and spiritual practice, leaning on a pile of self-help books, audio books, podcasts, long walks, and consistent exercise. I found EFT (tapping), EMDR (Eye Motion Desensitization and Reprocessing), talk therapy, group therapy, yoga, meditation, and essential oils. All have been helpful in some way, but none of these replace the need for an actual village of people to connect with, rely on, and work together to raise our children.

The emotional needs of my girls through this life transition combined with the 3-hour commute to my work in higher education created a scenario of constant racing against the clock and stressing out. It became so severe that I took a leave of absence and was treated for PTSD. During my leave, we had space and time together to begin healing, and we were all much better off after 3 months. A re-org and mass exodus at work meant I'd rejoin a toxic scenario where employees were being forced out. With this in mind, I made the decision to strike out on my own and work for myself from home to continue our healing and to be available for my girls more consistently.

Initially, this made an instant positive impact on our family and reduced the crazed dashing. The downside is how hard we've had to work hard to create connections in a diverse community that tends to separate into cliques instead of the mingling that we were excited about when we moved here.

It's been over two years now, and I count myself lucky to have found a dear friend, another single mom, who swaps babysitting, and I've had her daughter for overnights to give her a break. My neighbor now swaps childcare time with me and is able to be there if I'm not home the minute my daughter gets off her bus. I've recently connected with moms who are new to the area and I'm beginning to know what it feels like to have a village. It's been a huge relief to me, and my daughters call one of their friends a sister. They love this new sense of connection and feeling included.

As women, I think we can support each other regardless of the disparity of income, marital status, religious, political, and cultural differences. And as mothers, we have perspectives and challenges to share that can positively impact how we are with our children and family.

Sometimes just having another parent tell you that they've been there, that they understand you without judgment, is all it takes to lift the guilt or anxiety of daily struggle. This allows us to be more present for ourselves and our children, and beautifully reinforces the idea that we are all connected—something so many of us yearn for in the current climate of divisiveness.

Author Bio:

Stephani Roberts is a proud solo mama of two energetic and creative girls ages 4 and 9. She hosts two podcasts and a live streaming video show based on empowering women to break free from societal expectations that keep them stifled and step into an Audacious mindset. As a Digital Strategist and Video Marketer, Stephani leans on her 20 years in Information Technology, higher education, and start-ups to help mompreneurs and small business owners leverage the power of video and storytelling to connect and attract clients through social media.

Website: **www.stephaniroberts.com**

The Single-Mother Struggle Is Real
by Jana McMullen

Single motherhood is hard! That statement surely requires an exclamation point. I never aspired to be a single mother. On that note, I'm fairly certain that the majority of women have that similar lack of aspiration. When I think back on the desires I had for the future, in my early twenties, I am 100 percent certain that at no time did the thought "I bet being a single parent would be kind of cool" enter my mind. I can also say that I never thought that I would have gone through a divorce by the age of twenty-eight either. Forget being divorced, I never even anticipated being married by the age of thirty, and yet take a look at me now! Married and divorced all before I hit the big 30. I guess one could look at this in a glass-full sense: "Wow look at all you've accomplished in the love department. What some don't even accomplish in an entire lifetime, you've managed to cycle through in a handful of years!" Note my dripping sarcasm in the matter. I'm not bitter, I swear. I love being a single mom. Maybe if I keep saying that over and over it will ring true?

No, really, I love being a mom. I could do without the "single" in front of that title, but if the option was single mom or no mom, then I choose the former. Not only do I love being a mom, but I am pleasantly surprised that I feel the way I do about motherhood in general. I understand that many of you reading this connected with the idea of being a mom at a very early age. You pushed that Suzy doll around like she was your very own. You burped her, you fed her, and you rolled your eyes when she wouldn't stop crying. You felt fulfilled as a mother... and you were six. Well here's a breaking news fact for you, I was never that girl. I was never the girl who wanted kids... ever. Sure, I wanted the lifelong partner who would travel to exotic lands with me. I wanted the one who would spend Saturday nights with me on the couch as we fell asleep to the sound of Dateline in the background, surrounded by half-empty Chinese food boxes and empty bottles of wine. But nowhere in that picture did I imagine that the wine-induced sleep would be interrupted by a seven a.m. wailing human alarm clock that was sure to induce a hangover headache the size of Texas. Nowhere in my mental picture of my future adult life did I imagine playing the role of soccer mom, attempting to make bunk beds (which are impossible to make I might add), or spending three hours on a Friday night turning the living room back into the living room, post couch fort. Those thoughts held not even an inkling of possibility in my mind. But if we're being honest, I am so happy that I'm not the only one who has influence over my mind's direction. Thank you sweet Jesus for taking the wheel of the bus that was steering my mind. Had I remained on the "my life, my way" bus ride, I would not have experienced half the joy that I've experienced in the past six short years, and that I am sure of.

Single motherhood is hard. Have I mentioned that? Well, I'm going to say it again. When you're a single parent, you don't have the option of saying "I'm just running to the store because we're out of milk" when we all know that's code for "I just need a break from my life for a minute or I'm going to explode." You don't have the option of playing good cop, bad cop. You are, and will always be, bad cop. You don't have that person to bounce punishment ideas off of, or help coordinate pick-up and drop-off schedules, or serve as an extra hand when one child needs help with math and the other has a science project due the next day. You never get to say the phrase "your turn." For those of you who do get to say that phrase, you have no idea how lucky you are, even if it ends up being your turn. Just being able to say it releases a sense of satisfaction unlike any other. Being a single mom means that you do it all... solo. Oh sure, you have people that offer to help and sometimes you have people that just help without the offer (those are the best kind of people), but at the end of the day, it's all you, girl. I know what it's like to lay your head on that pillow at night and feel accomplished that you rocked out that day. I also know what it's like to then roll over and have that feeling of accomplishment be followed up with the reminder that you have no one to share that feeling of accomplishment with. Single motherhood can be a lonely island. Sure, the island is covered with monkeys (aka your children), but let's be real, even the monkeys will ask you to peel their bananas for them.

I am only six short years into my motherhood journey and yet I have learned more about myself in the past six years than I did in the twenty-six years that came prior to them. I have learned that the dreams I had for my life prior to having children dwarf in comparison to the dreams I now have for us, for myself and my children's own path to parenthood. I have learned that thinking about "us" takes me to a whole other level of fulfillment than the thought "me" could ever take me to. I have learned that the best things in life come when you least expect them to, and I am reminded of that each night as I attempt to tuck my mini me into her nightmare of a bunkbed. Single motherhood is not easy, but I'll be darned if it isn't rewarding. You get to take credit for all of the passed spelling tests and all of the "here, let me hold the door for you" comments your child makes. You get to spoil them without answering to anyone else. You get to let them stay up late to watch old reruns of Fresh Prince of Belair with you. They won't even judge you for your choice in 90s television because they will think it's just as awesome as you do. You get to watch them grow, and know without a shadow of a doubt that you are helping influence them, you're helping them grow into the person they will become, and that person will be amazing.

Single motherhood comes with a large weight of responsibility, and it is not for the faint of heart. I can promise you, though, that if you are ever faced with the reality of single motherhood, that you will surprise yourself, and you will rise to the occasion. You just need to be prepared to let Jesus take the wheel for a day or two, or three, or four. I am confident that my motherhood journey will take me down many untraveled roads and probably up a few creeks, but I am looking forward to the adventure, even if I have to lug all the travel gear myself.

Author Bio:
Jana McMullen is a life and entrepreneurial coach for mothers. She is a divorced, single mother to one child, an exact replica of her six-year-old self. She loves to travel, write, read, and collect hotel-room keys. She resides in both British Columbia, Canada, and Coeur D'Alene, Idaho,yet she considers her future home to be somewhere on a beach.

Motherhood: The Initiation from Girl to Goddess
by Michelle McMillan

Some women step into motherhood already having experienced life and already knowing who they are. They may have already finished college and focused on careers for some time. Or maybe they explored the world a bit as a single young woman before deciding to settle down. Perhaps they got married and took some time to truly experience their partnership before becoming a mother.

I was 18 and had just graduated from high school when I first saw those two pink lines that indicated that I was pregnant with my first child. A million thoughts ran through my mind, most of which were based in fear, anger at myself, and a bit of embarrassment. My life at that time revolved around going out with friends, spending time with my boyfriend, and lots of partying. My future plans had focused on what college I was going to attend and figuring out what I would be "when I grew up." The idea of being a mom had not yet been anywhere on my horizon. Yet here I was, with a new life beginning to grow inside me. I took a deep breath, put my hands on my belly, and said "hello, little guy." It was time to start making new plans—to quickly figure out what kind of mom and woman I wanted to be and how I might get there.

The next eight months were not particularly easy. My boyfriend stuck around, but he was quite overwhelmed, and dealt with it by going out more with his friends and drinking. Obviously, the news created some stress within my family, and my mother and I argued fairly often about this mess that I had gotten myself into. I worried quite a bit—about money, what kind of mom I would be, what labor and delivery would be like, and how I could teach a son to grow up and be a man when I was still just a young girl myself. However, I quit some bad habits, cleaned up my life a bit, and started looking more to the future. I spent most of my time focusing on how to be a good mom. Knowing that I wanted to be in a healing profession and that I wanted to provide for my son, I enrolled in a nursing program and planned to start a few months after my baby was born.

Attending Lamaze classes as a teen, with my grandmother at my side, was informative and awkward. In a room full of several couples in their 30s, I was definitely the youngest there. All my own doubts and insecurities reared their ugly heads, as I imagined the judgement from the couples around me. Where was the father? How could I have done such a thing? What kind of mother could I possibly be at that age? But as I felt my son move in my belly, my fears and insecurities were put on hold, and I somehow knew that it would all be all right. One thing I learned in that class served me well going forward, and that is to just focus on my breathing. Doing so doesn't just help with labor and delivery; it helps with life!

I was amazed at the idea of life beginning and growing inside my womb. Labor was scary and painful, but I focused on my breathing and took it one contraction at a time, just as I had learned and practiced. I remember the feeling of power and accomplishment as I gave that last push, and out came this wet, squirmy little being! And when I held my firstborn son for that first time, it felt as if I could reach out and touch the galaxies just by looking in his eyes. I could literally see and feel the power of creation that had come from within me, and I was so grateful in that moment! It hit me that my life isn't what other people necessarily saw it as. My life was to be whatever I wanted it to be... and how exciting that felt!

Life was still quite challenging for me for the next several years. While juggling the needs of my son, I went to nursing school during the week and worked full-time nights on the weekends as a home health aide. Thank goodness my family was very supportive during that time, as I could not have made it without them. After my son turned two, I married his father, which added more to my already full plate. Two years later, shortly after finishing nursing school, I discovered that I was expecting another baby. At that time, RN jobs were difficult for new grad nurses to obtain, as all the hospitals only wanted experienced nurses. So, after my daughter was born, we packed up and moved across the country and far away from our families so that I could finally get a nursing job.

Three more years passed, and we had another son. We had some good times, but things were quite difficult. During those years, I was just functioning in a fog of being focused on work, paying bills, trying to meet the needs of my kids and husband, and keeping up with household needs. My identity was so merged with my roles of wife, mother, nurse, and provider, I still didn't know who I was as an individual and as a woman. As time passed, the struggles and the distance between my husband and I became too wide, and I ended up initiating a very ugly divorce.

Because I had not really taken the time to find out who I was yet, my divorce process forced me to do so in a brutal way. Past traumas that I hadn't yet dealt with came up to the surface to be healed, and it did not look very pretty. I made many different choices during that time, some that I regret. They say everyone goes through a dark night of the soul. My soul went through a dark decade as I fought the life lessons thrown at me, as well as my own reflection in the mirror. The mistakes I made during that time led to my firstborn adult son deciding to cut contact with me. It was a dark, painful time, and there were times that I honestly didn't believe that I could survive. However, it was my children, the life that I wanted them to have, and the hope that they inspired in me that kept me waking up each morning and moving forward each day, despite my many missteps.

During that dark time, I had my fourth and final child, another daughter. I was no longer working overtime, so I had the opportunity to really be there to experience and enjoy the different stages of her early development. And as she grew, so did I! She taught me to slow down and to pay attention to the smaller moments, as those can be the most miraculous. She taught me to see the light again.

Through all of my experiences as a mother, I saw how precious life is, and how important it is to nurture the relationships closest to our hearts. I learned that I am human and imperfect, and that I will still make mistakes, but that I can learn from them. I learned how to apologize. I learned to love myself fully and completely. I learned that I am a much better mother when I take time to nurture myself, and that it is OK to do so. I learned about patience, gratitude, and unconditional love, and how practicing these qualities makes the world a better place, starting in my own home. I learned who I am—not just in a role as a wife, daughter, mother, or nurse—but just as myself... as a woman... as a Goddess with the power to create. I realized my power to wake up each morning and create a new life, with the new day, just by changing the way I look at things. I began to chase after my own dreams and passions, the things that lit me up inside. In doing so, I found true peace and joy.

Some women step into motherhood already knowing who they are. But my journey of motherhood was more of an initiation—of breaking down what I thought I knew and rearranging my life in a way that taught me about myself. Motherhood started me on a journey of empowerment and showed me the power I have to truly create my life. And I wouldn't trade my journey for the world.

Author Bio:
Michelle McMillan lives in Arizona with three of her children (ages 7, 17, and 20). Though she worked as a nurse for more than 20 years, Spirit took her on a wild and wonderful journey, landing her

in a far different place than planned. It has been said that "The love of Michelle's energy can be felt from across the world." Indeed, this energy is palpable as Michelle shares her stories and uses her gifts of healing, mediumship, and soul coaching to show others what is truly possible and how to create the lives of their dreams.

Website: **www.KaliHealingCenter.com**
Email: **KaliHealingCenter@gmail.com**

Enlightened Parent
by Lydia Samuel

There is a popular saying, "Kids don't come with an instruction manual." It is so true, but also so obvious that they don't need a manual in the first place. Why? Simply because we learn a lot from them instead of the other way round—that is if we realign with our intuition. That's my story.

When I was pregnant with my first, I was very excited and had a long script in mind about what would be my first words to her after she was born, what would I tell her everyday as she grew up and what would I advise her so as to help her in this challenging world. Little did I know that this script of mine would soon be trashed.

I have heard that having kids is a life-changing experience. It indeed was and all for good. As she grew up and I made a decision to consciously listen to my inner voice, I just let her lead my way. The very fact that she loved staying in nature more than anything else taught me how disconnected I was with nature. I never had to tell her to water the plants, feed the birds, get grounded in the grass, etc. since those were like her innate nature and she came preprogrammed with those thoughts and feelings. That was such an eye-opener and a profound experience for a mom who wanted to teach her that food grows on plants and water comes from rivers and lakes and not from a supermarket. It just felt like she already knew everything that I wanted to teach her. It just proved to me again that I was the one who needed lessons on realigning back to my intuition.

One of those rushed-up busy mornings, I was almost at the verge of losing my patience when my daughter was late to school but wanted to catch a butterfly and was refusing to get into the car. I was so close to yelling when my inner voice asked me to follow what she does. She was just running behind the butterfly describing it for me, saying, "Mommy it's yellow with blue dots, looks very beautiful. Is that a monarch?" I had no idea.

I said, "let's look it up on the Internet."

She said, "No, momma, let's follow it," and there she found a few more really vibrant and beautiful colors. "It doesn't look like monarchs, ma," she said, citing a remarkable difference between monarch and other butterflies. I was stunned because I never even realized that she was actually paying attention to the books I read to her. Every single thing I did and said made a huge impact on this beautiful, tiny human being who was looking up to me like I was her encyclopedia. Little did she realize she was teaching me beautiful lessons to get back to my intuition.

Children are like sponges. What we do impacts them more than what we preach. It is the actions that matter. Even today I regret saying things to her that I should not have when I see that getting passed on to her younger sibling. I tell her, "No, that's not how to treat him, mommy might have said that to you accidentally and I'm sorry about it." Life was such a huge roller coaster ride when God sent her to our family, and it only has made me a better person. I'm so grateful for her in my life, since she taught me life's valuable lessons of listening to that quiet inner voice and realigning with my intuition, re-prioritizing and recalibrating my goals in life.

The second one came along with another amazing round of life lessons. I was 5 months pregnant with my younger one and an appointment with a holistic dentist made me realize I have been mercury poisoning myself and the little one that I was carrying now. In addition to that, the dentist said based on the amount of heavy metal poisoning, there was a high possibility that the baby might have neurological disorders. That moment I badly wished there was an option for me to turn back and give him a clean environment for his nine months inside me and start off over all again. I ran from pillar to post to mitigate the situation. I had thankfully decided to take a long break from the corporate world at that time. I thought I would use this opportunity and not leave one stone unturned to see how I could bring him whole, pristine, and unscathed from my doses of mercury.

It was discovered during my labor that he was a face up, but I decided to go with natural birth without epidurals or any other intervention. I was warned multiple times by the hospital staff that it was better to opt for a C-section and go with pain medications, but after my 5 months of research when I was pregnant with him, I realized the risk was totally not worth it and opted for a natural birth. He finally came out after much struggle and there I was high in oxytocin touching my newborn and feeling him for the first time. Tears of gratitude rolled down my face when I saw him whole and he was already holding my fingers. My maternal instincts immediately told me there was no neurological damage whatsoever, and he was whole as I wished.

I still was skeptical what else could have happened to my child when I was unknowingly dosing him with mercury from my dental amalgams each day. The answer came 2 weeks later when he suddenly turned colicky and was crying for hours. I was so desperate crying along with him and unable to take his pain away from him. I had no clue what was happening to him. He slept only 3 hours for the whole day and was crying and in so much pain the rest of the day. The pediatricians had no clue. They said let us put him on some antihistamines and Benadryl to make him sleep. Let us also inject the toxic cocktail of vaccinations into him so he doesn't get infected by the "so-called" deadly diseases. That was the last day I stepped into a pediatrician's office. The mama bear in me which was so sleep-deprived and mad at the dentist for putting those toxic things in my mouth was desperate for answers.

I did hours of research at night and assured everyone at home even though he was in so much pain I couldn't let him go the conventional way. I needed to get to the bottom of it. The answer to my prayers came in the form on an amazing homeopath that we met in Toronto. She was ready to take up the case even though he was just 2 weeks old, and over multiple discussions we decided where to start and what the protocol should be. He had myriad of issues, ranging from low stomach acid leading to acid reflux and candida overgrowth. There were no supplements or herbal tinctures available for a baby that young. The little guy had to be on 9 different herbs and supplements for that period and he was only thriving. That was followed by another year of roller coaster trying to get his candida in control and after almost 2 years of his life he is whole, pristine, way ahead of his schedules, the most kind and awesome human being ever.

It is a testimony to our faith in God and how nature's pharmacy is so powerful and it only has positive effects. The side effects to his treatments are that he bounces off from any sort of infection or fever in a day. Praise be to God alone! What a joy, and I saw firsthand the body healing itself when you provide the right inputs. I only wish I knew what I know now, before my first one was born. I could have prevented her consuming a lot of junk the first three years of her life. But after a long time now I'm out of my guilt for ignorance and I do the right thing by detoxing her and filling her with loads of goodness from nature's pharmacy, hoping someday she will thrive like her brother.

I guess I'm into a tribal parenting mode now, the term I learnt from a blogger. I grew up in a big family with both grandmothers, one grandfather, and an aunt. It was a common thing in my generation back home in India where I co-slept with my mom until I was 10. Sounds weird, right? But she never forced me out, and it was that decision of hers and the outcome that made me think I'd do the same for my kids and I stick to it. It brings in a lot of moral and emotional support and you always know your parents will stand up for you no matter what. If I think about it now, I guess I took it for granted that there was always someone home to listen to my banters, answer my questions, give a shoulder for me to cry on, and make me the emotionally strong person that I'm now. I hope someday I can pass on to my kids the same cultures and traditions that made me the person that I am now.

Author Bio:
I, Lydia Samuel, am a mom of 2 amazing kids, and my life spins around them for the most part. It was because of them I got super passionate about a healthy lifestyle and realized what the difference is between barely living and thriving. I'm a computer science engineer by profession. But I suddenly found my bigger purpose, my calling when I was helping my little one heal from a heath crisis. I realized how amazingly the human body can heal itself given the right inputs and I also realized I'm more inclined towards research on health topics and helping friends and family figure out the root cause of their health ailments. Someday I hope to help people beyond friends and family achieve their health goals.

Growing with Grace
by Merianne Jackson

I remember repeating the words "I'm having a boy," over and over my head for the entire nine months. I'd only known the world of pink and little girls, so this would be completely new territory I was exploring. The range of emotions were from excited, to scared, and then to elated. I had the usual aches and pains, but overall a good pregnancy. Then on a beautiful March morning my Andrew came into this world and I had no idea how he would change my life.

As a baby he was quite normal. He was happy and healthy; and I was truly in love. As he grew into a toddler, I started noticing things such as not talking, minimal eye contact, and above-normal hyperactivity. Several times I shrugged it off, saying he's just a boy, and it must be normal. But that feeling in my gut just wouldn't go away; I knew something wasn't on track. I had him evaluated by several professionals. Outcome was that he had some speech delays and ADHD. I didn't know what a challenge this would be for me, but I knew I had no choice. I began researching everything I could find on ADHD. I had so many questions and so many doubts. I knew that I would be his number-one advocate and it was my job to do what I could for him.

Along the journey I didn't realize how this would actually affect me. You see, when you deal with a child with ADHD, you learn a lot about yourself and ultimately you grow.

The reality is that I can say I'm a better person today because my son has ADHD. One of the first things I had to grow in was compassion. I had to understand what was really going on with him and the fact that he had no control over it. I had to mentally put myself in his shoes and feel what he was feeling and grow my compassion for something that he didn't ask to have. I have now learned to use more compassion in my daily life and it's become a tool that's made me such a better person.

Another wonderful way that I've grown is in my patience. Patience is a nonnegotiable when dealing with ADHD. You are dealing with a child who does not have the ability to stay still or focus. Patience was hard for me—I can barely handle the supermarket line—so yes, he stretched me. I've now learned to ground myself and to take deep breaths. I never knew I could do this. My life was about the rush and getting things done quickly. Andrew has given me the ability to slow down. He has given me the remarkable gift of growing in my patience.

Another part of this journey that I'm grateful for is my ability to trust myself and go with my own intuition. As a mother I've had to learn to trust myself. When you have a bunch of medical professionals and educational staff tearing you in one direction and your gut tells you it's the wrong way, it takes strength to stand your ground. They're professionals, what do I know?

It takes strength to listen to that inner voice and know that you as a mother are making the right decision for your child. I can now say that I know what's best for my son and I don't care how many degrees or accreditations you have, you can't tell me otherwise. I've been able to sit at a round table listening to groups of professionals tell me what they think of my kid and how difficult his life will be or how he really isn't going to be able to function unless I do exactly what they tell me and still stand my ground with conviction.

I must say the most valuable lesson my son has given me is the ability to love unconditionally with grace.

When I look at my son I see nothing but a remarkable, smart, creative and happy human being. I wouldn't change anything about him or anything about my journey as a mother to him. I am eternally grateful for this experience growing me into the person and the mom I am today.

Andrew is now nine years old and running for student council. It doesn't matter if he wins or loses, he's already a winner in my eyes.

Don't Be Too Proud to Admit
by Janie Saylor

October 18, 2013, 9:38 a.m.:

Noticing the incoming call, it was Jake, my son. What the heck was he doing calling me at this hour? He was supposed to be in class at school. I'd spoken to him previously about using his cell phone from school; he knew it was prohibited. Nothing in the world could have prepared me for what I was about to hear… "Mom, I need to let you know I won't be able to contact you in any way for 30 days. I'll be in drug rehab." He was 17.

I was completely blindsided. It felt as if someone had physically knocked the wind out of me. I pried for more information, but he only had time to reiterate what I wished I hadn't heard the first time, let alone a second. He disconnected and I sat in complete silence as the words I'd just heard finally sank in. With one deep breath I tried to gather my thoughts, but the only thought that mattered to me at the time was, "How could I have not known?" Tremendous guilt came over me. "What kind of mother wouldn't know her son was using drugs?" The abundance of tears that began to fall on that autumn morning stung my eyes. My heart felt broken.

Somewhere along the line I'd failed my son.

His father and I had divorced ten years prior. We'd shared physical custody of Jake and his older sister until four years previous, when his sister, at age 16, and he at 12, made the decision to stay at their dad's full time. I was crushed by this news. I knew I could fight it in court… but I also knew that even though I knew their dad had told them horrible lies about me, I couldn't bring myself to put them through that. I didn't want them to hear what I would have to say in court. Not to mention I was still scared out of my wits of their dad and his manipulations. He'd told me he'd fight me in court for full custody when I first began contemplating divorce from him years before. There were several more threats that followed. At the time I was so used to the manipulations, I believed them. I was naïve and I didn't know the truth... so I let them go. At the time we still lived in the same small town. I made a point to see them every single chance I could, which could never have been often enough for me. I didn't share with them the depression I fell into after their decision, I didn't think it was necessary for them to know how deeply this decision had cut me.

Looking back, I'm now able to see the fact that I did what I thought was best for them by letting them go. The decision to not share with them my hurt, I still feel was a wise one. They were far too young to hear some of the things I had to say, and I didn't feel, at their age, it was necessary to express my pain to them. They still needed protection.

Late October 2013:
Somehow, I'd managed to survive the pain I had within myself as well as the pain I was feeling for Jake. What would make him so unhappy he thought drugs were the answer? I'd raised both of my children giving them age-appropriate information about drugs and alcohol. When I felt they were old enough to know, I told them that addiction ran in both mine as well as his father's family. Their dad had started drinking again shortly after our divorce finalized, but even during the years their dad wasn't drinking, during our 14-year marriage, he was still unhappy and manipulative, but I never told them their father was an alcoholic. Again, I felt I was protecting them.

Jake's therapist had made an appointment to speak with me. I'd have the first opportunity to see or talk to Jake in more than two weeks. As I drove to the rehab that day, I wanted answers. Was he okay? When did he start using? What made him start using in the first place? More than anything I knew I needed to apologize for not knowing. I felt like a horrible mom.

During this appointment, I learned Jake had been using drugs and alcohol since he was 12. I cried and apologized profusely for not being there for him and because I didn't know. The words I heard from my 17-year-old boy's mouth made me realize a couple things... He'd said, "Mom, please don't blame yourself for not knowing, and there's nothing you could have done to change what happened. Don't you see? I was so addicted it was actually easy for me to hide this from you." I realized the wisdom of his words. Although I wasn't convinced that it wasn't my fault and that I should have known, his wise words somehow comforted me in that moment.

One of his assignments from his counselor was to write a letter to each member of his family and explain the part they'd played in causing him discomfort in his life. The letter I received from him still rests in a small box in my room. To this day, reading his letter makes me cry. Not because he expressed all of the pain I'd caused him, just the opposite. He wrote about what I'd taught him. He explained how much he'd learned from me and he hoped someday he could be as much of an ideal person to everyone around him as I was to everyone around me. He did explain some areas where I'd gone wrong, but his main focus was on everything I'd done right. It was the most heartwarming letter I could have ever received.

January 17, 2016:
Flash-forward to this year. Going through rehab in 2013 was the first of four rehab stays over the next three years. Jake, now 19, called me in the afternoon from college and told me about the trouble he'd been having with his roommates. He said he was sad. I told him, "It sounds like you need someone to talk to. If you ever need to talk about it, day or night, no matter the hour, call me." He nonchalantly stated that I'd said that many times in the past. "Yes!" I told him, "and

you've never taken me up on it!"

That very night, about midnight, he called. He completely unloaded his emotions and expressed his need for help with his addiction. Over the last three years, I had aligned myself with many, many people in the addiction and recovery community. I'd become an advocate helping others who were in need because of their or their children's addiction. Now, I had connections. After our long talk, he agreed to let me call in some favors, and I was able to get him into an out-of-state rehab facility in Pompano Beach, Florida. This time he'd be in rehab for at least 60 days, possibly 90. A far cry from the 21-27-day stints he'd had at facilities in our state. He called me on a Sunday, and by the following Saturday he was on a plane to Florida.

March 5, 2016:
I was on a plane to visit Jake at rehab in Florida. His counselor had expressed that if there was any way I could get down there and be a part of some of Jake's therapy sessions, that great strides could be made. That turned out to be an understatement. I participated with him in several sessions, a small group session, a large group session, and two individual sessions.

In our small group session, his counselor asked us to move our chairs to the center of the room to talk to each other. These were the most powerful moments I'd ever had with my son so far. He asked me questions about the marriage, about my life. It was different now. I felt it was okay to tell him some of the things I'd never spoken of; he had the support of his peer community and his counselor to help him through anything after I left. This couldn't have been a more perfect opportunity. We aired our feelings. Shared our thoughts. And both cried... A LOT! But we came out of these sessions with a brand-new relationship. He told me he felt horrible for thinking the way he had about me all those years, blaming me for certain situations. I told him I couldn't care less what he thought of me prior to this day. The only thing that mattered now was what we did with this newfound information and our new relationship.

He spent almost 70 days in Florida and is doing quite well now and our relationship is something a mom only dreams of.

I have advice I'd like to share from my experiences here:

- Always love your children NO MATTER WHAT... And tell them those words every chance you get... And be prepared for whatever, NO MATTER WHAT that might be. It will get very trying.
- Be honest with your children from the beginning in age-appropriate ways. Don't unload your "dirty laundry" on them just to get back at your ex or for any other reason (you'd be surprised how many people do). If you want them to be open with you, you need to be open with them and share your goods and bads (within reason) along the way. And hopefully, someday you'll be able to tell them more.
- Begin sharing information about drugs and alcohol with your children, in age-appropriate ways, from a young age every opportunity you get. Even a three-year-old can learn they're not supposed to take medicine unless you give it to them.
- Educate yourself with the signs of alcohol and drug addiction. It's very easy to sit back and claim the "NOT MY CHILD" role. Please, don't be this person. Addiction knows no boundaries.
- Addiction is a disease, NOT a choice. The first time they use, that's a choice, but after that, it rapidly is no longer a choice. When your child says they want to stop... It's not that easy. Get them into a program that has mental-health counseling as well as substance-abuse counseling.
- If you suspect your child may be using drugs or alcohol, DON'T BE TOO PROUD TO ADMIT IT! Reach out. Ask for help. Believe it or not, addiction is everywhere. Shame and guilt is what keeps people from discussing it. There are many support groups, both online (Facebook) and in person. Get yourself some answers and

help even if you aren't able to get help for your child at this time.

Author Bio:

Born with a positive attitude and the ability to see life from a different perspective, Janie Saylor is a trained life coach with a BS degree in Psychology and a focus on the field of Positive Psychology. As the author of The Road You've Traveled: How to Journal Your Life, Janie has been involved in the self-development field since 2001 and is determined to research, study, and continue to help herself and others to flourish in their lives.

Facebook: **www.facebook.com/BecomeUniversity**

I Choose Love, Not Fear
by Joslyn Bryan

Motherhood was one of those blessings I never thought I would experience, yet I found myself the mother of three boys who were perfect right down to how each little freckle was placed upon their baby-soft skin.

Life seemed complete. It seemed like I had it all together from the outside looking in. As the years progressed, though, I just couldn't be the woman my husband at the time expected me to be. The anger turned to abuse, not just to me but towards my children as well. As a mom, you never expect someone who is meant to love and protect you to turn on you, but that is what happened. I remember one night I got the children and myself in the car while he was out and we just drove away. It was then or never, and I knew if I wanted a better life then that was my chance to make it happen.

The days and weeks following were a blur of emotions. I knew I had done the right thing for my children; I felt relief, like I had a chance for us to be happy. There were days were I still felt emotions of fear, guilt, and sadness, but I knew if we went back, nothing would ever really change. I knew that no one can change unless they want to change themselves. I couldn't heal him, so I turned to healing my children instead.

We spent the following months rebuilding our lives. I wanted to show my children it isn't what happens to you in life but how you react that counts. It taught me that if you want a better life, then you will find a way to make it happen.

Becoming a single mom taught me fears were just thoughts, and that being a single mom doesn't mean I am broken or we are broken as a family, it means we did what we needed to do to become whole again.

The cycle of abuse has a way of creeping in from one generation to the next. The environment we raise our children in becomes a foundation for them to base their lives on. To break the cycle, we must know within ourselves that we can support ourselves, we can make our children grow up knowing love is the answer and that we can be worthy of a better life.

I'm so grateful my children now know how to make choices from love and not fear and to know that violence and control are not the way to happiness.

Being a single mom taught me what real love is. Each and every moment since then I have used that to fuel my soul to guide them into living a life full of love where they can reach their full potential and break the cycle in our family once and for all.

Author Bio:
Joslyn Marie is the founder of the Soulfire Technique, a personal and spiritual development method that helps women discover and stay connected to their own personal and spiritual practices. This technique helps women to connect to their inner guidance, abundance, and life purpose, creating a life of balance and flow in every aspect. Joslyn Marie is a certified International Coach, Spiritual guide, and meditation teacher. She has also trained in many healing and personal-development techniques including Theta healing and NLP to help women free themselves from limiting thoughts, beliefs, and patterns. Her passion is to show women how to embrace themselves as a whole.

Facebook: **www.facebook.com/joslynmariesoulfire**

MINE
by Leah M. French

My daughter, Mia, came to me late in life. I would tell you that I waited to have children, but that just isn't true. I avoided having children, in whatever possible way. My own miserable childhood cured me of any notion I had of ever being a mother. But when I was 20 I learned I was having a baby boy, and it scared me to death. I had no maternal inclinations. Early in the pregnancy I had chosen a family to adopt my son. We worked together on things like choosing a name, and I invited the adoptive mother into the delivery room so she could be there when her baby came into the world. All along, people made me feel as if I was doing a wonderful selfless thing giving my baby to a childless couple. But that changed once he was fully separate from my body; there was a turbulent stampede and barking to "get that baby out of here!" I heard him let out his first cry while being made to feel like that was more than should be allowed. I never saw him. I didn't understand it then; I do now. Over the years we had sparsely kept in touch, but when I visited him or spoke to him as he got older, I felt unfairly judged. I loved him, although we were very disconnected.

I failed at every kind of relationship I had. And so my relationship with Mia's dad was a disaster from the start. It was a violent, three-and-a-half-year mind game. I got very sick from the stress of it. My hair fell out. Lymph nodes throughout my entire body swelled. Lumps formed in my skull, which were painful to the touch, and my psoriasis flared terribly. I began to use a healing guided imagery CD we had made for my mom when she was dying. This was my first experience with meditation, which guided me through self-healing and then to visualize myself on a path 5 years in my future. There is only one purpose in telling you all that, which is: although I had no reason to imagine anyone other than familiar faces, I repeatedly saw myself walking hand in hand with a little girl. Every single time I used the disc, she was there. I had no idea what it could mean, since I wasn't harboring some secret desire to bear children, even still in my late 30s.

A few months passed and I had reached my limit within this toxic relationship. I ran away. I recall starting my period that morning, and after walking miles to a friend's house, the bleeding stopped. That night, the first night on my own, I dreamed I gave birth to a baby girl. And so it was, as I would learn a week later that I was pregnant at 37 years of age.

I was pregnant with no support system, no job, and nowhere to live. I didn't know what I was going to do or where I was going, but I knew the universe had chosen me to be this baby's mother. And I suddenly realized I needed this baby. When my mother passed away 3 years before, everything in the world became superficial and temporary. I had no truly unconditional love anymore. And nothing else mattered. I wholly believed that life without love wasn't worth living and this baby was my lifeline.

But as time went on, I didn't feel any closer to this life that was growing inside me. I thought something must be wrong with me. I was worried that I was that rare mother who would reject her offspring. I was bouncing around from house to house, and whoever would take me in. My brother kicked me out and disowned me because he believed I would just end up going back to the baby's father. It was hard to find stability. With still no vision of future, she came.

But the moment they placed her in my arms, everything changed. My fears about not being able to love this child vanished, and when we locked eyes, my capacity to love was amplified tenfold. Any concerns about how we would survive were replaced with only knowing that we somehow would. Literally everything changed. It's a completely magical experience, an instant transformation, a rebirth. What I am describing is something only other mothers can really understand. I went on to experience a honeymoon period with the love of my life for 3 whole months.

After a brief stay in a shelter, I took Mia to live closer to her family. I was shocked to learn they had no knowledge of her. Her father led me to believe we would co-parent, and in the meantime thwarted any effort I made at disclosing her birth to his family. But when I returned, he made no effort to see her. For a time his family played a role in Mia's life, but ultimately have had little involvement.

Once my emotional honeymoon was over, Mia and I were staying with friends. Then it came time to go back to work, and all my previous fears came crashing back to me. Everything I thought I had come to terms with from my childhood began to haunt me. I started seeing a therapist. I had always known I suffered from depression since early childhood, but I learned that I also had been struggling with a pretty severe anxiety disorder. I wanted to work to support my daughter, and I wanted to go to school to build a future, but my mental health was making it impossible to do much more than keep myself and my daughter alive. I had panic attacks at the thought of trusting her in the care of anyone other than myself. My sole purpose had become to be this child's guardian. It was so bad that my therapist believed he could not help me further and referred me elsewhere. It would be another 4 years and 3 therapists before I would be properly diagnosed with Borderline Personality Disorder. And finally I would need yet another new therapist who specialized in personality disorders and Dialectical Behavior Therapy.

Having children makes you aspire to be a better you. Being responsible for someone else makes you want to be more responsible. Suddenly you care about what everyone is eating and being a good role model. So it was not long after I was finally able to begin making sense of myself that I started to hear my calling. I knew I could be a fantastic Life Coach. For the first time in my life I followed through with my desire to further my education and even expanded my ideas of how I am to be of service in the world. I have earned a degree in Mind Body Transformational Psychology. I finally have a clearer vision of the future and I'm about to continue my education to augment my skills and my purpose. Were it not for my daughter, I would still be aimless. She made it necessary for me to learn how to follow my bliss so that I can pass that knowledge on to her and hopefully send her into the world with a bigger, brighter vision than I had.

To say that my journey as a mother has been an easy one would be another lie, but my journey is not over. And as it has been said by many before me, it's all worth it. Almost 6 years ago, my daughter came into my life and turned it upside down. That was necessary so that I could shake loose all the bits and pieces that needed fixing. There are days when I can't tell which of us has it more figured out, her or me. And sometimes it feels like I do more yelling than laughing. But when I take a breath from criticizing myself, I see this perfect creature standing before me calling me mama, followed by intense pure insight and wisdom beyond her years, and I realize I am doing something right. I love her more than anyone could love another thing in this universe, I am sure of it. And she loves me. In spite of all my shortcomings, she still thinks I'm the best mom in the world. Well, at least on most days.

Author Bio:
Leah is a recent graduate of Southwest Institute of Healing Arts and has earned her degree in Mind Body Transformational Psychology. She specializes in Life Coaching, Holistic Nutrition Coaching, and Hypnotherapy. She is currently on the path to augmenting her education in Art and Music Therapy and Yoga Instruction. Her goal is to travel all over as an agent of change,helping to bring balance back to the world.

I Knew We'd Need Each Other
by Kendra E. Laguna

7 pounds, 14 ounces, 21 inches long... born at 1:10 a.m., July 29, 2007. After 21 hours of labor, they laid this silent, blue-eyed baby boy on my chest. We named him William, "Will" for short. I distinctly remember looking right into his eyes while the nurses, doctor, and my husband bustled around the room. He looked right at me and I had an overwhelming sense of knowing... knowing him, this little baby. Looking into his eyes, I thought to myself, *I know I know you, but I have no idea who you are.* They took him and cleaned him. His father, we will call him "Jay," stood next to him, tears in his eyes. Thinking back now, I am not sure if they were tears of joy or fear. Fear that he did not know how to be a father, that he had lost his own father at the age of 5 to suicide. Fear that he would have the same fate. The truth is, that day, in the delivery room, as I held my son, I never, not once, felt as though he "belonged" to both his father and I. I always felt like he was mine alone. I understand how that sounds horrible. That a child is the creation of two people, that he belonged to his father as much as he belonged to me. I struggled with the feeling for a long time.

The first year of Will's life was not easy on my marriage. My husband began having affairs and things were deteriorating fast. My instinct was to protect Will, to make sure that I fixed everything that was wrong, I needed to make sure my family remained intact. It was exhausting. In March of 2008, my now ex-husband and I had planned a family trip to Arizona to visit my parents. For a week before we left, Jay continued to pick fights with me; the night before I told him that no matter what, Will and I would be getting on the plane and going to Arizona to visit with my parents. The next morning, at 3:30 a.m., Jay decided that he would join Will and me on the trip. We arrived in

Arizona on March 17, 2008, St. Patrick's Day. As we unpacked, Jay just lay on the guest bedroom bed; he wouldn't talk, he wouldn't look at me. After HOURS of no communication and taking care of Will alone, I approached Jay and asked him what was wrong. His answer set in motion a transformation in me, as a mother, that I was unaware was possible. "What is going on? What is wrong with you?" I asked.

"I want to kill myself, I cannot shake the feeling that I want to kill myself," he said, looking straight into my eyes.

Panic set in, but a panic that I have never felt before... I was driven to stop whatever it was that was happening. I took Jay to the nearest ER and decided to leave William with my mom and dad. Jay and I waited for a psych consult for 8 hours; by this time, I had been awake for 32 hours straight. Finally, the psychiatrist entered the room. I don't remember much of the discussion; however, I do remember the doctor asking Jay if he "had a plan." All I could think was "a plan! Really? This guy can't plan a lunch!" Jay's answer stunned me...

"Yes, I had a plan. I had been picking fights with Kendra all week leading up to this trip. I was planning on not coming, I was going to kill myself in the living room and leave a note on the front door so that when she came home she wouldn't come in and find me."

After that the room blurred. I remember saying through tears "but we have an 8-month-old son!" WHAT WAS HAPPENING? I know that they were still talking, but all I heard was the sound that the Charlie Brown teacher makes... wahhh, waaaa, wahhh... Then I heard a voice, a male voice, it came from directly in front of me, he said, "HE WILL BE LEAVING YOU AND WILL ONE WAY OR ANOTHER, SO YOU BETTER PROTECT YOURSELF AND WILL NOW."

Fast-forward a few months, I had completely shut down. Will was my ONLY focus.

Being his mom, his stable parent, his constant, was what consumed me. Jay decided to join the military, a decision that I supported, foolishly thinking that it would "fix" our family. He and I could move away with Will and be the family that I longed for. Of course the "voice" played back in my head like a record with a skip in it... "HE WILL LEAVE YOU AND WILL...." I knew I needed to be Will's protector. I suggested that Will and I move to Arizona while Jay did his Basic Training in the Army and then continued to Officer Candidate School. Jay agreed.

On September 2008, Will and I drove the 1700 miles to Arizona. My head told me not to leave, but my heart was telling me this would be the best decision that I would ever make, not only for myself, but Will as well. October 2008, 10 days after our two-year anniversary, Jay told me he wanted a divorce. I was beyond crushed... I had a baby boy who needed his dad (or so I thought). I cried all the time. Will, then only 15 months old, would come sit by me and pat my back. I remember one night after a very long and intense conversation that Jay and I had, I was in the fetal position on the floor, crying so hard that I couldn't see. Will was about 18 months old, he sat down next to me, took my face in his hands and said, "It OK Mommy, no cry, I here." It was then that a light bulb went off... I was looking into those big blue eyes, the eyes that I knew so well the day he was born; I felt a shift in my heart and in my soul. I was DONE crying, done being weak, done with all the drama. My little boy needed not only a mom, but a mom that could be strong and show him that giving up was NEVER an option. I held him and told him that I was "sorry for crying so much," that I was "sad because I wanted what was best for him." Little did I know what was happening to me was what would be best for him.

In March 2010, I met a wonderful man. He treated Will like his own. Jay had dropped out of the picture totally, not even sending a birthday or Christmas gift to Will. We married in December 2010. I did struggle with whether I was doing the right thing by Will. Was this the right guy to be his dad? Would Will question about his biological father? I did not have those answers. What I did know is that no matter what the question, I would answer it to the best of my ability, an honest, not sugar-coated answer. When Will was 6 years old, his little sister was born...he always wanted a sister. He is an amazing big brother; I am a proud mother. He has grown into a fine young man, now 9 and half years old, in 4th grade. Does he ask about his biological father? Yes... he has many questions, questions that go unanswered because Jay has not contacted him in 5 years. The one thing that astonishes me is how Will processes and thinks about the world. When he was 6, we were sitting at the breakfast table, eating his cereal. He stopped, looked at me with those eyes, and simply said, "Mom, do you know why I chose you?" I responded, "No, I am not sure what you are talking about." To which he said, "You know, when you are up there (pointing to the sky) and you get to decide who will be your mom. Out of all the girls that want to be moms, you know why I chose you?" Astounded by what he said, I answered, "No, buddy, why did you choose me?" His answer? "Because I knew that one day we would need each other." Oh, how right he was.

Author Bio:
Kendra Laguna is a Speaker, Intuitive Counselor, and Medium. Using her own life struggles, she encourages and empowers those who are looking to rebuild their lives. Using her holistic approach and intuitive gifts, Kendra is like a best friend that is easy to talk to and helps you navigate through life's hills and valleys. Her passion is helping others by having honest and open conversations. She connects on a level that is unlike traditional therapy; using her Mind, Body, Spirit certification, Reiki training, and her ability to connect with those that have passed,Kendra gives her clients a new compass to navigate life.

Website: **www.kendralaguna.com**

Raising Healthy Kids

Clear Your Own Childhood Trauma to Raise a Healthy, Empowered Leader
by Karen Langston

I think it is interesting that those who want to teach children must become an educated professional and yet anyone can have a child. This was something I thought of often as I went through school to become an Early Childhood Educator.

When I had my daughter 23 years ago, I was filled with excitement and fear, wondering how much my life would change. Once I held my daughter in my arms for the very first time, I instantly fell in love. In that moment I let her know that I would forever love her, care for her, and protect her from harm. Instantly I forgot what my life was like before her, and I can't imagine my life without her.

When I was in school, one of the teachers said "a baby that is picked up every time he cries, cries less." Before I had a baby, I thought this was the most ridiculous thing I had ever heard. Of course the baby cries less because you are chronically picking it up every time it cries. I still had a lot to learn.

Essentially, if you tend to your baby's needs, baby does cry less because they learn to trust they are in a safe environment, they are protected, and their needs are met, creating security. Babies are intuitive, and if they feel safe and secure, this is their first level of development of self-esteem and the ability to relate positively with others.

What we have learned over the decades is that a baby's emotional well-being is developed in the first 5 years of life, when they are learning to trust their environment and have their needs met. This helps your baby to develop compassion, empathy towards others, to trust their intuition, develop a positive self-esteem and positivity towards others, tools that become a part of their lifelong success.

Like all humans, your baby wants cuddle time with you. Think about the one person that you like to cuddle or hug with. Do you feel safe, secure, and loved? There is no difference with your baby; all babies want the same thing you do: comfort, security, and love. So tune in, pick your baby up, love them, and play a significant role in their development. Your hugs are creating our future leaders.

There is almost nothing more rewarding than baby's first steps. It is an exciting time. My daughter started pulling herself up on furniture at about 7 months. Marteen walked behind the wagon until after her first birthday. I was in fear she was never going to actually walk. I put her to bed one night, a usual ritual, and sat down to do some work. About ten minutes later there was Marteen standing in front of me with the biggest smile of pride. I was stunned and could not say anything. As I quickly recovered from my shock, I picked her up and praised her. It was an incredible experience that left me thinking about how these first steps were symbolic of the rest of her life— where would these first steps take her in years to come?

Sometimes I wonder about what Mother Nature was thinking. Why can't babies talk at birth? Wouldn't it be great if your baby could say "please change my diaper" or "I am hungry." It would make parenting so much easier.

When my daughter was learning to talk, I found that she was frustrated because she could understand us but lacked the words to express what she wanted. I had taken a course on sign language and decided to teach Marteen. She had about twenty words: milk, cookie, cat, dog, apple, Dad, Mom, and so on. What was interesting is she would make sounds as if she was saying the word while signing the word with her hands what she wanted. Her first sign language sentence: "Mommy I want milk please." This instantly took the frustration away. It was the most effective communication tool for her at the time. As she learned how to say the words, each sign word was no longer needed and was quickly forgotten.

I could not help but cry tears of joy, sadness, and wonderment as I walked my daughter to school for the very first time. I had no idea I would be so emotional. Where did the time go? How did this helpless infant grow so fast to be her own individual little person?

As much as we want to protect them, we must let them go so that they can come back to us for encouragement and support. This is also the time where I believe that if you have given your child the most positive rearing to this point, it is going to pay off. If your child feels a good sense of love, security, and bonding from infancy, they will be excited to separate from you and explore their new world in confidence. Having a solid foundation allowed Marteen to explore this new experience knowing that she could look back, see our open arms and encouragement to move forward.

Once reality has replaced fantasy, children develop emotionally, physically, and cognitively in leaps and bounds. Unfortunately, this is when they get their first taste of peer pressure from friends. They may do some things that they are not sure about and are looking for someone to trust, and that is you.

Your child is interacting with friends and peers of all different backgrounds, and you can no longer control who they are interacting with. You can, however, have control over who they go to when they really need some help. You must open the lines of communication. This is when your role changes from parent to a coach, guide, and friend.

We must let our kids go through their identity phases. If they want to experiment with hair color, clothes, makeup, let them. Jump in and give them a hand or take them to an expert. The more we allow our teenagers to explore, the more they figure out who they are and what they really like. If we keep telling them they can't do things, the more repressed they become, and the more problems of rebellion and acting out you are going to have.

I am not saying that you let your teenager do whatever they like. However, if you have an open relationship with them where you can discuss and negotiate, your teenager is going to feel like they have been heard and empowered. You are going to feel like you are being heard and still in control.

Part of why we repress our teenagers exploration is because of our own upbringing. Think back to when your parents disapproved of something you were doing as a teenager. How were your parents dealing with the experience? What did you do? Now think about you as the parent; what are you disapproving of and how is your internal teenager reacting? Break the cycle and learned behaviors; let go of your past.

My work as a Somatic Intuitive Trainer has taught me that most of us are living in a world that is filtered through past hurts and traumas. Just look at the last United States presidential election. When it comes to raising emotionally healthy children, we have to let go of our past hurts, wrongs, mistrusts, and wrongdoings regardless of how horrific they are. If your child is doing something they are not feeling right about and they come home to share with you and you yell, scream, freak out, or get upset, they learn quickly "I can't trust my parents to support me."

Do you know the definition of insanity? Extreme foolishness or irrationality and, to quote Albert Einstein, doing the same thing over and over again and expecting different results. In order to be fully present and react in the present moment, we must gain the tools to release our own doubts, fears, and hurt to truly accept our children for who they are.

When you think about it, the only training we have for raising children is what we observed firsthand growing up as a child. Which brings me back to my point: those who want to teach children must become an educated professional and yet, anyone can have a child without any education. I think we all need to clear ourselves of our stored traumas before having children.

You have the power to change. We just have to want to change and really become the guide we need to become. We have to put our emotions and judgement on the back burner and empower our children and give them the trust they are looking for.

This trust starts the moment your baby is born: the warm blanket, the warm heartbeat of mom, the food, meeting their basic necessities, and the love of both parents. It is crucial to their development. Pick up your baby when she is crying, it is her only way of communicating. Babies want love, and we are on this planet for one thing: to be loved. Pick up your baby and love them.

Allow your toddler to explore their world in confidence. Be their support. They will take a couple of steps and look back; hold your arms out, let them know you are there for them and encourage them to go further. This allows them to trust the world around them and to fall back on you for support, not just as a toddler but when they are a teenager figuring out who they are and as a young adult when they are ready to soar. They too will look back; hold out your arms and encourage them to take the next step.

Support, encouragement, and love does not cost any money. You do not have to be rich to love your child. Just love your child unconditionally and without judgement. Your child does not need your gadgets, big houses, and fancy cars. They only want your time, love and devotion, support and guidance. Children are not materialistic; we create this in our children in much the same way we teach hatred, prejudice, and judgement. Teach your child by your actions; love them unconditionally.

We all have skeletons in the closet we do not want our children to ever have to witness or experience. Fix your past, let it go, and see the world through their eyes instead of your wounds. Share with them that you are not perfect. Show them you are here to keep them safe and to support them. Allow them to come to you with any concerns no matter how bad, knowing you will coach and guide them without judgement.

The more we support, encourage, and love our children unconditionally with no judgment, the more positive, conscious young adults we will have in this world. Your child, my child, our children are our future leaders. Let's give them tools to really change the world and end the suffering, pain, and conflict. All it takes is for you to pick your baby up and meet their needs, love them, and make them feel safe. Ditch your past traumas and start fresh. Talk to your child so they will want to talk to you and listen so that will keep on listening. Give them the encouragement to soar, because they know when they look back you are there with open arms to encourage them to go further.

Author Bio:
Karen Langston is a an Internationally recognized Certified Holistic Nutritionist, Lifestyle Educator and Speaker training Health and Wellness Professionals who want to truly help clients, increase revenue, and become the expert in their community.

Website: **www.KarenLangston.com**
Facebook: **www.facebook.com/HealthyGutAdvisor**

A Gluten-Free Mom
by Puja Agarwal

Being a mom is not an easy task with all the hard work and patience that it takes. I never knew that till I became one. Over the years I have come to realize that I never thanked my mom for what she did for me—I took her perpetual presence in my life for granted. But today as I write this article I cannot thank her enough for everything that she did for me as my mom.

My journey of being a mother started way back in August 2005 when my daughter was born. Like every other mom in this world, I did my best to provide her the best of everything in every facet of life as a baby, toddler, or kid.

I would take outmost care in providing her a balanced diet, and deep within I lauded my efforts and always thought she was getting what I thought was best for her as a growing child in terms of nutrition. Hailing from a North Indian background, I would cook the most nutritious food, which included lentils, beans, veggies, and whole wheat tortillas called rotis. But still she had health issues. I initially thought them to be a normal part of childhood, but when these symptoms persevered or went away for some time only to come back, I started to ponder about what was wrong with her. Whether I was giving her something that was triggering the advent of these symptoms and causing them to flare.

Being in the United States for quite a while, I was already aware of something called "food allergies," but I had not come face to face with them. I decided to see a pediatric naturopath for my daughter, who ordered food allergy tests for her and as expected she was diagnosed being gluten sensitive and she was supposed to be kept off wheat.

That was the day when the real challenge came up! The arduous task of being a mom gets all the more difficult when you have to take up an unconventional path. Till now, the cooking was effortless, spontaneous, and never involved too much thought process, as I followed what I had seen my mom do for our health and well-being and I was following suit. But now my life changed and every meal became a challenge. Wheat is an integral part of the north Indian cuisine. We can't think beyond wheat. If I don't use wheat, then what do I cook, was the biggest question. What would I give her for lunch in school?

Would I be able to cook a palatable gluten-free meal for my daughter? Moreover, this was just the tip of the iceberg called "gluten-free life." I had so many thoughts racing in my mind about other challenges as well, like what would she eat while going out or at birthday parties or get-togethers. My brain started to work fast. Apart from cooking, I also had the onerous task of counseling my daughter and coaxing her to give up her favorite things. She was just a 9-year-old.

The Internet was the first step in my journey of being a gluten-free mom. I read umpteen number of blogs, articles and reports on this topic. I consulted my doctor and a few friends whose kids had similar allergies. Everyone had their piece of advice to offer. With so much food for thought, I had to undergo the gigantic task of choosing what was best for my daughter. I started to plan recipes for her which were gluten free as well as wholesome and filling. I was doing what I could to traverse this path, but every now and then a thought or rather self-doubt prevailed on my mind, which was another challenge to overcome. I would question myself, Am I being a good mom? Am I making the best choice for her? There was no one to counter or validate my thoughts, and I tried to curb them but they kept coming up every time.

I will admit that previously at one point I realized that I too was allergic to wheat, but since it was an indispensable part of my conventional cooking, I never seriously gave a thought to leading a wheat-free life. But now when it was a question of my daughter's health, I immediately decided to do away with it. The next step I took was to read the list of ingredients for everything that I bought, and honestly speaking 80 percent of the stuff had wheat in one form or another as an ingredient. Even most of the India snacks which I assumed to be free of wheat had wheat gluten in them.

Planning and executing a gluten-free diet was much more challenging than I had anticipated. Packing a filling and wholesome lunch box for each day of school was difficult, at least for the first few days. Like every other kid, my daughter loves to eat out, and Friday was the day that was fixed for eating out, but with these new regulations in force, her choices were narrowed down and she had to give up so many favorites. It was really heartbreaking for me to talk to her about her health issues and choices and about why she needed to give up cakes and pizzas at birthday parties. I also had to keep reminding her about it.

Coming from an Indian background posed one more challenge for me, and it was handling peer pressure. The concept of gluten-free life is still alien to Indian society. Back home, my family and even my parents did not conform to my way of thinking; they do not accept the fact that over the years the quality of wheat has degenerated due to genetic modifications. Same went with my Indian friends who would just brush off the idea of a gluten-free diet. Too many people telling me the same thing indeed had an influence on my psyche, and I would ask myself if I was really on the right track.

There was another aspect of this nonconformity with the idea of being gluten-free: sometimes I had to deal with the pity and sympathy that people around me felt for my daughter. When we would be a part of any celebration and my daughter would say no to delicacies like cake, pizza, roti, pasta, or samosa then there would be so many sympathizing hearts who would approach me and tell that it's really sad that my daughter is missing on all the good stuff. Being a mother, it would hurt me and make me guilty over why my child should suffer from all these allergies and give up all this stuff. Though I very well know that I am not alone in this journey, still the thoughts would crop up and I would brood over them for a long time. People expressing all kinds of opinions make things more difficult for the mom and the kid who are already having a hard time adjusting to this new gluten-free way of life.

So I took on the challenge of making me and my daughter impervious to people's opinions and comments. I started discussing her food choices with her. I wanted to empower her so that she does not get affected by people's comments and is able to overcome them. I started educating her on better, healthier choices. I continued to read lot of articles and books on gluten-free diets and recipes, the challenges involved, and how to overcome them. It was overwhelming to know that there were so many people out there who were gluten free.

It has been an ever-evolving journey, and I have come a long way in this one and a half years of being gluten free. Now, the gluten-free way of life comes naturally to us and we do not hesitate to say that we are gluten free. My daughter, who turned 11 in August, is in perfect harmony with her gluten-free life and she even feels proud when she says no to cakes, pizzas, quesadillas, and the like!

Author Bio:
Puja Agarwal is a full time mom, a self taught artist with a passion to live a chemical free life. Her Dream is write a book which can make life a bit easy for moms dealing with food allergies . She runs a Facebook group called Taste of Gluten free India to educate Moms about gluten free and vegan living.
Facebook: **www.facebook.com/groups/223567118089126**

Shopping
by Kimberly Spair

Yesterday, I was out shopping with my 20-month-old son, who was happily sitting in the stroller with his hand in a snack cup full of peas. He was chatting, observing everything around him, and stuffing his face between saying "hi" and "bye-bye" to everyone that passed us. One older woman stopped us to talk with my son; she admired his smile and his eyes. She then turned to me and said, "I feel sorry for him." I looked at her puzzled (he looked pretty darn happy to me), and she said, "he's eating peas for a snack," and "he should be eating cookies or cheerios at his age." Of course, I froze in the moment and smiled at the woman and kept walking.

As I finished my shopping trip, I thought about all the times my son is singled out by family, friends, and strangers because he eats a healthy diet free of processed food. He prefers fruits and vegetables over anything else. He has never been given a powder, formula, or "food-like" substitute, and often, when handed a "treat snack," he hands it back to us asking for fruit.

This makes people feel sorry for him?! We are not ones to ever comment on what other parents feed their children. This is none of our business, and we don't try to educate them. SO, why do people feel it's appropriate to try and make our son a spectacle?

This child has two parents dedicated to making him homemade "goodies" packed with vitamins and nutrients, so he never feels deprived at a social event. His little cooler is always full to the brim with beautiful, colorful, healthy food. He eats REAL food! Why is this so strange?!

I cringe when I hear people single him out by saying "he can have this because it's 'organic'." We are not food-obsessed; however, the human body can only recognize food and does not understand what to do with chemicals, preservatives, or "food-like" products. These are not things we choose to give to our growing and developing child. Somehow, parents have learned to turn a blind eye to the childhood obesity and disease rates in the United States. This couldn't possibly have anything to do with what we feed our children.

Our son has the experience of visiting the farm and co-op several times per week where we buy our organic produce. He knows where food comes from. He doesn't look for food in a hot pink box in the cabinet. Of course we have our favorite restaurants, he gets snacks, he gets treats, but YES we are particular about what he puts in his body.

He is a kid, and when he's off to school I am sure he will venture into some foods I would rather not know about, BUT, for now, we can give him a foundation. A foundation built on whole foods, and a solid immune system. Then we can pray that the choices he has learned to make will carry him through a very happy and healthy lifetime.

I am never one to ridicule or put another parent down; we are all doing the best that we can. This is our priority over many other material things. BUT when someone tells me my son needs a "treat" or that he or she feel "sorry" for him, I invite them to spend a few days with us and see how much LOVE and FUN we have creating amazing and nourishing meals together as a family.

Author Bio:
Kimberly is a Certified Holistic Health Coach, Speech Pathologist, and Yoga Therapist. Her mission and passion is to empower moms by encouraging them to trust their inner wisdom about the health of their children. This includes helping moms become their best selves

so they can maximize the potential for healthy development in the lives of their families.

Kimberly takes a nutrient-dense whole-foods approach, and believes in using food as medicine to obtain optimal health and enable the body to detoxify naturally.

Website: **www.reclaimersofhealth.com**
www.integrativebeginnings.com

On Food
by Margot Freitag

I recall the fear that I might never be a mom. I remember the notion that I might not meet Mister Right and I may never have toddlers hanging on my leg. That was long ago. I have since been blessed with a great husband and two beautiful, amazing, smart and witty kids, now entering their teen years. It has been a whirlwind. Just a moment ago I was changing diapers and pushing a stroller, sleep-deprived and energized by an incredible, endless love for my babes.

The fear of not having children morphed into the fear that they might choke or not wake up or get hurt or kidnapped. We got through those years unscathed. But the fears ebb and flow. There are, I have discovered, endless dangers beyond my control. We must be fiercely strong and protective, confident, and equipped in order to make our way through this sea of uncertainty.

It turns out there are some things we can do to provide a safe haven for our children. I have learned that the most significant protection we can offer is a gift that is something we have quite a bit of control over. This is the gift of good health. When we empower our children with a strong body, a clear mind, and standards that value healthy living, it's then that their sense of self and their identity in a crazy world becomes solid.

I was a sick kid. I struggled with asthma, allergies, and chronic fatigue. I was overweight and fought an uphill battle with yo-yo dieting. I was physically unwell, and so I was mentally unwell. Preoccupied with body image, thigh circumference, and pant size, I couldn't think clearly, because I was relentlessly starving... or stuffed. I was addicted to nasal sprays and heavily medicated with asthma inhalers, inhaled steroids, and I was frequently puffed up on Prednisone. High school was a wash. I struggled with self-esteem, I was chronically insecure, and didn't like myself or my life very much. While my brother went on to Oxford and then law school, I bumbled around in a mental fog.

In short, it was the proper food that saved me.

As you can imagine, I wanted to ensure my children did not experience what I had. While my health improved significantly through diet and lifestyle changes when my children were small, I was not doing everything right. I was still using asthma inhalers daily when I was a new mom until the fateful day that everything changed. It was the day my little boy was diagnosed with asthma. He needed a "daily inhaled steroid," they said.

I knew what we needed to do. I had been blessed with an incredible nutrition teacher a few years prior who had taught the merits of a plant-based diet, but I had been resistant to giving up the things I loved. In a single sweep, I made the changes, cleared the cupboards, and embarked on clean, whole foods, plant-based nutrition. My little ones cheered when I told them they no longer needed to eat chicken or fish. They cried when I told them they wouldn't be having cheese. That was the beginning. I pursued a formal education in the field to complement my careers in health care, fitness, and education. Before long my children were thriving on plants. The asthma inhalers have been sitting at the back of the kitchen cupboard for years now. They are never used. There are rarely colds or flus, and our home is healthy and happy.

My children have a solid sense of self, and they feel good about the way they eat, not only for their own health, but for the health of the planet and for all of the animals (oh, how they love animals). They understand why we eat the way we do, how we are connected to the larger "whole," how our choices have a ripple effect... and they are downright proud of it.

A students and top athletes, there is no question that my children are eating right. Yet we are persistently met with conventional ideology. The norms of animal foods and processed foods are intertwined with our education and health systems. Schools and hospitals pave the way for animal agriculture to push their products on our children and on families, despite the clear evidence that they are unnecessary and dangerous, hard on the planet, and devastating for the animals we love. Healthcare providers worry about calcium and protein, illustrating over and over that they too are victims of conventional wisdom.

Our fears as parents must lie now in the future of today's children, eating more dairy, meat and processed foods than ever before. Cancers, type one diabetes and other autoimmune diseases, inflammatory conditions like asthma and allergies, heart disease, anemia, constipation, skin conditions including acne and eczema, depression, obesity, and more leave parents grasping for answers. Mothers and fathers worry so much about protecting the health of their children, yet little guidance is available on the simple solution for most of these conditions, which almost always lies in the food. And so it goes, the dangerous foods, the cause of the health issues we fear most for our children, are perpetually pressed on us through the professionals we highly regard.

Speak to your children. Empower them with the freedom to question everything. Let them know that just because everyone is doing something doesn't make it right. All children need more plants. Given the opportunity, children will make choices that are aligned with their core values. This improves not only their health, but also their sense of self.

When I let my children make the connection, they chose the path of compassion and self-care. This approach has allowed them to thrive. Rather than hiding the truth for the sake of convenience or tradition, giving our children the option to eat a healthier, plant-based diet sets them up for success. Good health, strong, fit bodies, mental clarity, a solid sense of self, an awareness of conventional thought, a sense of interconnectedness and compassion... all abates our fear. Our best work as parents may be to set our children up for a happy, healthy, well-balanced and optimistic view of the world. Perhaps we can achieve this by providing fuel that creates happy, healthy, well-balanced and insightful children.

Author Bio:
The shift towards clean, whole foods vegan nutrition was the answer for Margot in eliminating a lifelong battle with asthma, allergies, chronic fatigue and yo-yo dieting. Through her careers as a Registered Massage Therapist specializing in soft tissue and joint rehabilitation, Certified Personal Trainer, Teacher, and Nutritionist, Margot could not ignore the gap in our health and education systems when it comes to understanding the power of nutrition. Margot has had the good fortune of training with leading nutrition researchers of our time and is certified in Plant-Based Nutrition through Cornell University and the T. Colin Campbell Foundation. Through her tailored programs, Margot educates and supports her clients to take charge of their health and their destiny.

Website: **www.taigawholehealth.com**

The Golden Age of Breastfeeding
by Lashonda Neal

If you've been a breastfeeding mother (or the spouse of one), you're probably well aware of the dedication involved—the long hours, lack of sleep, the insecurities, the worries...the pure exhaustion of it all. Yet you do it. You do it because for you, there is no other option. You made a commitment and you're seeing it through to whatever goal you set for yourself. For me, that goal was six months. That six months quickly turned into a year, and before I knew it, I had made a decision that would prove to be one of the most significant choices in raising my daughter. I decided to allow my child to self-wean. A lot of faith, information, and science went into my decision, so it was not made lightly. And although I sacrificed in ways I never would have imagined, I'm incredibly content with where full-term breastfeeding has brought us—for my child, myself, and my family. As many moms can attest, there are very distinct stages of breastfeeding. And while these stages are very similar between breastfeeding moms, each mother has her own unique experience with these different "eras." My daughter and I had our own unique journey, and one of the most beautiful stages I can recall is the beauty that was breastfeeding a toddler.

My baby girl went through SO much on our four-year breastfeeding journey. It started with the all-too-common worry over milk supply, followed by diaper "output" drama (I seriously had pics of baby poo saved on my phone). From there, we had food allergies, slow weight gain, a two-week nursing strike, elimination diets, thrush, clogged ducts... You name it, we dealt with it. But on top of it all, there was immense, immeasurable, indescribable joy.

Breastfeeding saw us through the good, the bad, and the teething. Through developmental milestones, sleep regressions, illness, and more. I won't lie, though. There were many times when I have been "touched out" and exhausted, but quitting was never an option. There are lots of very important reasons why, but the bottom line is this: most of the doubts moms have about natural feeding have been planted in our heads for a reason. (There's an entire history behind that.) These doubts and hurdles didn't make my child any less deserving of the food she was meant to have, the food that was made for her, and these doubts certainly were not going to beat us. So on we went! Through everything, breastfeeding was our baby girl's comfort, nourishment, stability, and protection.

And then we were there. The Golden Age of our breastfeeding journey.

Shortly after our daughter turned two, we entered a magical stage of nursing. The toddler era. We had finally made it past the developmental superhighway, and nursing was just comfortable and absolutely lovely. Gone were the worries over diapers, weight checks, and latch issues. While nursing still had incredible nutritional value, the main focus had changed, and it was now mostly about connecting. We would just kick back, snuggle up, read a book, sing (she hummed), and if I was lucky, I might have gotten a chubby foot in my mouth. Of course, there were times when I didn't want to nurse when she did, and that was all right, too. I would simply say to her, "Not right now." And more often than not, she replied with, "OK," coming back to ask me later (and a toddler's "later" is 3-5 minutes, but still...) It really was one of the most enjoyable parts of my day. We got to connect in a way that she still needed, yet she was developed enough to understand the concept of waiting. It was bliss! And in that bliss, I learned so much, like learning to slow down and make time for the most important things. And as she grew closer to weaning, I understood even more the importance of doing what I know to be right—despite what the world around me might say.

I had no plans on nursing as long as I did, but I am so glad I did. No one told me how beautiful it would be to nurse a toddler. No one told me how perfectly natural it would be, later during the weaning stages. No one told me how it would strengthen our bond and my resolve to always be what my children need. And no one told me how absolutely wonderful it was going to be. So I'm telling you now. If you're considering nursing your child into toddlerhood, go for it. There are some rough milestones, and breastfeeding is a great tool to get baby through them. Once you're past them, though, you're in for a new and beautiful experience.

I'm so happy with how far my child and I have come. I love that I didn't force her to get to this place before she was ready and that I got to go through the weaning experience with her. Full-term breastfeeding may not be for everyone, but I have absolutely no regrets and all the gratitude in the world. I know that God had this planned out long before I existed, and I find absolute beauty and joy in what he's given us.

Although our breastfeeding journey has come to an end, I look forward to the next eras in the lives of my children. From birth, through toddlerhood, until my days on this earth have ended—I will never give up on them. I will be everything they need me to be—always.

Author Bio:
Lashonda is a full-time working wife and mother, living in Phoenix, AZ. She is committed to instinctual and gentle parenting and helping her family navigate through life with Christ as their guide. In addition to breastfeeding advocacy, Lashonda is also passionate about childhood development, education, and creating a safe and healthy environment for her family.

Website: **www.thenealproject.wordpress.com**

Imagine
by Jyl Steinback

Imagine - making a difference in every child's life YOU touch!

Imagine - educating the "Whole Child" through Their Mind, Their Body and Their Emotions! Healing Them From the Inside-Out and Making Them WHOLE!

Imagine - a child having unconditional love FOR THEMSELVES At the very beginning of their life

Imagine - teaching them how to be Resilient!

Imagine - giving them the power to empower themselves!

Imagine - transforming families, as we know it today!

Giving our children the tools to thrive and blossom into Happier, Healthier Adults

Loving Themselves First and All their Life will be That Much Easier

I do believe with all of my heart and soul WE ARE THAT CHANGE!

As MOM'S WE have the Tools to Give This Amazing Gift

To our children and To Their Future

TOGETHER WE WILL Create a Circle of Wellness That Last a LIFETIME!

Let's ALL Reach For That Highest Star!

Let's Dream HUGE

WE ARE THAT DIFFERENCE!

LET'S CELEBRATE OUR CHILDREN'S FUTURE!

TOGETHER WE WILL "BUILD A HEALTHIER FUTURE FOR OUR CHILDREN"

THE FUTURE OF OUR WORLD!

Author Bio:

Mom of 3 amazing children, Jamie, Scott and Adam (son-in-law) - all spreading their mission of health and wellness in their special and magical way. Jyl Steinback is passionate about changing the face of education as we know it today and heal children from the inside-out (mind, body and emotions). She founded Shape Up "US" a 501c3 non-profit, The Hip Hop Healthy Heart Program for Children™ A Healthy Literacy Curriculum and Clap4HealthSM a National Fitness Campaign to get ACTIVE, GET HEALTHY and BE HAPPY!

Fierce Mothers Grow Healthy Families
by Lisa Robbins

As a mother of three children, three grandchildren—one more coming soon—three granddogs, two grandcats, and a grandbearded dragon, it is critical and most important to me that they all have proper nutrition, otherwise they could end up like the rest of the "poor" people and pets, who aren't aware of how important proper nutrition is to the quality of their life. It is imperative to me that all members of my family have access to excellent nutrition to keep them healthy and balanced throughout their lives.

When I grew up in the 60s and 70s in Southern Ontario, Canada, my family had access to healthy local foods, mostly farm fresh, during late summer: greens, berries, apples, plums, tomatoes, cucumbers; to early winter: turnip, potatoes, carrots, broccoli, spinach. We had Maple Syrup, yum.

We ate a lot of peanut butter (with hydrogenated fat) sandwiches on white bread with margarine and berry jam; bologna and mustard on white bread; and cheese spread from a jar on white bread. These seemed to be our favorites. Cheesy pasta from a box was a frequent lunch in our home, smothered in sugary ketchup.

Sometimes we splurged during camping trips on eggs, fresh white baguettes, and a large hunk of crumbly white cheddar cheese.

Sometimes we made Fish'n Brewis with soaked hard bread (very, very, extremely hard white chunk of wheat bread), "scrunchins" (tiny fried cubes of salted pork fat), and soaked, salted codfish. Drained and fried up, sprinkled with salt and pepper, it was the ultimate winter "new-fie" comfort food. My family added mashed potatoes to stretch the dinner further.

Every now and then my mother cooked a whole corn beef, chicken or turkey. We went to the Chicken restaurant and had French Fries smothered in barbeque sauce and apple pie for dessert (pastry made with hydrogenated fat shortening).

We drank glasses of pasteurized milk every day, sometimes chocolate and strawberry, usually made with liquid, artificially flavored corn syrup.

We ate hot dogs, bacon, plastic slices of cheese, hamburgers, canned tuna, white rice, oatmeal and canned corn and peas. We enjoyed fruit pies and pastries made with shortening, candies, potato chips, and chocolates made with hydrogenated and modified fats and lots of sugar.

Thankfully there were a few healthy foods tossed in the mix. Still, though, all these toxic additives were clogging up our livers and gall bladders for many years.

This was city living in the 60s and 70s. We lived in Toronto, and my mother was a self-taught cook. Her food was delicious and she taught us to cook early on, before we were 10 years old.

So we were lucky and we were not. We had access to healthy food and still our entire family was sick and overweight by middle age, mostly caused by over consumption of congestive, allergen-type foods. We had addictions to dairy and sweet breads, and ate excessive sugars and too many foods fried in damaged and altered fats.

Who knew how these foods were clogging up our filters (livers)? We sure didn't. We just thought it was our lot in life to be fat and feel terrible. It was inherited. Okay, that's not a joke; we really thought that was true and kept eating whatever we wanted, never connecting our health to what we ate. After all, who didn't have a milk mustache in those days?

So I learned the hard way about how and what to eat because of chronic illness and early deaths in my family. It became very important to me to teach my children what changes were crucial if they wanted to live a healthy and happy long life. I went back to school and studied to be a Holistic Nutritionist. Ha, they couldn't argue with me now, or so I thought! Looking back now, of course it was the best thing I could ever have done.

I didn't learn about healthy foods until about a third of the way through raising my children, and they had picked up a few bad eating habits. Here are some of the crazy things I've done to stop my kids from eating things that make them sick.

I began writing with permanent black marker on anything brought into our home that was some modified version of safe and real food.

I started writing: "Toxic," "Cancer Causing" and other such profanities, all over their toxic groceries. "This will make you sick," "Are you kidding me?" "Please Take Me Back," "Hormone Imbalance," "Mood Swings," "Just Say NO to GMO!" "NO GMO," "Infertility," "GMNo," and my all-time favorite, "Who Bought This $*&%?"

My youngest daughter loves doing things like dipping homemade cookies I make with awesome healthy ingredients into a fresh bucket of cheap icing made with hydrogenated fat, then smiling wryly as she poisons her own body in pleasurable defiance. Argh!

When any of my children and their spouses, even their very close friends, bring a snack containing some toxic ingredient, after they have their fill, I secretly toss it in the garbage, sometimes replacing it with an organic version. A few times I've been found out. Still, though, it teaches them to look for alternatives to these products that don't carry the offending toxic ingredients, even if they hate me for it.

It took strength. I knew there would be backlash, and there was. One time Anna's boyfriend RJ admitted to joyously celebrating while cleaning out the refrigerator, saying with a smile, "Rotten, rotten, rotten..." as he tossed each fresh food item into the garbage, obviously my items.

"RJ bought them and they're his favorite, lime-flavored corn tortilla chips. Mom throws them all out and buys organic lime chips—SO GROSS!" — Anna

At first my kids would freak out at me and get angry, then gradually they began learning about problematic ingredients and reading labels. They started buying organic foods and really caring more about themselves and what they are putting into their bodies! Now their groceries are mostly organic, with lots of fresh produce, and dried and frozen whole natural foods. They've turned into amazing chefs who pepper their dishes with spices, herbs, and love.

I know this wisdom they carry about healthy foods will protect them and their own children and grandchildren and all future generations, and now they have a few funny stories to tell about what their parents did to them.

My story: my mother made me eat six peas when I was six years old and seven peas when I turned seven. I hated cooked peas so much I choked on every one. I love peas now.

My methods may not be the gentlest, and who has time for that anyway? Our children could be eating toxic ingredients and clogging up their own bodies, creating illness and disease, right now!

I did it and continue to do whatever I can because I care that much about my family. When my two-and-a-half-year-old grandson goes home from staying with me for a day or two, I can feel his parents' wrath (and smile secretly to myself) when he tells them he is not eating that cereal because "It's got g-mem-mo."

I say do whatever you can to change their minds and their lives, even if you risk not having their approval for a short time.

Eventually they will love you for it! Fierce Gra Gra (Grandmother).

Author Bio:
Lisa Gail Robbins, RHN, BScHN, CTT Author of The Cancer Journal Heal Yourself And Cancer Cure and Survivor Stories.

Website: **www.thegoodwitch.ca**
www.incrediblehealingjournals.com

A Collection of Poems For Mom's Soul

The Time to Be Happy
by Antra Bhargava

Faces peeping in at doorways
Little round cherubic smiles
Mischief bubbles dancing in eyes
Glittering drops of happy sweat
Squirmy grimy hands grip each other
The excitement too much to bear
Mom, may we come in
We have something to show you
No, darling, I'm too busy
That sudden dread of a moment lost
Spin around and grab that hope
Before it's lost to money's worth
Capture, hide away the clock
Slip not with sand or build with brick
Flow, merely flow, with their rhythm and beat
For disappear it will, and so quick.

Precious and rare that voice
Curious, keen, proud
Only for you
Where else does the world revolve
In sleep and awake attune
You are their axis divine
All to be gone, far too soon.

Poet Bio:

Antra Bhargava is a tough but fair business leader and a social changemaker. A Law graduate from the prestigious Trinity College, Dublin, Antra is also a qualified CA and Tax Adviser.

Antra has worked in various global roles and currently heads SuVitas, an award-winning and first-of-its-kind Transition Care Hospital which specializes in Neuro, Ortho, and Cardiac rehab— particularly for stroke, brain, and spinal cord injuries. Antra has been instrumental in setting up two social impact ventures: the PACE safety model based on her martial arts experience and The WoW Kitty, a social impact investors group.

LinkedIn: **www.linkedin.com/in/antrabhargava**

Autumn Leaves
by Cherrian A. Chin

Yellow leaves, red leaves, brown leaves, red and yellow leaves,
Rain leaf, reign leaves
Imagine a commodity for money
As precious as gold
Swept, sweep, swept in mounds
Bag leaves, scattered leaves, falling leaves
Yellow leaves, red leaves, brown leaves, red and yellow leaves
Rain leaf, reign leaves
Dry leaves and wet leaves
Rain leaf, reign leaves
Imagine a commodity for money
As precious as gold
Swept, sweep, swept in mounds
Bag leaves, scattered leaves, flying leaves
Swept, sweep, swept in mounds
Bag leaves, scattered leaves, falling leaves
No more leaves

Poet Bio:

Currently residing in Nevada City, CA, Cherrian Angela Chin was born in Montego Bay, St. James, Jamaica. She grew up in New York State and lived and worked in Japan for almost 20 years. She is also a mother of two children, instructor, and woodblock artist. She is a gifted artist with integrity who strives not for perfection, but for freedom of creative expression in work and lifestyle.

Dandelion
by Megan Heit

My beautiful little flower,
You look like the sun
You brighten my life, and everyone's.

Your roots are strong,
Embedded in the earth
You signify life, new beginnings, rebirth.

You do not brag or boast like the daisies or the rose
Illuminating the landscape with your delicate pose
Oh, little Dandelion,
You are wild and free,
Never growing in rows,
You are free to just...be.

There will be times
When you are not understood
But you will flourish in ways that only YOU could
Dig you up, they might.

Destroy you, no
Because even in the harshest surroundings, my love,
You will surely grow.

Let the wind carry you to new places
See everything that you can see
And when your seeds plant on mountaintops
You will spread the love that first grew inside of me.

Girl
by Sarita Talwai

When I am awake,
More often than not I tell my girl
To speak up
Speak out. Dream big,
Dream long.

Be loud,
Be strong.

That's what I tell my girl.

When I am not so awake,
Perhaps...sometimes,
I whisper to her
It is good to be quiet,
Unseen, unheard.

To be a part
Of a larger herd.

It pays
In many ways.

That's what I mumble in my head.

When I am awake
I mostly say,
Girl, don't hunch.

Don't slouch,
Stretch out.

Don't hide your pride.

Don't lose your stride.

You are one of a kind,
Girl, you are a find.

That's what I say, mostly.

When I am less than awake,
Words tumble in fear.

Don't stray too far, I want you near.

Don't laugh too loud,
Don't look so proud.

Know what to hide,
Hide what you know.

That's what I want
To tell my girl.

I watch my girl.

I know she knows.

My fears, my doubts
Are not hers anymore.

She sings and she hums.

She laughs and she thrums,
As she proceeds
To seize the day,
On the wing of a prayer,
And with her pepper spray.

Yogini Shakti
by Seema Kapur

Divine mixed Fire, water, air and then you
Emerged from Earth
Hey, captivating beauty
You are grand
You are wonder of nature
When clouds get a glimpse
Of you
They start pouring down
Dancing shiningly
Lightning gets crazy!

Your beauty is incomparable and unique
Bare and untouched
In you is
All creation!

You are earth
Sculptured in sand
Innocence is
Your nature
You scent this
Dried earth
With your fragrance
You shine with Simplicity
You fly with Wings Touching Everything
Your whole being Is
Like a harmonica
Your body flows like water
Rippling in waves

You are showering burning sparks
Every particle of Yours is ablaze
You are play of fire
You are Fire!

You move and twist
Wiggle and shake
Dance and circle
Kissing the earth!

What an uproar
Hey you naughty
Mischievous and playful Yogini!

Like rain of spring
So unpredictable!

Your deep sharp Glance
Your black, shiny Wild Hair
This gyration
This strut
You are Shakti!

Empowering, Opening to the Flow of
Divine Grace!

You are Shakti of Dharma
You are an Inspiration
Arising from Inner steadiness
Open and content
Sustaining all things
Without rejection
Holding essence of
All existence

You have the Universal power
Grace, love Deep inside
You are the Yogini Shake
In every woman

A Woman's Point of View
by Janie Saylor

I wait.

It is with great anticipation that I wait.

Somehow I feel...well, taller.

I can't explain it.

I never believed that old myth
About that "special glow,"
But it's true!

I lay my hand upon my stomach,
To know there is life. It's overwhelming.

I stand in complete awe of this miracle forming with each passing
day.

Though I'm afraid, worried, panicked at times.

They tell me it's normal. They... Doctors... Men, of course.

They always tell me how I feel.

How do they know?

What have they ever felt that could possibly compare
To the anxiety, the excitement, the aches...
The utter joy a woman feels.

The dreams a woman has during this...
This tender time.

Dreams which wake you up out of a dead sleep
Dreams that aliens just beamed you out of your bedroom window...
And since you're awake, you realize
That the desire for sex is surging through you...
Or is that the desire for Thai food?
Not sure.

Sometimes it's difficult to tell the difference.

He'd not be too happy if he heard me say that out loud,
So I try to be inconspicuous when it happens...
You know...
You wake up in the middle of the night,
You give him a gentle nudge,
He rolls over.

You kiss him passionately.
He responds and kisses you back.

That animal instinct takes over
And you manhandle him to the best of your ability
(Considering the large baby bump).

Rolling him over and climbing on top of him,
Embracing each other.

Then comes the moment of truth,
You recognize the urges you are having.

You lean close and whisper softly in his ear...
Will you please get up and order Thai food?

Shifting into Presence
by Kimber Bowers

Baby
You are a World
—All your own—
A world into which I
Sometimes (without warning)
Open and Fall...
The room is bustling around us
The world is spinning all around us...
But I Am Here...
Swelling in the joyful light of your eye,
In the wetness of your bib --
In the zealous fistfulls of soft "I love mommy"
Terry cloth shoved repeatedly into your eager mouth,
Gurgling with sloppy excitement until finally settling for just the fist
--
In the butt of your happy kicks falling carelessly against my arm...
Moment into moment into eons of You
Without notice of the bustle
Without racing to outrun the spin
Yes,
You are a WORLD all your own
Much lighter than any I've known
Into which I
Gracefully
Open and Fall...
Allowing the bustle of the spinning world
To spin on without me
Perfectly content

Not Ready
by Shannon Lanzerotta

Llama llama red pajama
Read another story, mama!
Little blue truck
Now we're stuck
Reading, reading, what the...

It's time to sleep
Don't make a peep!
No, we can't play hide-and-seek
Read again?
Maisy and friends?
I just want this day to end
One more book,
Then off the hook
Okay kiddo, Look
Mama needs to go to sleep
Okay fine, I'll sing.
Twinkle, Twinkle little star
What a tired kiddo you are
That's not how it goes? Maybe if I sing it slow?
No, no, no, no!
Singing's done, off to bed
Lay your little head...
A hug instead?

Aw, you're so sweet A kiss, for me?
I love you too, sweet pea.
A tear in my eye
I hug you tight

Can't believe one day you'll say goodbye.
Is it okay if I never let go?
What do you mean, "No"?
You're ready for bed? Eyes feel like lead?
What if I'm not ready yet?

Motherly Love
by Shyla Collier

A love that compares to no other

Dependency at its most

Hugs and kisses that melt your heart

Fun at its best

Happiness all around

Teaching at its finest

A purpose like no other

A bond that is unbreakable

The joys of motherhood

The Truth About... Children
by Cécile Correa

When your tree is fortunate enough to bear fruit,
your labor does not cease once you have delivered
those sweet lives into this world.

At that moment, you are assigned to lead your brood
not just through their stages of growth but way beyond,
as your labor only ends with the end of your life

But while they mature under your caring love,
they must bite into the sweetness of your own existence
so theirs can be whole, to appreciate the juiciness of life,

And while their roots must grow under your care,
the pot you nestled them in their first days
must be removed so they can grow without limitation.

Allow them to explore the wild and the soil of life,
and while you continue to guide them into the wilderness
do not let them fall into the traps you once fell into,

Those deep holes where you have encountered
the hostile darkness and lingering bitterness
that robbed you too soon of your juvenile spirit.

Become instead the guardian of their rawness
and their innocent thirst for life will blossom,
ripening a loving foundation for the world to cultivate.

The truth about children?

They are sweet beings who revive the sweetness of life.
They live now, in the present moment,
unaware of the days yet to come.

They are small beings expressing emotions
with such truthfulness that they remind you
of the freedom that comes from expressing yourself

So while you train them to survive life's deforestation,
they are actually teaching you that their loving, innocent nature
is the organic way to overcome this inhumane movement

For they have both the necessary energy and the will to do so
when you allow their virgin spirit to thrive,
and preserve the sweet nature they brought into this world.

Poet Bio:
Cécile Correa was born in the south of France, in la Côte d'Azur, and is originally from Guinea-bissau. She now lives in Qatar, in the Middle East, with her husband and their toddler, named Thibault. Writing has been her passion since she was little, and she has written countless poems since, along with a few movie scenes. Her favorite phrase is "La vie est belle."

Website: **www.cecilecorrea.com**

The Truth About... Parenting
by Cécile Correa

The word love can never measure
the depth of emotion your heart carries
once a seed planted and nurtured with care
finally breaks through into the light of life.

Have you realized it?

You signed on to a lifetime's duty
where under the shade of the family tree,
your infants will mature and grow
to be what they have seen you to be

So may your tree flourish with happiness
so all can see the beauty of life,
and may birds nest in your branches
so all can dance to the rhythms of life

And throughout your children's early days
with the wind's gentle sway
may you tenderly rock them to sleep,
and then when the wind angers
may you lovingly shelter them.

Then, as they grow to the prime of their lives,
open up and remove the branches from their way
so they will not bend but grow tall, and strong.

The truth about parenting?

At the core of your soul,
the word blessing itself can never measure
the magnitude of the quake you sense
the very moment your roots forever intertwine

Yet this blessing is too often hidden,
masked by trying compromises or buried beneath ego
until you uncover that as well as the teacher,
you must at times also be the student.

So take charge of your family tree
but only to reinforce the roots
watering them with unconditional love
to pass a loving legacy to the coming generation.

Prayer for Parenting
by Giuliana Melo

Dear Universe:

Being entrusted to take care of another soul is one of the greatest gifts. Thank you for this honor.

Please help me be the best parent I can be.

Grant me patience, understanding, tolerance, and kindness, and teach me how to be unconditionally loving like you.

May I always have faith and trust and listen in to your Divine guidance.

On those days that I am not my best self or the children are going through growth, help me to support them through the gift of compassion and forgiveness. And so it is.

Amen.

Tree of Life
by Priyankaa Gupta Agarwal

The above picture depicting a mother as tree of life protecting her children with the word mom written in different languages has been designed by Priyanka,a graduate of San Francisco Art Institute and founder of "Studio Chhavi." Priyanka has exhibited her work at Stanford university, Togonon Gallery, Market Street Gallery, Triton Museum in California as well as Indian art summit and Art Konsult gallery in India. Her work has received rave reviews in the San Francisco Chronicle and Time-out Singapore to name a few.

Website: **www.priyankasgallery.com**

Final Thoughts

Being a mom is more than giving birth, fostering or adopting a child. It's a blessing, a gift, a relationship that never ends and a love that never dies.

Motherhood, basically a 24 hour job is the greatest, hardest and the most fulfilling job in the world. Mother might be a simple word, but each letter of this word describes love, care, comfort, affection and sacrifice.

Mothers selflessly dedicate their lives to their children putting themselves last and somewhere lose touch with who they really are or who they want to be. This book will be your ally whenever you need that extra support or wish to connect with your emotions, and will help you process the changes as you go through your journey of motherhood.

Regardless of whether you have just become a mother or if you have been a mother for a long time, it is our sincere hope that you will resonate with the thoughts, fears and perceptions in this compilation from mothers around the world.

"Youth fades; love droops;
the leaves of friendship fall.
A mother's secret hope outlives them all."

Oliver Wendell Holmes

Praise For The Book

"For thousands of years, mankind worshiped the Goddess of Fertility. She was the symbol of loving pleasure, birth, creation and wisdom. This book is the celebration of Divine Mother in modern times."
~ La Belle Intelligence,
    European Journalist, Bestselling Author and Leadership Coach

"For too long the suffering and challenges that mothers often experience have been taboo topics. Without bringing their stories out into the open, each new mother with the same or similar predicament must blindly walk their way through their trial without benefit of the wisdom gleaned from those who walked before her. No longer must a mother feel desperately alone without hope of finding someone who understands her and her situation. The stories in "When You're DONE Expecting," breathe life and hope in to these once taboo topics. Other stories shine light on our shared insecurities and desire to be the best mom we can be. Read this treasure and feel connected to hundreds of mothers around the world. Revel in the triumphs of these moms and drink from their wisdom."
~ Nicole DeAvilla
    Mother of two, B.A., E-RYT500, RPYT, RCYT, is a Master Yoga Therapist, Mom Coach, Social Media Outreach Coordinator for 30 Second Mom and Best Selling Author, helping busy moms thrive in the high stake demands of our 24/7 culture.

"We Moms are the Difference! Let's celebrate our Children's Future!"
~ Jyl Steinback,
    America's Healthiest Mom, Executive Director, Shape Up US™

"This book is a wish for you to become a part of this wonderful and terrifying life called Motherhood"
~ Frank Shankwitz,
    Founder, Make-a-Wish Foundation

Resources

Website: www.parulagrawal.com
Amazon: amazon.com/author/parulagrawal

Please download your FREE gifts that come along with the purchase of this book from "www.whenyouredoneexpecting.com"

Online Magazine For Women: https://alphafemale.co
Retreat For Women: https://alphafemaleretreat.com

Books:
- Juicing For Healthier Families
- Viva la Cleanse
- Take Charge of Your Cancer